DATA DISTRIBUTION : MANAGING THE ENVIRONMENT

DATA DISTRIBUTION : MANAGING THE ENVIRONMENT

British Computer Society

Data Management

Specialist Group

Edited by

Richard Williams

Routledge
Taylor & Francis Group
LONDON AND NEW YORK

First published 1992 by Ashgate Publishing

Reissued 2018 by Routledge
2 Park Square, Milton Park, Abingdon, Oxon, OX14 4RN
711 Third Avenue, New York, NY I 0017, USA

Routledge is an imprint of the Taylor & Francis Group, an informa business

A Library of Congress record exists under LC control number: 92009265

Electronically typeset by

Richalis Limited, Meadow Thatch, The Marsh, Midgham, Nr Reading, Berkshire, RG7 5UU

ISBN 13: 978-1-138-61310-2 (hbk)
ISBN 13: 978-0-429-46365-5 (ebk)

CONTENTS

RESEARCH IN DISTRIBUTION

CONCLUSIONS

British Computer Society
Data Management
Specialist Group

DATE'S "12" RULES ON DISTRIBUTION : AN INTRODUCTION TO THE DISTRIBUTED DEVELOPMENT ENVIRONMENT

Richard Williams and Simon Holloway
Data Management 90

1 Introduction

It has been a basic requirement for many years that business users should be able to share and use the data contained within computer systems in any context or for any purpose of relevance throughout an organisation. The days of "stand alone" computer systems has passed, but many problems in Data Management still remain. The amount of time and money that is wasted by an organisation recapturing data already stored elsewhere within the organisation has compounded the problems associated with data value mistrust by businesses.

In the United States many organisations will not trade with other companies unless their data is delivered in standard electronic form, with internationally recognised definitions and meanings. It has been estimated that it costs an average US company up to $10 to process a paper invoice, whereas it is less than $2 for an electronic one.

The same problems occur within different business areas of the same organisation. If two departments hold data on the same subject (such as an individual customer) it must be consistent in its value. The only way to assure such consistency is for the data to be captured in a corporate context and evenly distributed to all interested parties.

This basic Data Management principle has already been responsible for many savings in time and effort within organisations. Yet to maximise the savings and improvement in accuracy, the capability to access consistent data values must be possible throughout the Systems Development Life Cycle. From initial analysis to implementation and beyond.

Common data definitions and standards are necessary for this to happen, and a number of fundamental problems and requirements for their use have been recognised. During development a project is normally worked on by more than one analyst, and any analyst can work on more than one project, often in parallel. In this way development support for projects must be multi-user in its nature. Projects may have their own set of activities, but they will undoubtedly share data with others. The costs of not sharing such data definitions are already clearly evident, and to overcome, this data must be maintained in a corporate frame of reference.

Hence, it can be clearly seen that data and meta data need to be shared and used by different personnel within an organisation throughout the development of a data processing system, from its original business conception, through its analysis, design and implementation and into production. It therefore becomes a fundamental requirement for systems developments to be undertaken with the capability of distributing data. It is argued that this may be best achieved by having a centrally held database or dictionary, but with distributed functionality given to powerful PCs with their own (possibly shared) graphics plotters and printers, generally known as a "Distributed Development Environment."

2 The Distributed Development Environment

To provide an environment where data, meta data and information can be shared between distributed users is more difficult than it first appears. It has been realised by users, as well as vendors, that an integrated set of software is required to achieve this objective, which includes at a minimum the following:

- Database Management System - to allow applications to share data;
- Data Dictionary System - to allow automated control and documentation of the data and the processes that use the data ;
- 4th Generation System - to allow for more rapid application development;
- Query Language - to allow end users direct access to the data resource.

The key, underlying software component is the data dictionary system. Everything in the new development environment hinges on the dictionary, even though data dictionary software in itself has changed little in recent years; the other software components are now providing the user friendly front end that hides the dictionary from the user. The task of maintaining dictionary objects is being automated by these other tools communicating directly with the data dictionary, as shown in Figure 1.

Guidelines or "rules" to support a distributed environment such as the one shown in Figure 1 are available for projects to use. A set of 12 such "rules" was defined by Date [1], and they are examined in detail in the following section.

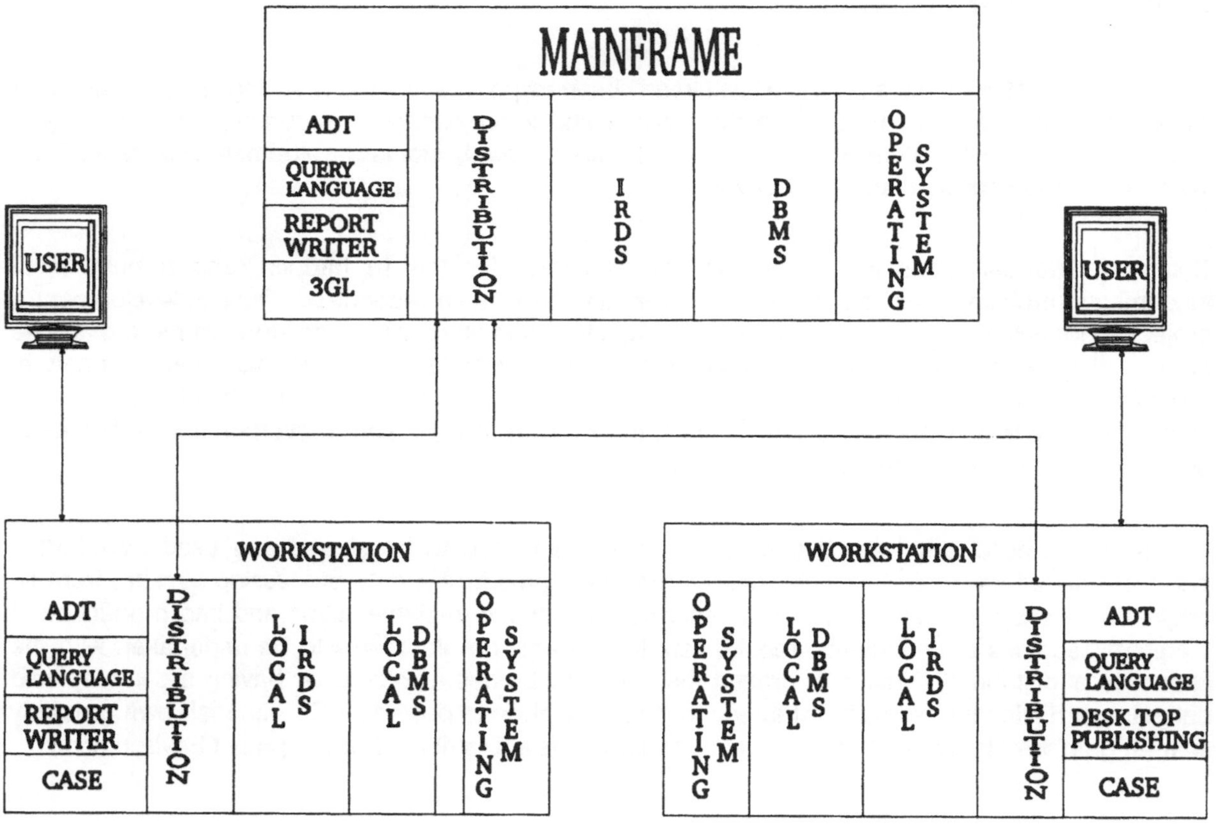

Figure 1 : The Distributed Development Environment

3 DATE's "12" Rules For Distribution

Date [1] established this set of rules to explain what a distributed database is and why it is desirable. He put the following caveat on the rules;

There is no such thing as the "ultimate distributed database system". Different users will attach different degrees of importance to different objectives.

Before looking at the Rules, it is important to understand what Date means by a distributed database system. He defines it as a system involving multiple sites connected together in a communications network in which each site is a database site in its own right, and a user at any site can access any data in the network as if the data were all stored at the user's own site. It is important to notice that Date evolved these Rules to support the production environment.

The advantages of distributed databases are summarised by Date as follows :-

It allows the structure of a DB to mirror the structure of the company, while simultaneously solving the islands of information problems;

Consequently, it is necessary to examine these "Rules" in turn to define what a distributed environment should conform to, and behave like, in respect to its users, regardless of their activities, location or role:

- Rule Zero :- To the user, a distributed system should look exactly like a non-distributed system;
- Rule 1 :- Local Autonomy - local data is locally owned and managed, so that no site should depend on some other for its successful operation;
- Rule 2 :- No reliance on a central site - there should be no central dictionary, query processing site, concurrency control or recovery control;
- Rule 3 :- Continuous Operations - the maintenance of sites, tables and the DBMS should not call for a shutdown of the network;
- Rule 4 :- Location Independence - users should not have to know where data is physically stored;
- Rule 5 :- Fragmentation Independence - users should not have to know about the fragmentation of the data;
- Rule 6 :- Replication Independence - users should not have to know about the replication of the data;
- Rule 7 :- Distributed Query Processing - the system should support multiple-site views and multiple-site integrity constraints;
- Rule 8 :- Distributed Transaction Processing - the system must be able to handle two-phase commits, concurrency and global deadlock;

- Rule 9 :- Hardware Independence - it should be possible to run the same DBMS on multiple, different hardware systems, and have those systems participate as equal systems in the distributed database system;

- Rule 10 :- Operating System Independence - it should be possible to run the same DBMS on multiple different operating systems, and have those systems participate as equal systems in the distributed database system;

- Rule 11 :- Network Independence - the system should provide support for LANs, WANs and other different network architectures;

- Rule 12 :- DBMS Independence - it should be possible to connect different DBMSs at different nodes in the same network, and to transfer processing between them.

These rules will be used by vendors as guidelines for product development in much the same way as the "12" Relational Rules have been used. Users, who are evaluating distributed systems, will use them as guidelines for comparisons between products.

4 Conclusion

As data is distributed, so must the data processing capabilities be distributed to fulfil Date's Rule 2. In line with findings on the reporting from dictionaries and CASE tools (CCTA [2]), which are distributed, this is just the same as for any distributed database and its associated applications. However, the introduction of CASE tools, which provides a further reason for controlled distribution of the data dictionary, introduces new requirements, which do not conform to some of Date's 12 Rules (Holloway [3]). In particular, site and location independence may not be desirable given the performance requirements of some data processing tools, and the need to maintain version control of complex objects. There is a need for a more comprehensive understanding of the Distributed Development Environment, with the increasing requirement of customers and users to access and use data at multiple sites. It is essential, therefore, to have a complete and comprehensive strategy to support such requirements. Dates "12" rules provide an important reference point from which to begin such work, because it is certain that such distributed requirements will increase in the future, and the data processing environment within which they are undertaken must be effectively managed.

References

[1] DATE, C.J. (1987) : "What Is A Distributed Database System?", The Relational Journal 1 & 2 .

[2] CCTA (1988) : "Data Dictionary Reporting", Information Systems Engineering Report 22, HMSO.

[3] HOLLOWAY, S. (1990) : "The Distributed Development Environment : CASE Tools And Data Dictionaries In Partnership," in Using CASE Tools In Systems Development, R.F.Williams (ed), Gower Technical Press, pp 25-40.

DEFINING DISTRIBUTION

DISTRIBUTION - MYTH OR REALITY?

Simon Holloway and Tim Warren
DCE Information Management Consultancy

1.1 Introduction

Interest in distributed systems initially arose from large decentralised companies who wished to decentralise their computing facilities. Early attempts were somewhat primitive and barely deserved the label "distributed system", but during the past 10 years there has been significant research effort aimed at providing sophisticated systems. The impetus for the increased research effort over recent years has come to a large extent from the great advances in data communications which have led to the widespread availability of cost-effective wide area and local area networks (WANs and LANs). These have made it economically feasible to transfer messages (queries, responses, mail, etc.) from computer to computer at different locations. Distributed database technology represents the merging of two major technologies: database technology and data communications technology. This paper sets the scene for this publication by putting forward some definitions of terms used in the distributed world, and looking at some of the myths and realities of distribution.

1.2 Definitions

Distributed IT/IS is a major classification of IT/IS methods, in which two types are possible:

- *Distributed processing*. Execution of an application program results in the program using CPU (central processing unit) cycles on more than one CPU in a network of processors. Program A on CPU 1 may call subroutine B but request that it execute on CPU 2 and within the same recovery scope as A; the processing performed has been distributed. The single recovery scope means that the resource changes performed by program A and subroutine B must be fully executed or neither set can be executed. In this way, integrity is maintained across the network.

- *Distributed data*. A single file or database is partitioned and the data partitions reside on different nodes (processors) in a network of processors. A bank may have a single checking account database with part of it in London and part in Edinburgh. Both sites can access the entire database regardless of the location of the data in the network.

1.3 Distributed Processing

Distributed Processing architectures are many and cater for communications between every conceivable hardware platform, from PCs to PCs on a LAN to Mainframe to Mainframe. Examples of distributed processing architectures include:

- *User Interface Front-end:* all processing and database operations on the mainframe, screen management, data entry validation, and help processing on the PC.

- *"Client-Server" Cooperative Processing:* processing and screen interaction on the PC, all database transactions go to a mainframe or a LAN-based database server.

- *Peer-To-Peer Application-To-Application Co-operative Processing:* a PC application doing both user interfacing and processing such as data entry of analysis cooperatives with a back-end application doing high volume data processing.

- *Host-satellite processing:* the application operates during the day with a complete database on the PC or on a LAN Server, uploading the transactions to a remote mainframe database at the end of the business day.

In this section, the author will concentrate on two of the above: Client-Server and Co-operative Processing. These are the buzzwords of 1990.

1.3.1 CLIENT-SERVER

There are two key aspects of a true client-server architecture. One is the ability to use workstations or terminal-based minicomputers to run applications that seemlessly access shared data management functions running on one or more server machines in a network. The second is the enforcement of data integrity within the database rather than relying on application programs. Client-servers allow the user to choose the most appropriate DBMS engine and 4GL for their hardware platforms and their culture. The real advantage of client-server architecture is that, providing the clients and servers operate in a standard manner over open networking systems, the server's operating system and the manufacturer are irrelevant.

1.3.2 COOPERATIVE PROCESSING

In a traditional, centralised application architecture, all processing is done on the same system including database management and user interfacing. The system may run on a PC, or on a mainframe or midrange system interacting with the user through a "dumb terminal". Cooperative processing is increasingly used to offload simple processing from expensive mainframes, to improve response time and user interfacing flexibility, and to make information locally available at several locations in a farflung business organisation. Cooperative processing services of several different forms are available:

- **Peer-to-Peer, application-to-application cooperative processing** through communications services provided in the development systems. This allows an application to communicate with another application on a mainframe, as shown in Figure 1 below for example.

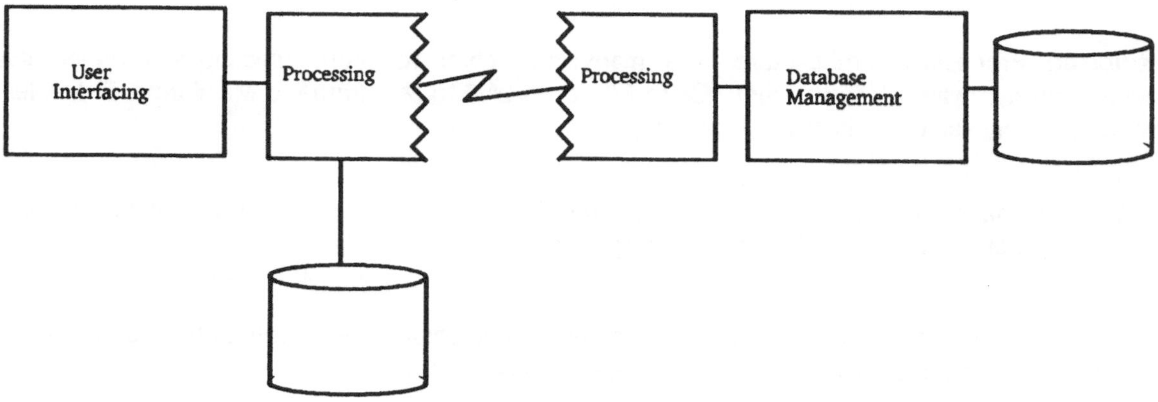

Figure 1: Peer-to-Peer

- **Remote function invocation** allows an application to request a service from another machine in a **server-requester** architecture. This allows a mainframe application to download the processing of user interfacing, data validation, and HELP on a PC workstation. **Transparent** remote function invocation allows the developer to build a system without concern for whether the service is provided in the same machine or another one, simply calling on the service knowing that it will be provided in one way or another. A pictorial representation of this is given in Figure 2 below:

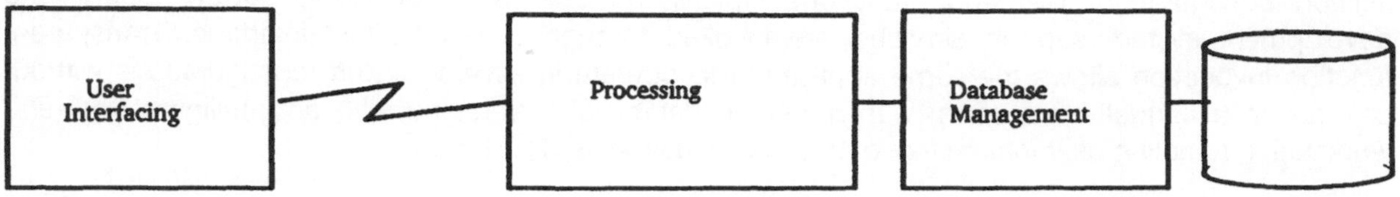

Figure 2: Remote Function Invocation

The **remote database access** functions of certain DBMSs also use a remote function invocation architecture. This area is covered by the work being done by the ISO on Remote Data Access (RDA). RDA is shown in Figure 3:

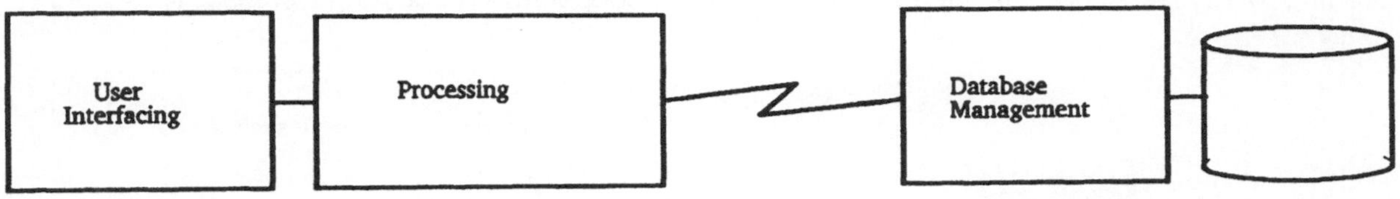

Figure 3: Remote Data Access

Distributed database processing allows an application to use a database without concern for integrity and transaction management regardless of whether the database is local, remote, or distributed across several systems. Figure 4 provides an example of the case:

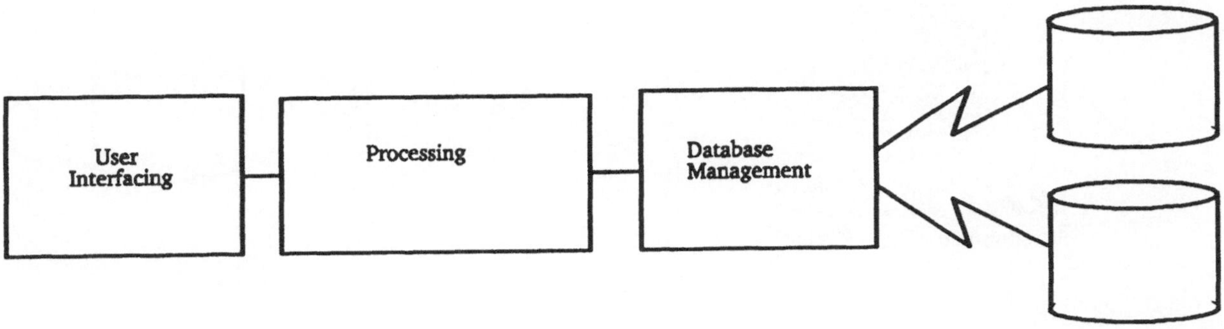

Figure 4: Distributed Database Processing

These forms of cooperative processing are all useful, offering different cost/benefit trade-offs, different levels of flexibility, and different sensitivity to network configuration. The distinctions between the different categories are somewhat fuzzy, but some general observations can be made. Application level cooperative processing provides the greatest level of flexibility and control for the developer: any processing may be done on either side, with or without a database. But it also requires the greatest development effort: the developer must build both the communications and the processing code on both sides and manage the cooperation between the systems. It is also most sensitive to changes in the overall system/network architecture: although technical details of the network configuration are isolated by the communications services, the application design typically reflects a certain configuration, requiring application changes when significant changes are made. Remote function invocation, including remote database services, insulates the developer to a greater extent from the network configuration. "Black-box" functions, typically not built by the developer but provided by the development system support services, are invoked through a well defined interface. Transparent function invocation allows the same application to operate in several system configurations without change: in a centralised system, with a remote database server, and with an intelligent front-end workstation handling user interfacing, data entry validation, and HELP.

Fully distributed database allows the database to be not only remote, but also distributed to several systems. This insulates the application completely from the network configuration: the system handles transaction management and integrity control across the network. This allows the system administrator to tune the performance of the system by rearranging not only the network but also the configuration data across this network, without requiring any changes in the applications. The transparent support of cooperative processing in the high level development systems can make this new technology significantly more practical. While cooperative processing offers many cost and efficiency benefits during operation, the cost of development and maintenance may be prohibitively high when done with traditional techniques. Since economic realities prevent us from discarding all our hardware investments overnight, most application systems need to support traditional centralised "dumb-terminal" architectures as well as the new distributed architectures. The developer is faced with building two systems, not one; far from reducing costs, cooperative processing increases it.

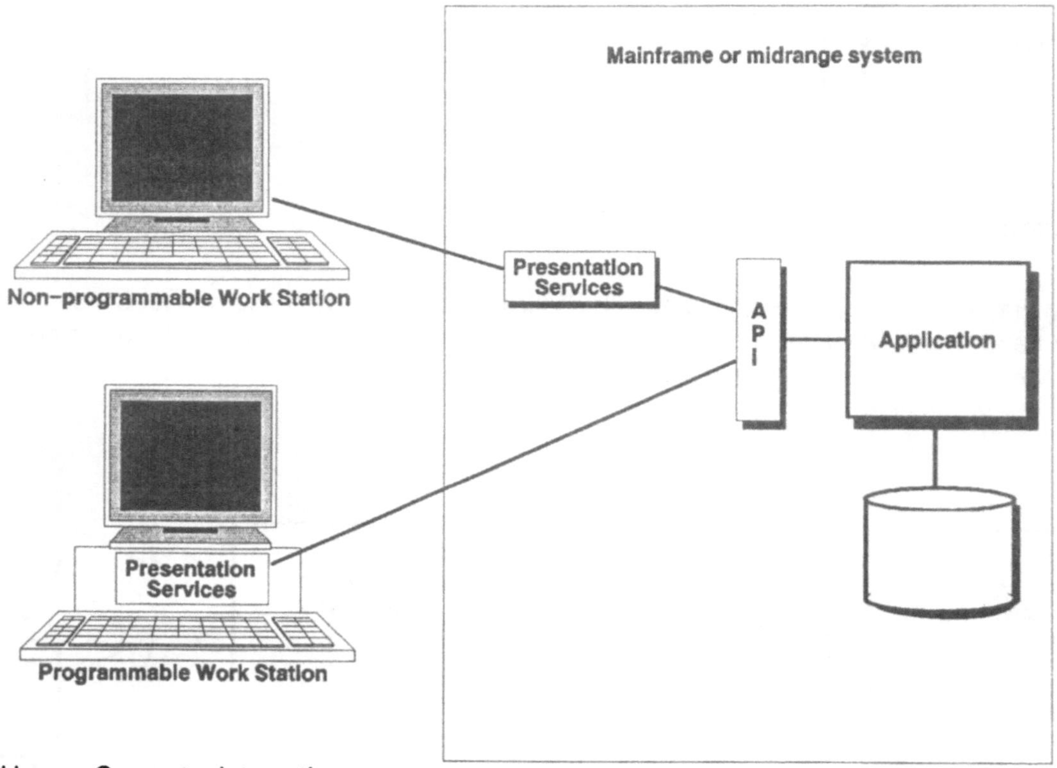

Figure 5: Human Computer Interaction

Looking at a front-end architecture, as shown in Figure 5 on the previous page for example, the application interacts with the User Interfacing Services (Presentation Services) through a common API (Application Program Interface) regardless of operating mode. The system determines if a specific user is connected through a dumb terminal requiring all presentation service processing to be done on the mainframe, or through a smart workstation which can take over the tasks of window and menu management, data validation and help processing.

1.4 Distributed Database

What is a distributed database? There are many diverse answers, depending on one's perspective. Inman and Bird [1] define a distributed database as a partitioned database where a network of database managers (DBMs) is involved in the control of the various partitions, and each instance of a data element is controlled by only one database manager in the network. This definition is shown in Figure 6.

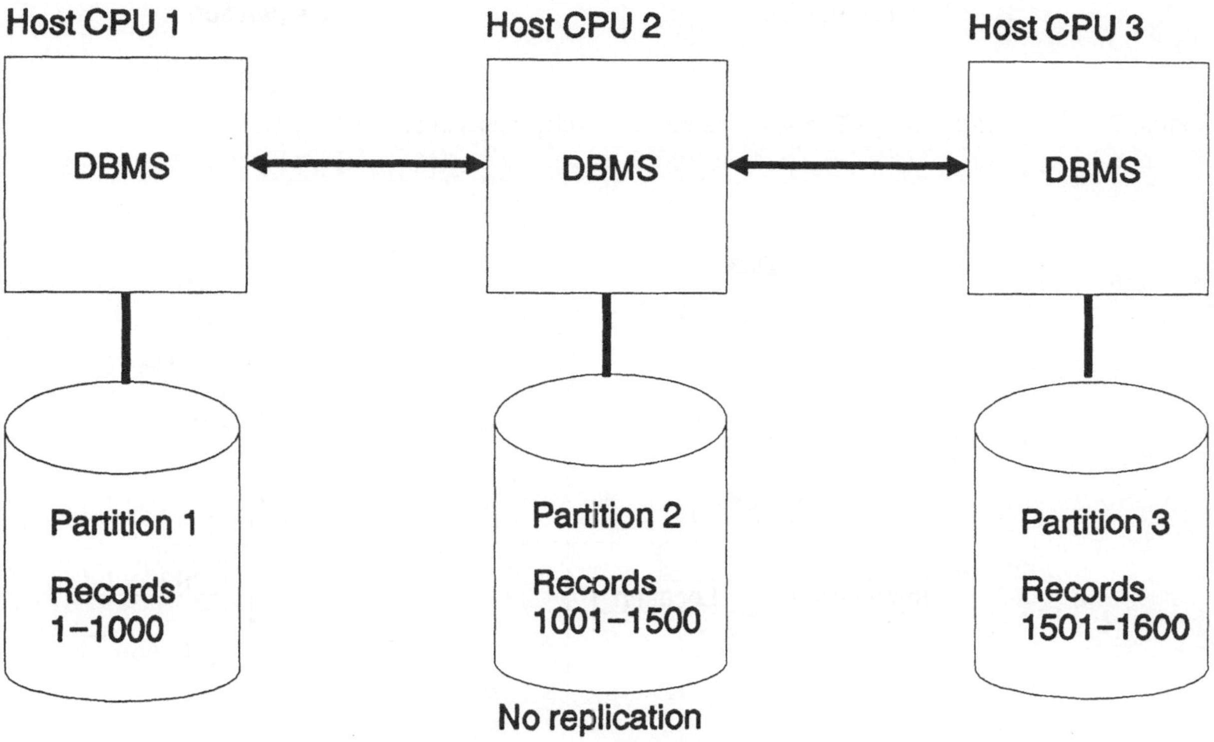

Figure 6: Distributed Database - a partitioned database with a network of DBMs

There are some related definitions:

- A database is partitioned if the contents of the database are grouped into separate sets, where each set can be manipulated individually from the others. Vertical partitioning, as shown in Figure 7 for a hierarchical database, requires that each partition contains complete database records. Horizontal partitioning, as shown in Figure 8 for a hierarchical database, allows the data to be split between the partitions along subrecord or segment lines depending on the database schema. Both vertical and horizontal partitioning may be used together in the same database.

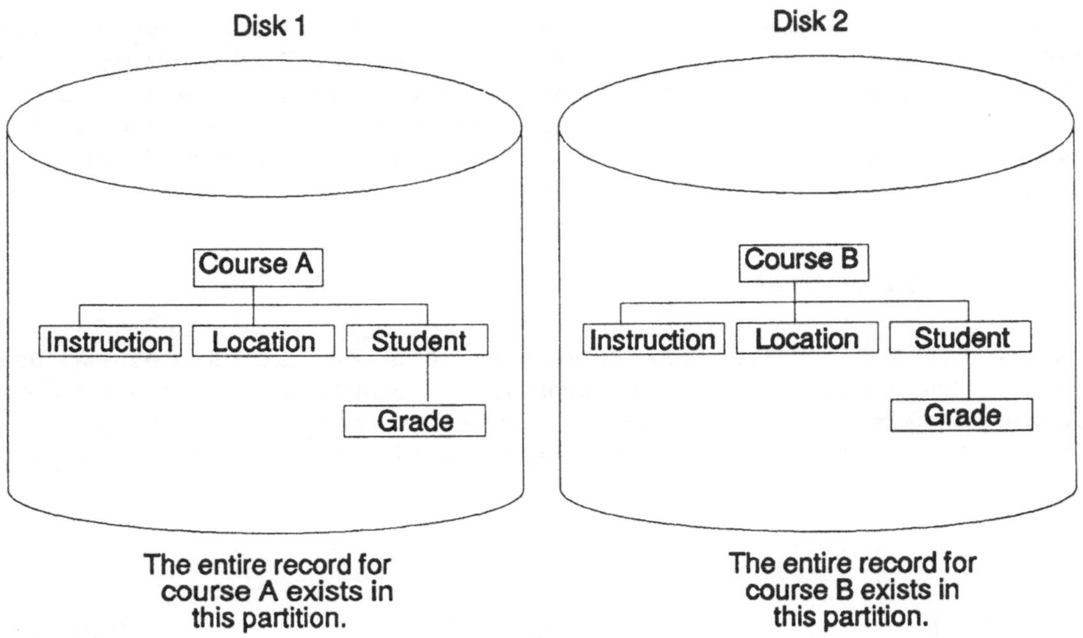

Figure 7: Vertical partitioning - The entire record hierarchy exists in each partition

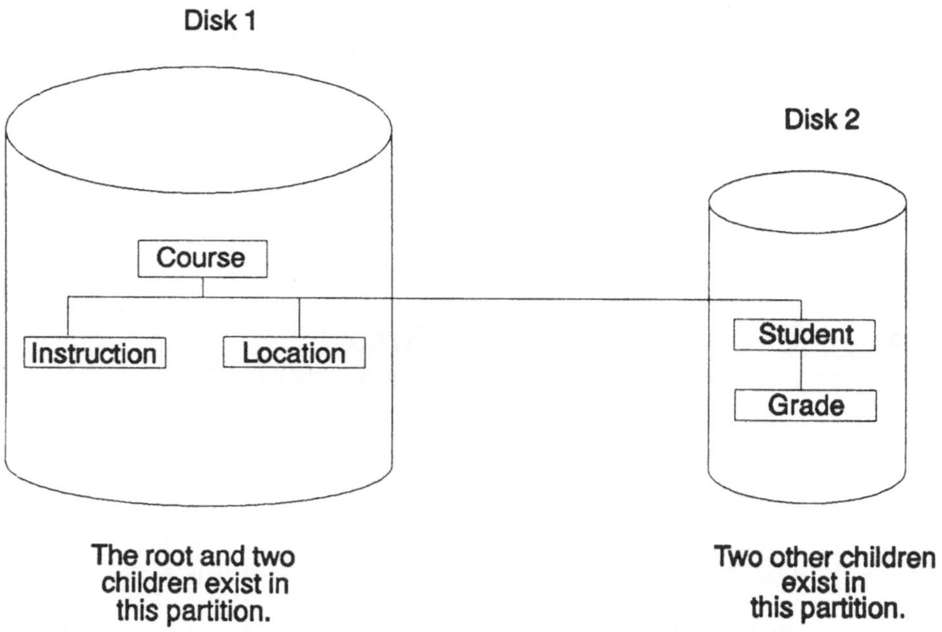

Figure 8: Horizontal Partitioning - Only portions of the record hierarchy exist in each partition

- Any given data item may exist in more than one partition, in which case there are multiple copies of the same data. This is referred to as **replicated data.** Databases may be partitioned and replicated at the same time. Figure 9 (a) shows a non-partitioned, non-replicated database, (b) shows a partitioned database without replication, (c) shows a replicated database without partitioning, and (d) shows a partitioned replicated database.

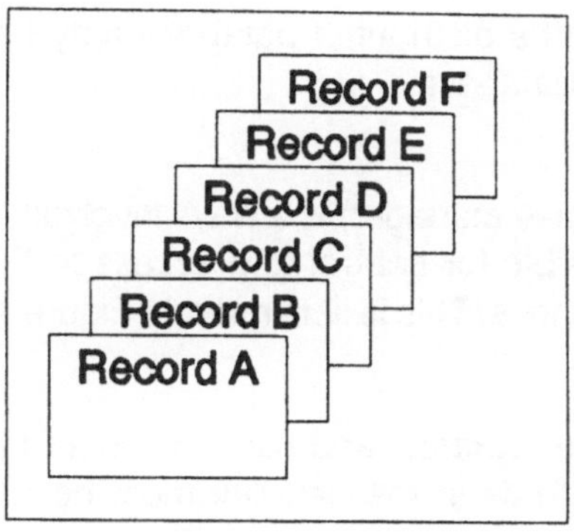

(a) No partitioning, no replication

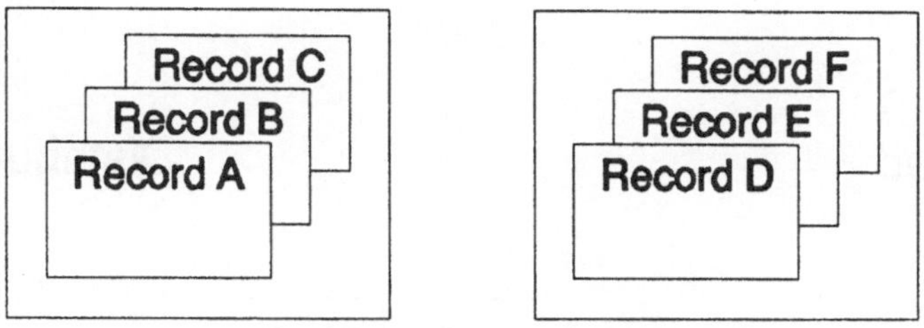

(b) Partitioned, no replication

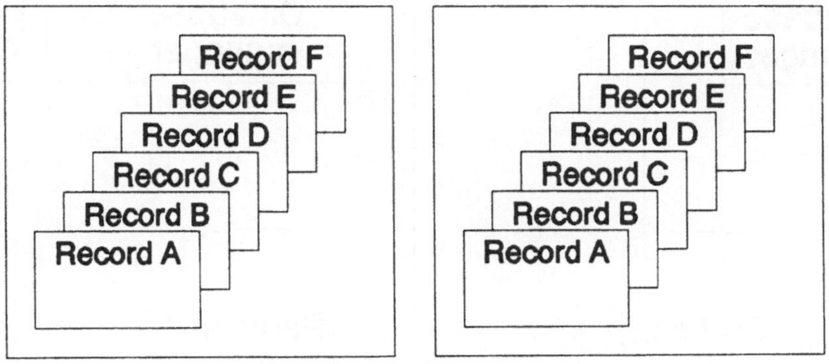

(c) No partitioning, replicated

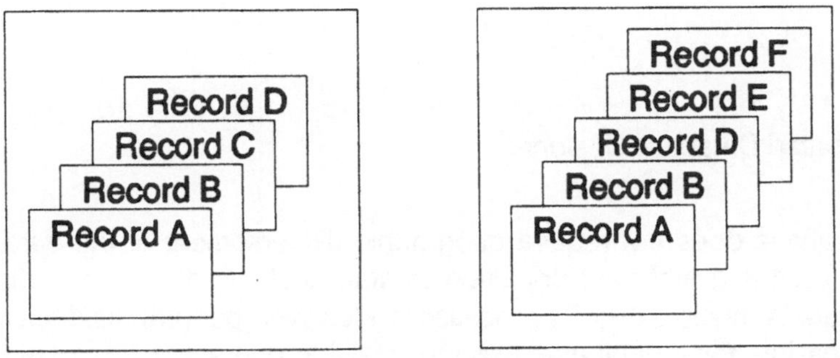

(d) Partitioned, replicated

Figure 9: Partitioning and Replication

- The individual partitions of the distributed database may be intersections of, or unions with data from other partitions of the database.

- More than one DBM (database manager) is always involved in the control of a distributed database. If only one DBM is responsible for control and access to the entire database, the database is not distributed but the processing is. This is illustrated in Figure 10.

- Only one database manager controls and has access to a given data item instance. Requests for the data item from other DBMs in the network must be routed to the owning DBM. This is also illustrated in Figure 10.

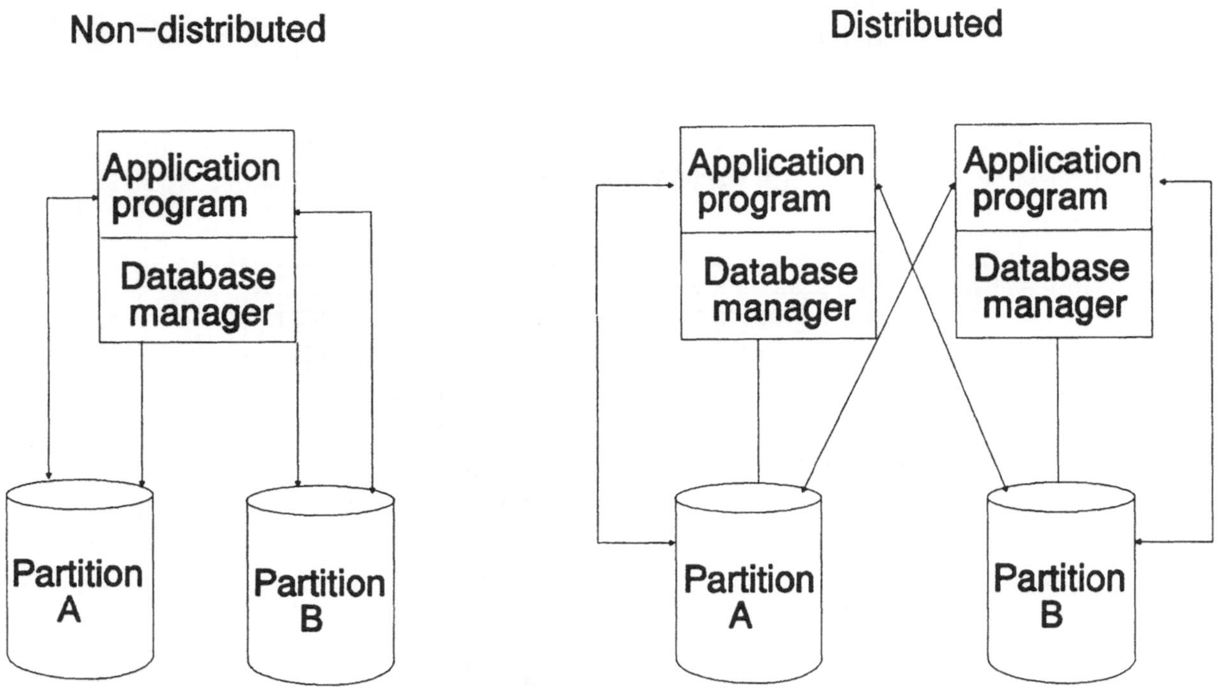

Figure 10 : Distributed Database Designed

A distributed database does not require geographic dispersement of the data. However, geographic dispersement of data is a sufficient condition to state that the database is distributed, since no one DBM could execute in multiple disjoint processors. However, geographic dispersion is not a necessary condition. It is possible for a database, existing totally in one site, to be partitioned and managed by multiple DBMs at that same site. Many of the benefits and problems with a geographically dispersed database also apply to the single-site distributed database. Indeed, most of the distributed databases in existence today have all database partitions within the same computer site.

1.5 Why Distributed?

Dividing a database into partitions and then controlling the partitions by the use of independent networked DBMs is a complex and resource-intensive function. In many cases this complexity and added cost is offset by the benefits accrued:

- *Application processing efficiency.* The data can be moved closer to the point where it is to be used most often. This is referred to as taking the data to the work.

- *Increased data availability.* Failure at any subset of the DBM network nodes still leaves the other nodes and their partitions available for use. If some or all of the data is replicated, then the entire database can remain available even when some nodes are not available.

- *Organisational flexibility.* The database may be partitioned according to departmental units within the organisation (i.e., corporation, university, etc.) and each organisational unit can have complete control over its portion of the database. The organisation is not forced to centralise the data resource due to IT/IS constraints.

- *Increased data accuracy.* Moving the partitions closer to the source of entry and usage of the data may improve the chances of correct, true and timely data.

- *Network-wide access. Any user, with the necessary security clearance, can access any database regardless of its location in the network subject to performance considerations.*

- *Increased capacity.* Multiple DBM network nodes can handle a higher volume of work than a single DBM on a single processor complex

- *Simplified system expansion.* Nodes can be added to a network more easily and with less disruption than is the case for a single centralised system.

- *Improved performance.* Since the data is usually closer to the work and, therefore, to the user, improved response times are likely. If the data is not optimally located for performance, it can be migrated to the node where it is needed. This data migration in the network may be on temporary or permanent basis.

Distributed databases are useful in operational systems and decision support systems. Operational systems benefit from the increased capacity and flexibility. Decision support systems can effectively share the database with operational systems with less performance impact and by using different hardware than the host. For example, the operational system may be using large mainframes, whereas a manager uses a personal computer to access a subset of the database that has been distributed to the personal computer itself.

1.6 The Challenges That Must Be Faced

There are several complex issues that must be adequately handled by a full function distributed DBMS. Most of the complexities arise out of the need for the applications to perform updates of several different databases or partitions that reside in different nodes of the network.

1.6.1 SITE RESOLUTION

When an application program issues a request for data, the DBMS software must locate the data, access it, and pass it back to the requesting program and user. Locating the data in a centralised system is straightforward. The target database table or view is passed to the DBMS by the requesting program, and the DBMS either owns the data or it does not. In a distributed database environment, the DBMS must first recognise that it does not own the data and then determine the owning DBMS. This process of determining which DBMS owns the data is referred to as **site resolution.** Site Resolution determines the node DBMS combination that should be contacted. This convention enables the daisy chaining of site resolution processes and can reduce the complexity and size of the site resolution process in any given DBMS. Site resolution can be accomplished using a combination of techniques not suited to the data and application requirements:

- *Table lookup.* The target database and partition names are used as operands of a node-DBMS table lookup. The key of the requested record may also be used. The table is kept current with the network configuration.

- *Catalog.* An advanced and sophisticated version of the table lookup.

- *Hashing.* The target node-DBMS is determined mathematically by using a hashing or randomising technique that produces consistent results across the network.

- *Dictionary node.* A node or group of nodes in the network are defined as dictionary nodes. As such, they will provide any other node with site resolution answers, partial or complete.

- *API specification.* The application program interface (API) to the DBMS provides an application specification capability wherein the program can assist with or totally determine the node-DBMS to communicate with.

Site resolution requires network definition information, DBMS system information, and application-dependent information. This diverse set of requirements can make this task a most burdensome part of the design and implementation of a distributed database system.

1.6.2 DML PERFORMANCE DEPENDENCIES

The choice of a data management language (DML) for a distributed DBMS can have significant impact on the performance of the internodal data requests. DMLs can be divided into two groups: DMLs that handle records and DMLs that handle sets. A record DML makes available only one record per data request. DL/1 used with IMS, is an example. The application program issues a single DL/1 request and receives back at most a single database record. A set DML may return one or more records to the requester. SQL, used with DB2, is a set DML. The example of retrieving a specific record is also supported by a set DML. However, the program may request all the records within a key range in one request and receive them all back as a single response - hence the name set DML. In a distributed database environment, the choice of either DML for a single record request has little effect on performance. Both will perform site resolution for a single record, and both will access the network once for the record. For an application that requires a range of records and the range is known, set DML outperforms record DML considerably. The record DML in general performs site resolution and goes into the network once for each record. Optimisation techniques may be used to reduce the number of times that site resolution and network access is performed by a record DML at the expense of flexibility in the site resolution process. The set DML performs site resolution once for the entire set of records and goes into the network once for each node that is the product of the site resolution process.

If the entire set of records requested resides at one node, the set DML has, in the best case, eliminated n - 1 site resolution requests and n - 1 network accesses, where n is the number of records in the resultant set.

1.6.3 UPDATE PROCESSING

For a DML that requires an application-generated retrieval request before an update, site resolution is required for the update request. A DML that accepts standalone update requests requires site resolution after the parsing and validation of the update call.

Record versus set DML performance differences apply to updates in the same way as inquiries. However, the frequency of nonsingular set updates is less than for inquiries, and so the performance impact is not so acute. In other words, while it is common for an application program to request a set of records in one call to the DBM, seldom is more than one record updated by the application program in one DML call. Retrieval of a set of records is more prevalent than updating a set of records. Consequently, set DML performance approaches record DML performance for update activity in a distributed database.

When a distributed database has some of its partitions replicated, update processing requires that the participating DBMS be able to control the versions of the same data items. Network-wide integrity and synchronisation must be maintained in a distributed database with distributed update capabilities. These concepts are considered in the next sections.

1.6.4 SYNCHRONISATION

A DBMS maintains complete data integrity of the databases within its control. When a transaction program updates several database records as part of the processing of a single input transaction, the program expects that all the updates will be made by the DBMS or that none of them will. For the DBMS to do otherwise would leave the set of databases corrupted, at least from a logical data point of view.

This all-or-none DBMS process is referred to as **database synchronisation.** In a non-distributed environment, the DBMS owns all the databases accessed by the application program. Therefore, the synchronisation process is totally within its control. In a distributed database environment, the application program may have updated databases owned by several different DBMSs. A single DBMS can no longer control the entire synchronisation process.

A technique referred to as **two-phase synchronisation** has been developed to ensure networkwide integrity and effectively provide protocols that will allow the multiple DBMSs to work in concert during the synchronisation process. Since the word "commit" is often used in place of synchronisation, two-phase commit is sometimes used as well.

Essentially, two-phase synchronisation requires that each DBMS participating in the distributed database network perform its database updates in two steps. In the first step, the coordinating DBMS asks all DBMSs involved in a given transaction to prepare to perform all their database updates. The prepare phase requires that each DBMS determines whether or not all its updates can be performed. The coordinating DBMS demands a phase 1 response from each DBMS either indicating that it can or it can't perform its updates. The coordinator waits until a yes or no is received from all DBMSs.

At the point when the answers have all been received, no updates have been performed anywhere in the network. If any DBMS says no, the coordinating DBMS tells all the DBMSs to discard their database updates. This is called an abort. If all DBMSs answer "yes" to the prepare, then the coordinator instructs each of them to proceed with phase 2, which is called commit. The coordinator is not able to accept the inability of any DBMS to perform its updates after it has said "yes" to the prepare.

The two-phase commit then consists of a prepare-commit or a prepare-abort sequence. In both cases, network-wide integrity is ensured.

1.6.5 REPLICATION CONTROL

When replicating some subset of a database, the copies may be arranged in a hierarchy wherein there are one or more **primary** copies and one or more **secondary** copies. The primary copies are considered the masters. They contain the data that is considered accurate. The secondary copies may, as time goes on, become less accurate than the primary copy from which they were made. Periodic refreshment of the secondary copies from the primary may be required. The users of secondary copies do not have a need for current-to-the-minute data, or such timely and dynamic change may conflict with the need, such as in decision support systems. Alternatively, the copies may be viewed as peers. The true and accurate state of the data can be determined only by pooling the most current data from each copy. This synchronisation process must be performed by the participating DBMSs, but its invocation may be automatic or operator requested.

1.6.6 CONCURRENCY

The replication of some or all partitions of a database requires the study of concurrency levels. When a database partition is not replicated, all accesses are funnelled to a single disk drive where the partition resides. Even in a shared database environment, the multiple DBMSs still ultimately meet at the disk drive level. This has both availability and performance implications. By replicating some of the data, higher levels of database availability and performance can be achieved. With replication, multiple DBMSs access different copies of the same data items with the possibility of little or no common hardware and software. With this greater concurrency capability comes the need to maintain consistency of data. The DBMS must know which are primary copies and which are secondary copies. If an update is attempted against a secondary copy, the update must be forwarded to a primary copy site. An update to a primary copy must be immediately and uniformly applied to all primary copies or to none. Some replicated database management systems enforce a rule which says that no application program that accesses a secondary copy of a database can update it; it can only read it. This simplifies the concurrency-control issue at the expense of reduced function to the end user.

1.7 "And thus spake the prophet, and forthwith....."

Like all sectors within IS/IT, distribution has its own visionary prophet and guru, namely Chris Date. In 1987 at the VLDB conference in Brighton, and also at Relational Database '87, Date put forward his thoughts and visions for distributed databases. His "working definition" of a distributed database was "a system involving multiple sites connected together in a communications network, in which each site is a database site in its own right, and a user at any site can access any data in the network exactly as if the data were all stored at the user's own site." Thus in Date's opinion, a distributed database is a virtual database, whose components are physically stored in a number of distinct real databases at a number of distinct sites. Date saw that a distributed database was the solution to the "Islands of Information" problem caused by the moves towards decentralised computing. Whilst solving this problem, distributed databases allowed the structure of the databases to mirror the structure of a company.

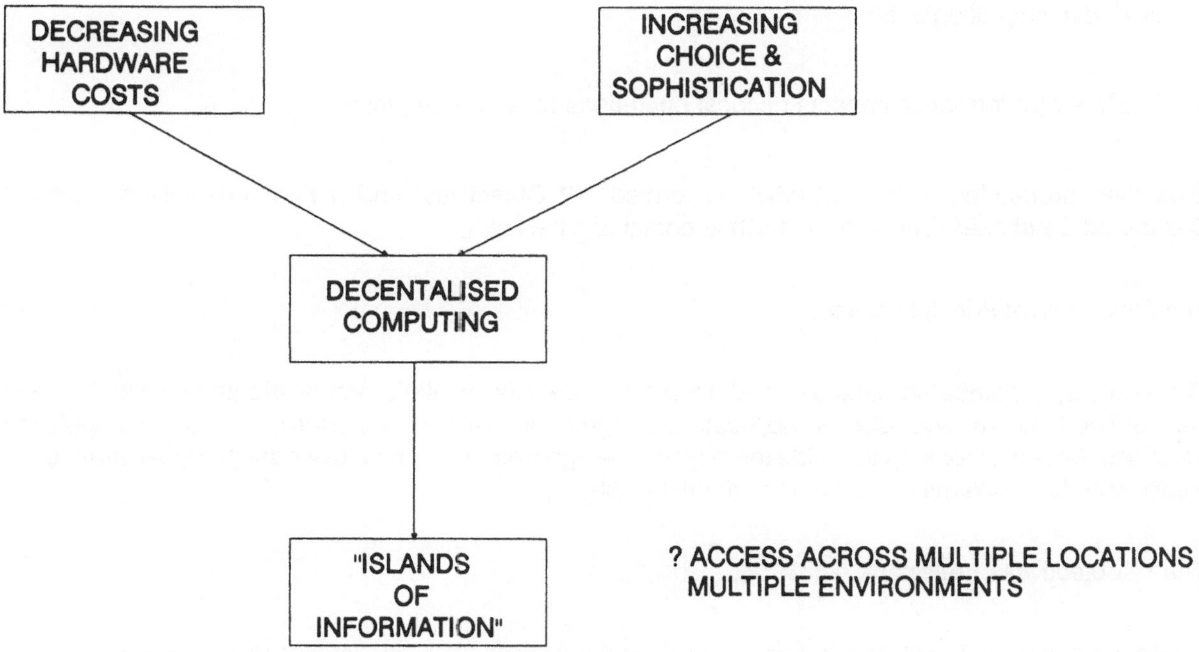

Figure 11: Date's Islands of Information

Date saw the following advantages for distributed databases:

- Local control for local data;
- Accessibility to remote data;
- Capacity;
- Incremental growth of data, its usage and resources;
- Availability of data and resources;
- Efficiency of data access; and
- Flexibility of response.

Unlike many visionaries however, Date did put forward some potential disadvantages of distributed databases:

- The implementation of the software to support the requirements is complex;
- The speed of data travelling on long haul networks is poor;

- The perioicial nature of organisations leads to political problems based round ownership and custodianship of data; and

- The likely performance impacts on local operations of remote requests.

Date then proceeded to lay out what he termed "12 Objectives" and a Fundamental Principle for Distributed Databases (The Tables of Stone containing the law).

The Fundamental Principle states:

"To the user, a distributed database system should look exactly like a non-distributed system." A user was defined as an end-user or application programmer who was performing data manipulation functions. Date was looking to divide the physical design from the conceptual design, by separating the issues and the problems related to the different levels.

The 12 objectives or rules are:

1. *Local Autonomy* - Local data is locally owned and managed. Security, integrity and storage representatives are locally controlled.

2. *No reliance on a central site* - This is a corollary of rule 1, but is important in its own right or otherwise there are likely to be bottlenecks, and certainly there is vulnerability.

3. *Continuous Operation* - The adding and/or removing of sites or tables should not interrupt the service at other sites, and should not involve any revision of existing applications or databases.

4. *Location Independence* - Users should not have to know where data is physically stored.

5. *Fragmentation Independence* - Users should not have to know if tables are divided into fragments for storage purposes.

6. *Replication Independence* - Users should not have to know if a given table or fragment of a table is represented by several distinct stored copies at several distinct sites.

7. *Distributed Query Processing* - The system should support multiple site views and integrity constraints. The optimisation process for queries should be distributed itself, in addition to the query execution process. Note a "query" in Date's words mean "any relational request".

8. *Distributed Transaction Management* - A transaction can be a unit of work, or a unit of recovery, or a unit of concurrency. There is a need to manage the integrity of the system as a whole in the case of failure. Date put forward a theory of how to accomplish this based on the use of two-phase commit and distributed deadlock and prevention and detection.

9. *Hardware Independence* - It should be possible to run the same DBMS on multiple different hardware platforms, and to have these systems participate as equal partners in a distributed database system.

10. *Operating System Independence* - To some extent, this is a corollary of the previous rule.

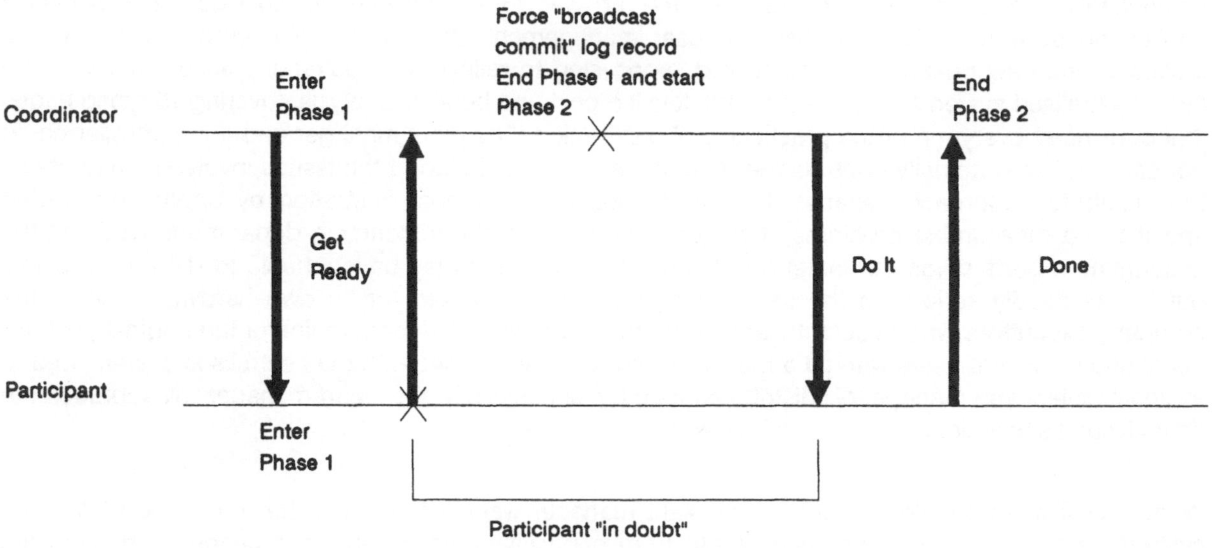

Figure 12 : Date's Two Phase Commit Diagram

11. *Network Independence* - In just the same way as the distributed database should be independent of hardware and operating system, so should it not be affected by the network management software.

12. *DBMS Independence* - The particular DBMS at any particular site should not affect the way which retrieval or update of tables is carried out. This should be equally true for both relational and non-relational DBMSs. Date recognised that an assumption based on strict homogeneity of DBMSs was too strong, and what was needed was a common interface.

Date's vision for distributed databases was not put forward as being totally set into tables of stone. He felt that it would need to be revised and added to over time. Unfortunately, like all gurus, followers sometimes blindly accept that there is no other way and miss the scope. One of the authors of this paper (Holloway [2]) looked at the applicability of these rules to what he termed the Distributed Development Environment. He found them not to be strictly applicable and suggested reasons for the necessary deviations.

1.8 Distribution : The Answer To What Question!

The first problem with distribution - and the reason it can cause such great controversy - is that most organisations have seized on the distributed approach as the answer to all their problems. The second problem with distribution is that managers and executives fail to understand the basic reasons for its initial marketing successes and are ignorant of the basic, underlying problems, which will usually lead to frustration, dissatisfaction and costly management blunders. Distributed processing in its original form was a good solution in search of a problem, and the IS world in the late 1990s had a wide variety of problems to solve. Reports from batch applications were consistently late, and user requests to upgrade batch applications were often ignored. On-line interactive processing did boost productivity and make possible a new range of business applications, but it also created its own unique set of conditions. Some on-line systems took years to develop and were partially obsolete by the time they were put into production. Others required so much additional CPU power that some lucky hardware vendors found an instant goldmine. Still other applications took so many highly skilled programmers to maintain or change that the true cost of on-line processing increased dangerously close to the "unjustifiable level". Although a significant number of on-line application systems did come through for the user with powerful interactive processing, IT/IS management teams still faced their own surprises and frustrations.

At the same time, the cost of computer processors dropped dramatically, and hardware vendors immediately proposed minicomputers as the answer to deficiencies in business and scientific application systems. IT/IS management, user management, and even senior company executives looked to the new buzzword of distributed processing to relieve the frustrations associated with the older centralised systems. No, it wasn't the detailed cost and benefits analysis covering 15 typed pages that convinced everyone of the practicality of distribution. The plant manager and the controller could not care less who actually controls the data, if they even understood the issues involved. They chose the distributed approach because it could reduce their personal frustration by apparently solving specific and measurable problems. If the computer was in the accounting department, wouldn't the accounting reports come out faster and better? That question may be laughable to IT/IS technicians, but it was deadly serious to the user management who pressed for its own hardware and to the company executives who reluctantly approved those requests. The bottom line of the original push for distribution was that users wanted a method to correct deficiencies with the centralised system, and to evaluate, select and manage this distributed function successfully, the smart manager will approach the entire issue as "solutions" rather than buzzwords.

What specifically does the accounting or plant manager want out of his or her proposed distributed system? "Better service" is not acceptable from a business standpoint, and neither is a rapid fire collection of fascinating but meaningless buzzwords straight from a hardware marketing representative. Distribution must be justified by concrete, measurable and well-defined objectives, not by theoretical platitudes that sound great over a drink but fail miserably when subjected to a business evaluation. Some valid justifications for a distributed system are:

- Reducing response time of the on-line transactions from six seconds to three;
- Extending the hours of operating to match the requirements of the operating unit;
- Producing the daily sales summary report three hours earlier;
- Providing interactive capabilities that the central system does not possess; and
- Producing an entirely new custom-made system to meet a specific need.

In each example, the cost per executable instruction of minicomputers, as opposed to that of large mainframes, was irrelevant, and the hotly debated question of centralised versus decentralised control of data was not important. The true issues of distribution can only be discussed if IT/IS management is willing to face the reason for favouring the distributed approach: Users perceive they can manage problem areas and bypass IT/IS with distributed processing. IT/IS technical and management personnel must document accurately each proposed solution to a specific problem from the user's viewpoint. Only when senior IT/IS executives understand which problems the users expect to be solved can they ever hope to correctly design a distributed system. It is a serious error for the DP management team to approve a £200,000 distributed system only to discover that the new hardware and software do not satisfy the frustrated users. Hardware to support a distributed environment involves far more than the purchase order for the original computer system, and any company planning for distribution must be aware of hidden expensive costs, such as netware, special software and maintenance.

1.9 Distributed Environments Of Tomorrow

Tomorrow's integrated information architecture needs to be thought of as a Co-operative Computing Environment (CCE) and not just a Distributed Computing Environment (DCE). A good way to picture a CGE environment is the analogy with most modern mini-computers. If you open up the box you will find several computers, a processing element, an input/output element, a memory management element, a number of processor elements, etc. These various elements are connected together by a high speed network or computer backplane; all the elements are designed to work and look like a single machine, but each element has a specific task. The level of co-operation and the integrity and speed of that co-operation delivers powerful mini computer performance. The CCE is an extension of the same principal outside the computer box. It uses high speed networks and computers but offers the potential flexibility to choose the elements that service your requirements best. The operation of a CCE can be thought of as a series of client and server relationships and represents a set of computer systems operating together as a single integrated whole. The server is a network-addressable processor or process that supplies the same service to other processors on the network. The client can either be another server (process) or a workstation that is providing the interface for the information to the end user. To build a Co-operative Computing Environment requires an imaginative understanding of what user requirements will be like as we move more and more to the use of information as a competitive weapon. We can try and define these potential user needs in three areas: applications resident on heterogeneous standards-driven networks; consistent transparent, secure access to distributed information; and natural, personal, intelligently assisted user interfaces. To meet these needs we need to develop evolutionary integrated information architectures that bridge the gap between current offerings and one that anticipates emerging standards and technical contributions. This will provide a framework for managing the CCE environment. We will need to de-emphasize the proprietary "complete solution" in favour of providing easy access to the combined power of networked, multi-vendor, standards driven solutions. This must encompass hardware, software and service. The development of sophisticated CCEs requires continued technological development in many areas:

- extensive, high speed networking based on standards;
- processors with flexible, open, scalable, balanced power;
- integrated data management with concurrent access to various database and data management models;
- code interchangeability across the network;
- workstation/server flexibility;
- integrated co-processors and integral multi-processing;
- high level use of instrumentation for network management; and
- user interfaces that make the workstations part of the society infrastructure just like the telephone or television.

Building a CCE requires the confidence that you can have the benefits of the traditional centralised, proprietary solution, the benefits of distributed computing and all the flexibility of picking the components that fit you best. It will certainly give you the best opportunity for Information Technology to support your thrust into the new global markets that we will all be operating in, whatever your competitive agenda is. Whether it is to achieve a global perspective on markets and competitors, let customer needs dictate strategy, structure and quality, focus on quality to reduce costs, use better information to manage and improve all business processors or build consensus and teamwork. There will be many potential areas to gain competitive advantage. For example, competitive differentiation could be achieved by acquiring better market intelligence, tightening relationships with customers and suppliers, creating new products and services, shortening the product development cycle and improving the quality of products and services. The revenue stream can be influenced by increased sales productivity and improved cash collection. Cost structures can be changed by the improved effectiveness of business functions (do the right things), the improved efficiency of business functions (do them well), and the gain of working capital (effective inventory management). Whatever business you are in and however wide your markets, the opportunities for commercial competitive advantage are there, though they are not easy to get at. The support necessary for this thrust for competitive advantage is the imaginative use of Information Technology, and the use of a Co-operative Computing Environment gives you the best chance of achieving these goals.

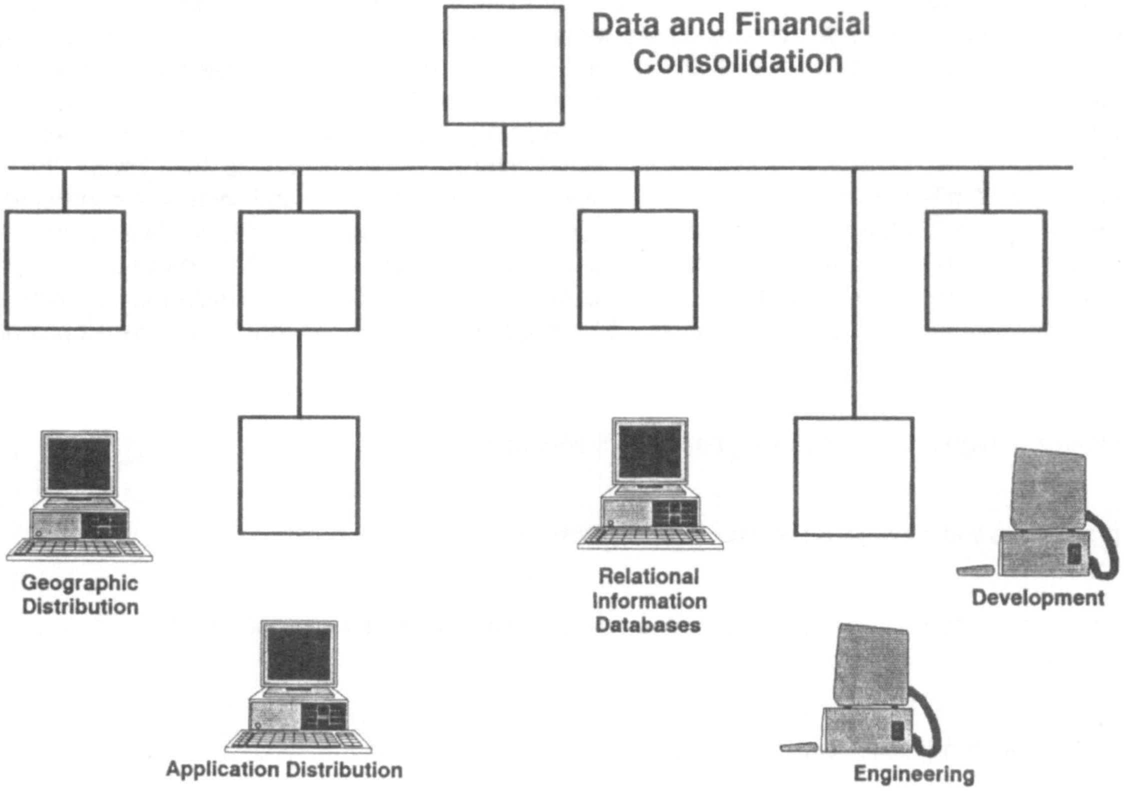

Figure 13: Co-operative Computing Environments

References

[1] INMAN, W.H and BIRD, THOMAS J.Jr. (1986) : The Dynamics of Data Base. Prentice-Hall.

[2] HOLLOWAY, S. (1990): The Distributed Development Environment: CASE Tools and Data Dictionaries in partnership. DATA MANAGEMENT 89, R. F. Williams (ed), Gower Technical Press, pp24-40.

DISTRIBUTION - SOLUTION OR PROBLEM?

Tim Bourne
Structured Information Analysis Methods

2.1 Introduction

"Distribution" is one of the newer buzzwords in our vocabulary, so perhaps it is worth exploring what it means. Like "relational", "object-oriented" and "integrated", it seems that anything worth buying nowadays has to be "distributed". But is that all there is to it? Is this really nothing more than sales patter?

In recent years there has been a trend towards the distribution of data and its processing in all but the smallest companies. In part this is due to the growth in the profit-centre management approach, which leads managers to want control of their own data. This is particularly true where the parts of a business have substantial autonomy from one another and from their head office, and where there is a significant geographical spread.

In the past some major corporations have opted for large central data processing centres, with a single central database and terminals spread over a wide area, or even worldwide. This approach incurs considerable communications costs, and potentially also exposes the business to the risk of communications failures or delays. Some form of distributed approach can reduce this risk, increase the resilience of systems and improve the responsiveness of the applications. There are those who would tell us that this trend signals the death of the large mainframe computer; it must surely be pure coincidence that they are usually those who sell smaller systems.

But perhaps there is something of value to be searched for here, some significant benefits which we should all be looking for. Maybe the trend towards distribution of applications offers us the promise of being able to build systems which will be better suited to the needs of the business customers. This chapter considers how applications can be built for a distributed environment.

2.2 Distribution As A Problem

It is certainly true that introducing the concept of distribution into the design of applications increases complexity, both of the resulting software and of the development task. With increased complexity comes increased cost, and we must be very sure that the benefits will outweigh this extra expense. It is also likely that a distributed solution will be more sensitive than a centralised one to organisational changes, which often involve the physical movement of responsibilities from one location to another.

2.3 Distribution As A Solution

On the other hand, there is no doubt that there are real problems to which distribution offers part of the solution. Where it is essential that continuous information systems support be available to a variety of locations in the face of communications or systems failure, some form of distribution of data is often inevitable. Costs can also be reduced if some data is held only locally, and a central database holds only data of corporate interest. Such an arrangement is also consistent with the growing trend towards management decentralisation; local management of information matches local management of other resources.

Another motivation for distribution occurs when it is necessary to make essential independent systems behave for some purpose as a single larger system. For example, the system of each credit card issuer is independent for some purposes; on the other hand, credit checking would be unworkable if they could not all be regarded as a single system when necessary.

Finally, the distribution of functions between subsystems is sometimes required because there is no single combination of hardware and software well-suited to all the functions of the intended system.

2.4 Types Of Distribution

2.4.1 DISTRIBUTED DBMS

Database management systems are now becoming available which can manage data distributed across two or more locations in a way which is completely transparent to the applications. As shown in Figure 1, the communication here is between the database management systems, each of which must know the location of all the data. There is as yet no standard to which such systems can conform; it is therefore necessary to choose between them very carefully. The choice of how the data is distributed is under the control of the database designer, usually based on the type of the data or on actual data values. Because the location of data is not known to the application, and the application logic is not known to the DBMS in advance, it is normally necessary for all the distributed nodes to be available at all times; this may be a problem in a widely-dispersed business.

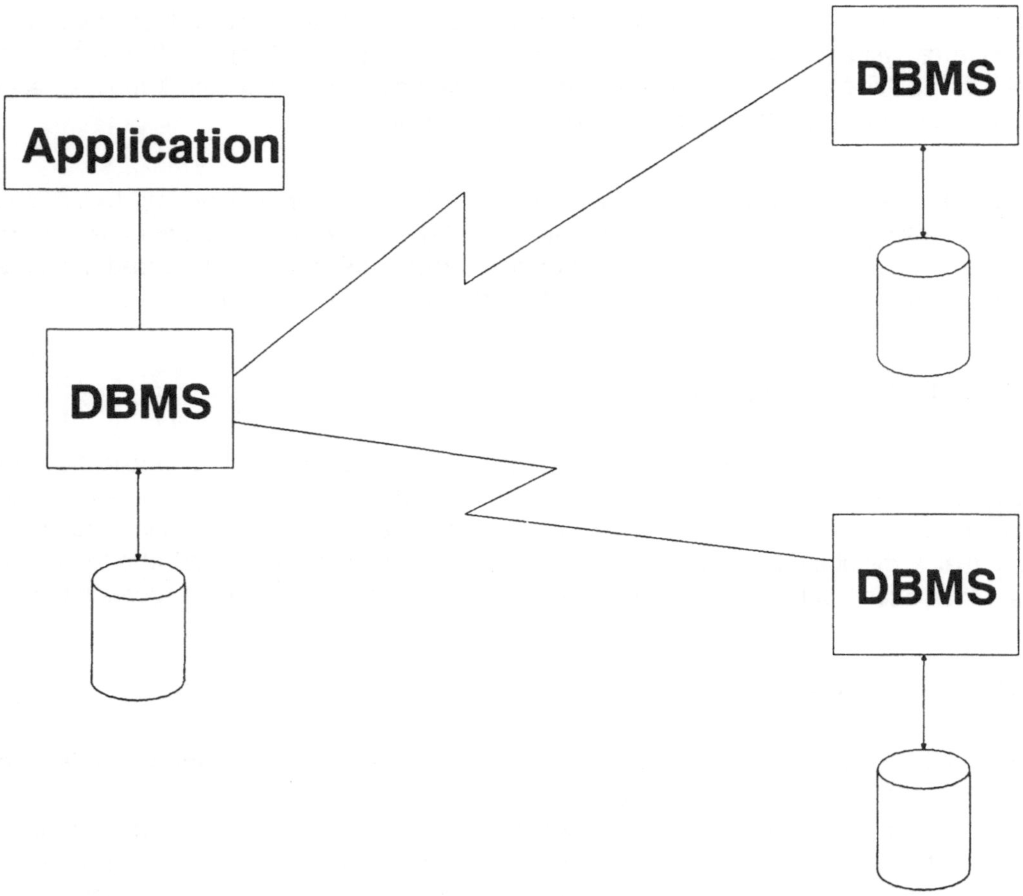

Figure 1 : Distributed DBMS

2.4.2 DISTRIBUTED DATABASE CONTROLLED BY APPLICATIONS

As Figure 2 shows, with this approach the application must be aware of the location of each item of data, and must request data from the appropriate DBMS or file handler. International standards are under development which will support this sort of remote access to relational databases in a controlled way. A key factor in managing secure updating of data across two or more locations is the availability of a two-phase commit protocol, which is currently not supported by most database management systems. This is necessary so that the application can be sure that if any of the updates within a transaction fails, all the other updates can be reversed. This requires a more complex version of the rollback facility described in Chapter One. The need for two-phase commit can be avoided if each transaction updates data in only one location.

Since the manner of distribution is totally under the control of the applications, the criteria for deciding where to locate each item of data can be much more flexible. This approach has been used in a number of applications, including for example several instances of distributed stock control, where each warehouse has its own system managing ts own stock, and a central system accesses all these to manage replenishment and reordering.

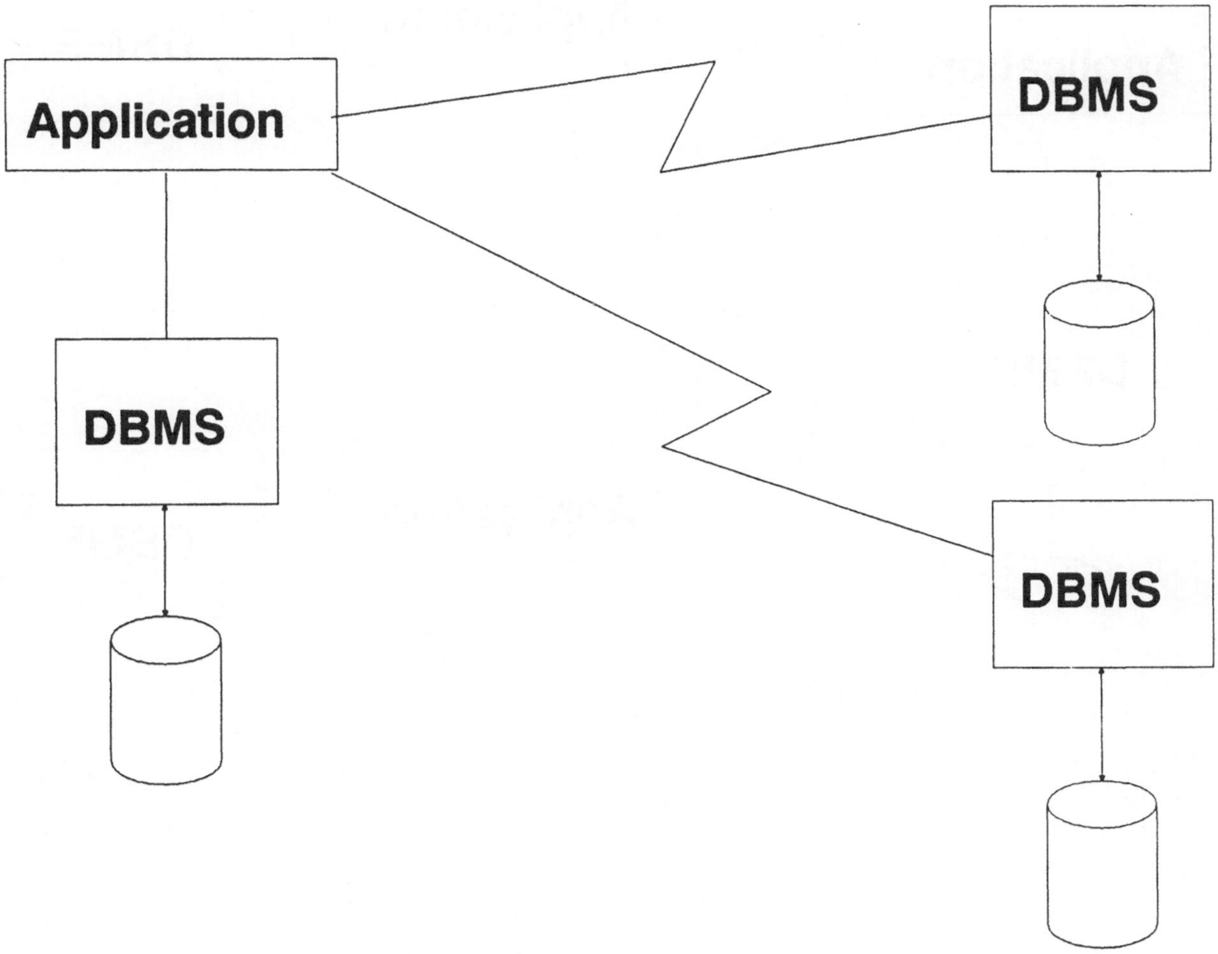

Figure 2 : Distributed Database Controlled By Applications

2.4.3 DISTRIBUTED PROCESSING

Here, as shown in Figure 3, the interface with the data at remote locations is through the remote applications. When an application determines that it needs some service from another location, it sends the request together with any relevant data, and waits for the response before proceeding.

The advantage of this approach is that the data at each location can only be updated by applications at that location, so there is less complexity. Each location can be served by whatever hardware and software combination is most appropriate to the applications and the workload, and the communication is always between applications. Since the requesting application waits for a response, the scope of an application may be impaired if some locations are not active.

Some reservations systems demonstrate the usefulness of this approach. It allows a single gateway system to support reservations terminals and provide access to other systems which manage specific resources; for example, an airline reservations systems may also act as a gateway to hotel or car rental systems.

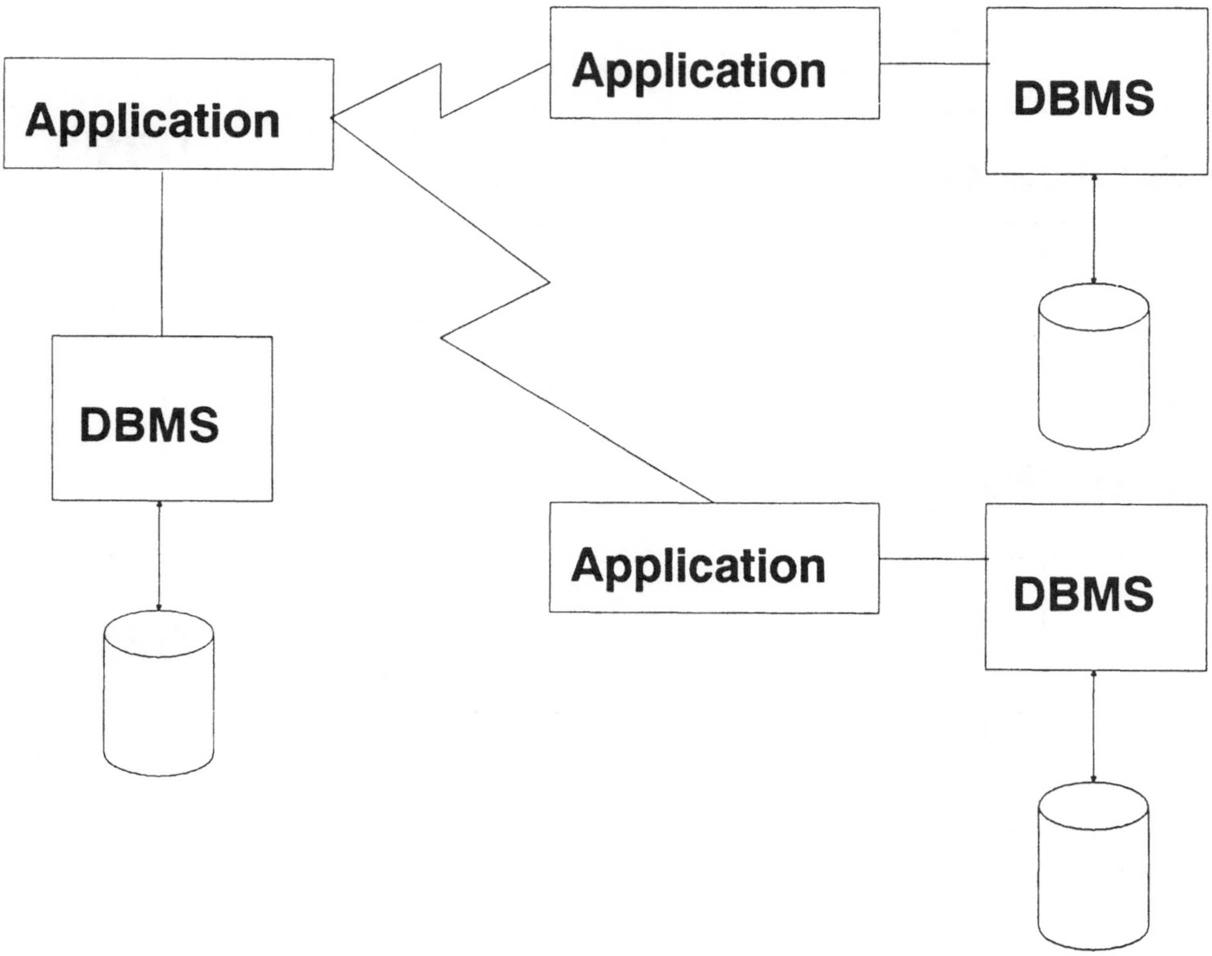

Figure 3 : Distributed Processing

2.4.4 DISTRIBUTED TRANSACTIONS

Figure 4 shows an approach which has been in use for some time, and is growing in importance. The essential difference from the previous case is that the distributed systems operate independently of one another, communicating asynchronously by sending transactions. The various forms of standardisation of Electronic Data Interchange (EDI) message formats will be of great value in promoting this activity, which is possible between as well as within corporations. An obvious example is the use of SWIFT protocols to transfer funds and give instructions for other financial transactions.

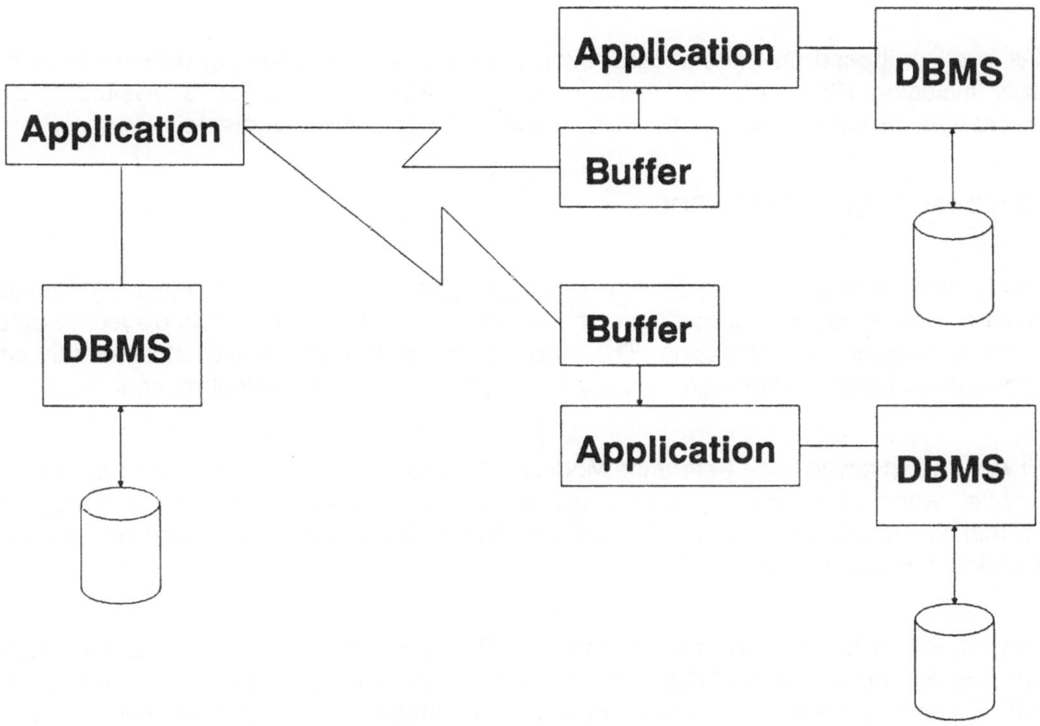

Figure 4 : Distributed Transactions

2.5 Standards Relevant To Distributed Systems

2.5.1 A FRAMEWORK FOR DISTRIBUTION

Within the last two years ISO has established a working group (ISO/IEC JTC1/SC21/WG7) charged with identifying areas of "Open Distributed Processing" where standards are needed. The emphasis is on the facilities needed for two or more independent systems to co-operate in achieving some processing objective. The first task of the group will be to create a "Reference Model" which provides a framework for positioning potential standards.

2.5.2 DATA MANAGEMENT STANDARDS

In the area of data management standards work has been under way for some time to produce a Reference Model for Data Management, again intended to provide a framework for identifying potential standards. The latest working draft includes new text related to the distribution of data and the processes which access data.

Further advanced is the work on Remote Database Access (RDA). When complete, this will specify a protocol whereby a process in one system can access a database in another system. A Draft International Standard covering RDA for SQL databases is expected before the end of 1990. Work will follow on remote access facilities for IRDS (see below).

A Framework for Information Resource Dictionary Systems (IRDS) has now completed most of the stages of standardisation, and is likely to become an International Standard during 1990. Work on the second standard in this field is well advanced, and is likely to lead to a Draft Proposal for an IRDS Services Interface by mid-1991. The relevance of this to distribution is that it will ease the use of common specifications in the development of distributed systems.

Work has been proposed on the standardisation of methods for exchanging data between standard databases, including IRDs, and the result of a "New Work Item" ballot is awaited. This would complement RDA facilities by easing the offline transfer of data between systems.

2.5.3 COMMUNICATIONS STANDARDS

The focus for work in this area is ISO/IEC JTC1/SC21 (Open Systems Interconnection). The scope of this committee now includes data management, in recognition of the central role played by data in any sort of communication or processing. The word "open" in the title is indicative of the emphasis on interconnection between heterogeneous systems, often under independent management.

The now well-known seven-layer Reference Model of OSI is the basis for all standards work in this field. In this model, which of course represents just one of many possible views, data management fits largely within the Applications Layer, the highest. Within OSI protocols are defined covering many aspects of data communications.

Finally, one specific OSI standard deserves mention. The standard on File Transfer and Access (FTAM) defines protocols for the transfer of data in "conventional" files between systems, and for access to data in such files. Lacking the data structuring concepts of databases, though, this facility is not directly relevant to the problems of most system builders today.

2.5.4 WHEN TO DISTRIBUTE

Several factors may indicate an opportunity to gain benefits by the distribution of data or processing. Sometimes the prime motivation is company policy: each profit centre is to be autonomous and manage its own data. This is fine in principle, but may make it very difficult for head office to pull together the necessary control information; here remote access to the local databases may solve the problem. It is also important to avoid creating a systems structure which is only appropriate to the current organisation structure; in many companies the organisation structure changes more often than it is economic to develop new systems.

As the cost of minis and personal computers falls faster than that of larger computers, there is pressure to move away from the large central computer and associated database. In distributing data it is important to distinguish between data which is essentially only of local interest, and data which has corporate significance and must be widely available.

The distribution of processing needs across time zones is a factor which can work either for or against distribution. Sometimes a single processing centre can deal with processing needs in, for example, the United States and Europe, since the peak times do not overlap, and total processing costs are lower. On the other hand, it may happen that processing costs are lower if a system is operated only during local office hours.

Distribution of processing is sometimes forced on us because a particular requirement can only be met by special-purpose hardware or software, so that a computer is dedicated to a single application. For example, it is currently the case that most requirements for graphical interfaces can best be met using personal computers, but these do not have the capacity to hold or process a large corporate database.

2.5.5 HOW TO DISTRIBUTE

Above all, it is important to avoid being dazzled by the wonders of what technology can perform. As we have seen, there are several levels at which distribution can be effective, and the choice is not easy. It is vital to be motivated by the intended benefits, rather than by the technical challenge.

A prime factor in the choice of approach will be corporate policy. The distributed DBMS is only viable if there is strong central management; departmental automomy tends to lead to a diversity of systems which prohibits this solution. The greater the degree of local automony, the greater the likelihood that some form of distributed processing or distributed transaction approach will be the best solution.

The need for resilience may dictate a system architecture in which most applications can continue operation even if some nodes are not available. Most forms of distribution can contribute to this objective, but distributed transaction processing gives the greatest flexibility. The latter approach is also indicated if different co-operating systems have different operating hours, or even days. For example, some form of transaction buffering is called for if different operating companies in different locations have to comform to different patterns of public holidays.

One factor which must never be ignored is the availability of the necessary supporting software. There are database management systems, particularly at the lower end of the market, which are totally inadequate to support distribution. It is very important to ensure that the security of the data receives sufficient attention.

2.5.6 WHETHER TO DISTRIBUTE

There is no doubt that the distributed approach, carefully followed, can lead to real benefits, in both systems and business terms. There is also an increasing range of technology available, supported by a growing collection of relevant international standards. As with database technology, though, it is necessary to sound a warning note: the biggest problems are not technical, but in managing a task of substantially greater complexity than ever before.

COMPLEX DISTRIBUTED INFORMATION SYSTEMS AND CASE TECHNOLOGY

James McFarlane
CREON Business Systems

3.1 Overview

The constant technological evolution and change of the 1970s and 1980s has seen the Information Technology horse pull the business and organisational cart forward at an ever increasing pace. As we enter the 1990s the pace of change is quickening to such an extent that the now enlightened cart is in danger of overtaking the horse in its ever more sophisticated demands.

In the words of Porter: "Technological change is one of the principal drivers of competition" [1]; this observation is never more true than now. There are many well documented cases where IT has been used by organisations to gain and maintain a competitive advantage [2], [3], [4] in the marketplace. Or where the strategic use of IT has produced complete realignment of whole market sectors, from the unanticipated participation of new market players in an existing and seemingly stable marketplace.

This paper sets out to examine whether the tools we are currently using to build information systems are adequate or sufficiently embracing to build the application systems which business and commerce will wish and demand we build in the 1990s. For the purposes of this paper I only propose to focus on the toolset which has been described by the term CASE, an emergent technology of the 1980s.

To be able to address our question of whether we have the correct CASE tools for the 1990s, we must first ascertain what are the likely new breeds of information systems and applications we would wish to build. We must therefore begin our search for some answers by trying to establish what will be the shape of business and organisational evolution and its IT demands in the 1990s.

3.2 Doing Business In The 1990s?

Much of what we read [5] and hear about at management seminars focuses on the issues surrounding the management of organisational change. For most organisations the traditional 5, 7 or 10 year corporate strategy plan has all but died an agonizing death. Most organisations are now faced with corporate strategy planning on a continual basis. Constantly trying to decide whether to rely on the creation of an offensive corporate posture, or focus on the implementation of a defensive corporate strategy, depending on which are the most important crisis issues of the day. With all this chaos in the markets, a number of reflections and observations have become quite clear, such that any organisation which ignores these, does so at its own peril.

The issues which will shape the organisations of the 1990s are as follows:

a. *Organisational size is no longer a guarantee for survival:* it is now an almost common weekly occurrence to watch multi-billion dollar organisations rapidly disappear, through either bankruptcy, acquisition or merger.

b. *Increased environmental turbulence:* is occurring at all market levels, from the effects of internal restructuring of political and ideological boundaries in Eastern Europe, to intra-market competition within niche marketplaces occupied by aggressive market players.

c. *Rapid erosion of competitive advantage:* is particularly true in the development of innovative products and services.

d.*Rapid obsolescence of knowledge:* is a constant challenge in all markets and is very evident in our own constantly evolving IT industry.

e. *Increased complexity of management decision making:* leading to the increased demand for support information, and very often ending in the management crisis of data overload and information scarcity.

f. *Customer requirement for greater choice:* leading to the demise of mass markets and mass market production techniques.

g. *Small players are successfully penetrating global markets:* creating a global presence of highly flexible and adaptive niche market players.

h. *Greatly increased demand for higher quality products and a faster market response:* resulting from a "life-style" based leverage from consumers.

i. *Increase in competitive threats from unanticipated quarters:* no market sector is now secure from market players who do not play by the established or agreed rules of competition.

All these issues and many more will change the shape, structure and management styles we have seen organisations exhibiting in the 1970s and 1980s.

It is true to say the organisations which successfully master the responses to the above reality will be the market leaders at the beginning of the 21st Century.

As the 1990s see us departing from an industrially based society to an information based economy, the shape of organisational survivors, winners and successful players in the 1990s may share the following organisational profile:

- smaller organisations with very flat management structures. Where service and product innovation is at the core of the organisational structure.

- Organisations which will be niche market creators and players.

- Organisations which will be highly flexible and adaptive, capable of responding to weak market input signals. With adaptable organisational structures, business strategies, management styles, products, technology and cultures.

- Organisations which will be highly quality conscious.

- Organisations which will be internationalist in market activity and penetration.

- Organisations which will have the ability to think, plan and implement strategically.

- They will have the ability to form strategic alliances with both consumers and suppliers.

- Inevitably these organisations will be those that will make creative use of Information Technology.

These issues will apply equally to both large, medium and small organisations. The largest structural upheaval and change will be in the biggest organisations, as they try to reorganise and position themselves to meet the realities of doing business in the 1990s.

To meet these goals and manage the frequent organisational change required, highly flexible management information systems need to be developed. These highly adaptive MIS applications will not exhibit the traditional life-cycle characteristics of inception, creation, development, maintenance, death and then possible re-birth. The information systems we shall build in the 1990s will be subject to constant evolutionary change, where functionality and utility will be in constant flux, depending on the prevailing market conditions and organisational change.

The consequences for IS development tools such as structured methods based CASE is quite clear. If the premise by which we have conventionally and consistently built our systems in the past changes, then those structured frameworks and method based approaches need to evolve or radically alter if they are to be of use to us in the construction of the information systems of the future.

3.3 Applications Of The 1990s

Paul Strassmann [6] makes the pointed observation that many organisations will depart from the management activity of cost justifying investment in information technology to support operational needs, thus linking investment to specific strategic goals, and applying information technology to the process of innovation within the management practices and business missions of organisations to raise their competitive awareness and strategic business goals.

As I have already indicated, the mechanism for change in developing complex information systems in the 1990s, will be derived from the turbulence in changing external environments within which organisations will conduct their business. The question still remains as to what kind of applications will be developed in the 1990s, and how will they significantly differ from those developed in the 1970s and 1980s.

To be able to answer this, we must turn our attention to the nature and structure of organisations, and more importantly, how various operational layers within the organisation utilise information.

In Figure 1 the use of information within an organisation may be structured as a pyramid. At each layer in the pyramid information flow and use of that information differs:

- *Strategic Information:* drives the corporate decision making processes within all organisations. The information at this level is highly unstructured, random in its format and content, and is transmitted randomly throughout the organisation through a variety of media and mediums.

- *Tactical Information:* supports the business decision taking processes within organisations. The information at this level is structured and quantifiable, usually of a known format and content, but is very often randomly processed by the organisation. This information is usually transmitted internally through known or identifiable media.

- *Operational Information:* supports the day-to-day activities of the organisation. The information at this level is highly structured and inherently non-random in format, content or occurrence.

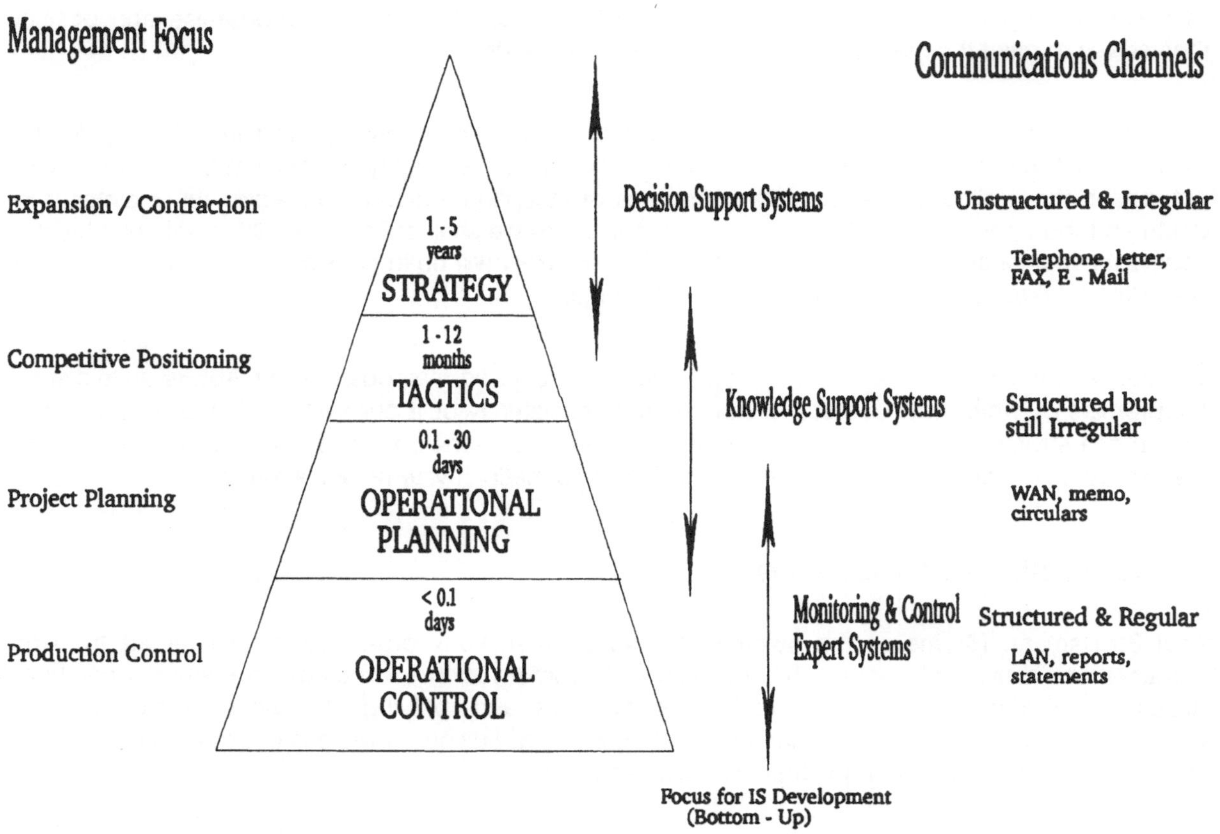

Figure 1: Organisational Structure

If we classify the information systems most organisations have built through the 1970s and 1980s we can identify that nearly all applications can be classified as systems needed for providing operational control, processing information and/or supporting tactical information requirements.

Although operational and tactical systems will need to be rebuilt and upgraded in the 1990s, the primary focus for developers of greenfield information systems will be to build advanced applications to support the types of information processes needed in the unstructured world of corporate decision making.

An Interesting feature of the focus for developing information systems over the past 20 years is that the bulk of the operational information processing systems built in the 1970s and early 1980s were based on the concept of centralised IT operations, with centralised information and data.

With the availability of cheaper hardware and the realisation of more productive development environments, the IT shift in the 1980s has been towards a decentralised IT policy within organisations and the creation of a decentralised base for both information and data. This allows operations to closely align the processing requirements of the tactical business operational units with its information needs.

There is now mounting evidence [7] that we will see in the 1990s yet another evolutionary shift towards another information structure, consisting of a centralised information base supporting corporate information needs, consisting of information derived from a range of decentralised IT platforms supporting the informational requirements of the local tactical business units.

The resultant challenges for application builders in the business world of the 1990s, will be to construct these highly flexible, adaptive and complex information systems, supporting centralised corporate decision making across a distributed network of tactical and operational information systems.

3.4 Enabling Technologies Of The 1990s

For those people who like to be considered as technology watchers, I think they would agree that the pace of IT change in the last few years has quickened remarkably, across a broad range of technological frontiers. The technological "watershed" we have now reached as we enter the 1990s means that the underpinning technology required to operate and support the advanced applications development programme outlined in the previous section is, or very shortly will be, with us.

If we focus on the technological needs of organisations operating centralised information systems from a decentralised operational base, on a national or international basis, the technological requirements are considerable. It is worth spending a few moments to consider the essential elements of these enabling technologies and their impact on the applications of the 1990s.

Possibly, some of the greatest advances in the 1990s will be in the dramatic change in price/performance ratios of new hardware platforms, and the long awaited revolution in digital network services.

Most major hardware vendors are already providing advanced RISC based architectures which will promise a price/performance ratio orders of magnitude greater than those which form the core memory based computer architectures of the 1970s and 1980s.

In the communications markets of the 1990s ISDN (Integrated Services Digital Network) promises to provide the communications explosion necessary to provide cost effective medium wide band computer-to-computer communications. The consumer, distributor and supplier relationships will evolve a whole range of EDI based networks. These private trading environments will pose new threats and opportunities for many organisations in the 1990s.

The inevitable deregulation of European PTTs is but another step in the direction of affordable global communications. Many non-PTT organisations [8], particularly in Japan, are now prepared to group together and undertake the construction of their own global networks for voice and data services. Privately owned and operated networks providing global services run by friendly and supportive national organisations which are closely tied, possibly pose a new wave of nationalistic based domination in the vulnerable economic market of global communication networks.

The recent formation of strategic partnerships between PTTs in Britain, America and Japan supporting traffic connections in the traded financial services markets will become more common.

As transmission speeds rise and deregulation drives competition, the cost/bytes of data will drop rapidly. This in turn will spur on the forms of communication which are an integral part of the corporate decision making process. Video-conferences will inevitably become one of the most cost effective business communication medium of the early years in the 21st century. Think of the possible consequences in international business travel markets if this type of communication becomes accepted and fashionable.

The traditional constraints and complaints of lack of processing power and connectivity will rapidly drop away as being a limiting factor on the applications development process. From a developer's viewpoint, some aspects of development which we currently undertake will change completely. For example:

- Database sizing for most applications will become an act of the past. As the cost of storage media and retrieval times drops due to advances in media technology and processor speeds.

- Time critical development environments will disappear, as processing speeds and power far exceed the real world application requirements which may need to be executed.

- As industry standards improve and become more universally accepted in all quarters, vendor domination in communications, operating systems and development environments will tend to diminish.

The focus on software development will be on the speed with which future applications can be developed. Productivity and market demands for dramatic decreases in software development costs will bring pressure to bear on the methods and tools we currently use to develop applications. The need for an explosion in automation of the software development process must now prove to be one of the last productivity barriers facing the IT industry.

3.5 CASE: A Historic Perspective

In a 1987 market survey report [9] it was indicated that the software engineering need for CASE products was overwhelming. The report found that in large software development projects (ie. 60,000 executable lines of code) the following situations were very often true:

- Large software development projects were typically costing twice as much as originally budgeted.

- These projects were typically delivered one year late, and 25% of all projects surveyed were never delivered at all.

- Maintenance of these projects absorbed two thirds of the organisation's software development budget.

The report indicated that the CASE market in the USA was worth $140 million and would grow to $1 billion by 1991. One year later another market survey report was indicating that there were some 600 products within the market claiming to be automated CASE tools. The paradox is quite apparent if CASE products of the late 1980s were truly and conclusively the panacea for all software development problems. We could justifiably claim that we had solved the software development crisis.

It is quite clear, however, that as with all emerging areas of technology a certain amount of market hype about CASE often clouds the true representation of the actual situation. Coupled with the natural reluctance and scepticism of most IT managers not to rush out and buy this years "hot" product but to wait until the technology settles, the problems of developing large applications are likely to continue.

Another observation which was quite clear is that there are now a considerable number of software products claiming the technological status of CASE. I believe the definition of what constitutes a CASE product requires some clarification before we continue.

If we track the historical evolution of the combination of software development environments and methods or working practices by which software is developed, we may establish a more precise definition of what constitutes a CASE product. Figure 2 shows a potted history of applications development environments, and the corresponding methods of software development or working practices used from the late 1960s to the present day. The main focus in methods and tools to support the software development process has revolved around our appreciation of software development as an assembly line set of procedures, providing developers with a series of discrete steps for undertaking applications development. This has brought about the emulation of these sometimes manual techniques for system analysis, design and construction in an ever increasingly automated environment.

Our belief that complex applications and systems may be constructed using the principles described by the term "lifecycle" has focused on being able to improve the quality and productivity within the software development processes.

The principles surrounding CASE have evolved from our requirement to create an automated software development environment. Surprisingly perhaps, the term CASE is a relatively recent occurrence in this area of information technology. With its roots in the ideals of engineering CAD/CAM, the majority of today's CASE products are based on, or around, the encapsulation of methods or software development practices, procedures and techniques within an automated environment. CASE products are themselves just software applications, to varying degrees of sophistication.

Originally, CASE set out in the form of "analyst workbenches" was used to provide computer based automation and support for analysis and design activities within the software development "lifecycle". As time passed this automation has spread to code generation and programming support environments, and more recently lead to the integration of standard project control procedures within an automated environment and framework/methods of working.

To progress the definition of what constitutes a CASE product, I feel we must state what may be considered the minimum principal set of properties a CASE product must consist of, in order to set it apart from the whole range of software productivity tools which claim to be CASE tools.

The minimum set of properties contained within a CASE environment are as follows:

- CASE products must adhere to the ALVEY definition of software engineering principles. ALVEY defines software engineering as the computer aided application of science and engineering principles.

- Quality of product output must be the touchstone of a CASE product. A CASE product must provide a definition of quality based on metrics and formal system construction logic.

- CASE products must provide lifecycle support for the principles of software engineering.

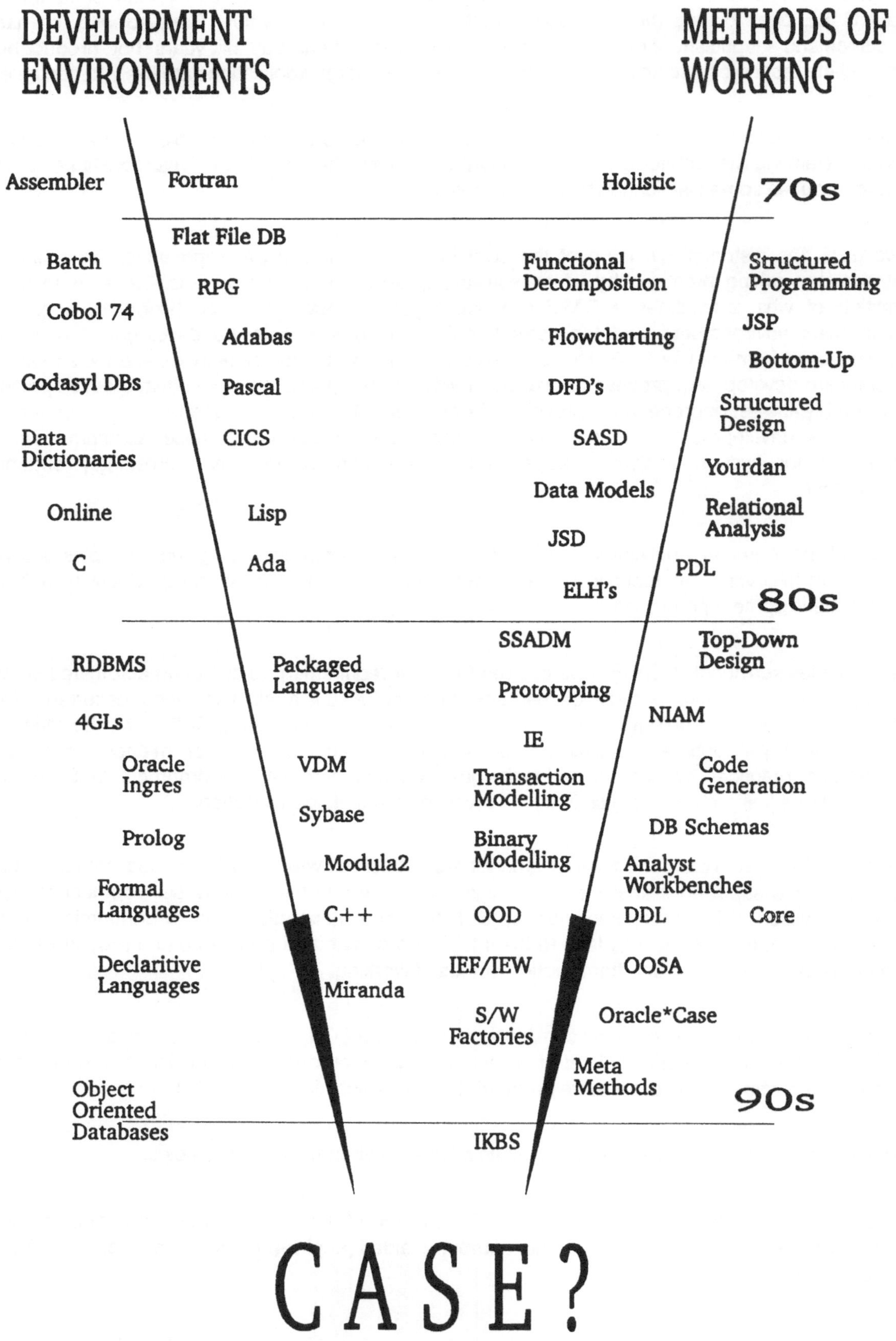

Figure 2 : The Evolution Of CASE

- CASE products must support requirements capture, analysis and specification.

- CASE products must support the formal process and data oriented approaches to systems analysis and design.

- CASE products must support the physical design and representation of systems along formal rules and logic.

- CASE products must support the act of system and application construction along the engineering principles of modular fabrication from a pre-defined set of sub-components.

- CASE products must provide a multi-working environment for teams of knowledgeable users.

- CASE products must provide a set of quality and configuration control procedures to allow for multi-working and audit trail traceability.

- CASE must aid in the act of software development complexity management from a number of viewpoints along established lines.

If we were now to apply our more rigid definition of CASE to the 600 plus products in today's marketplace, the number of products which could justifiably claim the title of a CASE product would drop to a very small percentage of the original market population.

The remaining major problems with the majority of the small number of remaining CASE products in the marketplace is that most CASE products do not have the qualities I have already outlined as being completely necessary for building the applications of the 1990s. Most contemporary CASE products and methods are built around software engineering theory and techniques designed to solve the problems of the 1960s, 1970s and early 1980s.

To truly meet our needs over the next decade, we must move away from many of the purely structured production line ideas and techniques embodied in structured analysis and systems design methods. A continual evolution in existing methods and techniques provides only the limited prospect of achieving step-by-step increase in software development automation. What is needed are newer concepts to be added to our understanding of methods and working practices, and the development of more advanced tools to support these new methodological ideas.

3.6 CASE: The Future - Evolution Or Revolution?

When we consider the current activity in the recent spate of new CASE product offerings [10], [11] we can, in the main, only detect a "more of the same" type of evolutionary picture in the CASE marketplace.

If, as I have advocated, we are to look for a revolution in the CASE marketplace, from which direction is that revolution likely to come from?

What will be the new horizons we must set for that CASE revolution?

What are the critical issues in information systems research [12]?

The answer to some of these questions may lie in the following.

3.6.1 CASE BASED BUSINESS RULES

CASE products will need to support the fundamental processes by which business rules and decisions are undertaken. Only from these may we determine the identifiable needs for the development of complex systems. Management and control of systems development through CASE by adopting systematic software metrics to deal with complexity management will be required.

CASE based techniques will enable IT strategists to classify both applications and development tools, and operational environments within which applications may be developed and operated. There will be the requirement to relate certain kinds of application's development with particular management development strategies within a business and organisational perspective.

This will probably take the form of a front-end CASE environment based on expert systems, which will integrate and extend the ideas and concepts prescribed in techniques such as SLIM and COCOMO.

3.6.2 EXTENDED SOFTWARE ENGINEERING PERSPECTIVES (ESEP)

CASE based products will need to support a considerably extended notion of software engineering principles. This will be done by including a range of system development perspectives not just in the information domain, but also in the system and organisational domains [13].

There are a whole range of domain perspectives upon and through which systems can be modelled. Those perspectives could be active during each component phase of the traditional development lifecycle of an application. The perspectives describe the types of information a developer will need to collect and assimilate. We may show by example the types of information which could be collected and analysed during a business analysis phase of any complex IS development. The perspectives now provide us with the ability to support and analyse the following development activities:

- *Function perspective:* relates to the identification of business activities that directly support the objectives of an organisation, those activities which are related to each business activity, and their interested groups.

- *Data perspective:* relates to the identification and definition of information resources, data classes, primary objects and the relationships between those objects.

- *System perspective:* defines the business systems, information systems and the complex inter-relations of systems within a problem domain. This allows us to establish an information systems architecture within an application.

- *Rule perspective:* relates to the business rules regarding products and or services; prices, sizes, delivery times and acceptance procedures are all rule-related objects associated in the business analysis phase.

- *Time and Event perspective:* defines the invocation points in the business process. Provides definition of a systems stimulus which responds to external events and interrupts.

- *Organisational perspective:* relates to the definition of the real world organisational activities linked to the logical definitions of the business functions, data classes and their attendant systems.

- *Process perspective:* is the sequencing of information transforming activities which lead to a clearly defined product, from order to delivery of that product or service to a customer.

- *Change perspective:* involves the study of the problems, possible solutions and alternatives for implementing IT and IS applications within the organisation.

- *Business and strategic goal perspective:* involves the study of the nature of the business and its goals. Undertaking strategic analysis using the principles involved in value chains and competitor analysis and other techniques necessary to identify and focus on critical IS applications or innovations.

- *Communications perspective:* includes the business needs for communications infrastructures and architectures. Issues for consideration would include EDI, and, Distributed Networks at a national or on a global basis, how the organisation communicates internally and the information flows within and between focussed business areas.

By undertaking to view information, organisational and systems development through a series of perspectives over the "lifecycle" phases of a development we can create a Meta framework or method within which future CASE products will operate and support our development and construction needs.

3.6.3 PRACTICAL ISSUES FOR ADVANCED CASE PRODUCTS

The CASE products of the revolution must adhere to the principles supporting the "Open Systems" architectures. Architectural considerations are paramount in preserving an organisation's investment in the applications developed from CASE products. "Time to ultimate obsolescence" will be one of the watch-phrases. To this end, CASE environments must be capable of constructing systems which have the following critical success factors:

- CASE produced applications must be host environment independent.

- CASE produced applications must be database platform independent.

- The CASE tools themselves must be method independent.

In addition, CASE products must be able to connect and interconnect with other established system development tools and environments such as:

- Project management and control tools.

- Quality and configuration management tools.

- Documentation production environments.

- Project and organisational cost accounting and control methods.

- System performance assessment tools, etc.

Currently, I do not see any of the latest CASE products from any of the major CASE vendors addressing more than a few of the above revolutionary issues needed in the systems development world. Until these issues are addressed across a broad front, evolution not revolution will pervade the CASE marketplace of the 1990s.

3.7 Conclusions

In this paper I have laid out the arguments and described the need for change in the methods and tools we have to adopt for the development of information systems in the 1990s.

I have indicated that in the near future it will be business and organisational needs not technological advances which will drive the development of ever more sophisticated and complex information systems. It is clear that the current industry response to the likely challenges manifest themselves in the prospect of an evolutionary advance in the current technology rather than any revolutionary next step. I have advocated that if we are to meet those business challenges of the future we need to broaden and deepen our range of system development methods, tools and environments.

I would like to close my paper by setting a new goal for CASE products in the 1990s. I believe we should focus on developing CASE based products which will enable us to truly meet the software engineering challenges of developing complex information systems. The use of CASE, should in the future enable us to declare in advance of constructing a system:

- *How much it will cost?*

- *How long it will take?*

- *And that we can deliver the required systems to our customers expectations?*

These I believe are the challenges for CASE in the 1990s.

References

[1] PORTER, M. E. (1985) : Competitive Advantage. Free Press.

[2] McFARLAN, F. W. (1984) : Information Technology changes the way you compete. Harvard Business Review, May-June.

[3] KEEN, P. G. W. (1986) : Competing in Time, Ballinger.

[4] CANNING, R. (1984) : Developing Strategic Information Systems, EDP Analyzer, Vol 22, No 5.

[5] PETERS, T. (1987) : Thriving on Chaos: Handbook for Management Revolution. Pan Books.

[6] STRASSMANN, P. A. (1985) : Information Payoff, Free Press.

[7] BRADSHAW, D. (1990) : Around the world in a way that pays, Financial Times, January 1990.

[8] CARLYLE, R. (1990) : The Tomorrow Organisation, Datamation, February 1990.

[9] HEWETT, J. & DURHAM, T. (1987) : Software Engineering: Commercial Strategies, OVUM Report.

[10] HEWETT, J. (1990) : AD/Cycle, Software Europe 5, OVUM Report, February 1990.

[11] EDITORIAL (1990) : Trio State Their CASE, Multi-User Computing, January 1990.

[12] BOLAND, R. J. & HIRSCHHEIM, R. A. (1987) : Critical Issues Information Systems, in Boland, R J & Hirschheim, R A, (eds), Wiley.

[13] JONES, R. (1990) : The Holistic Approach , Software Development Monitor.

DATA ACCESS ISSUES

INTERNATIONAL DATA DISTRIBUTION

Richard Williams Ph.D.
Richalis Ltd

4.1 Introduction

4.1.1 THE EVER WIDENING HORIZON OF CUSTOMER NEEDS FOR DATA

The development of data processing, management and distribution over the past 20 years has been remarkable to say the least. Significant changes have occurred in not only the way in which customer requirements for data access have been addressed, but also the purposes behind those requirements.

Twenty years ago data processing was a relatively basic activity, with large, central processing units supporting simplistic administrative functions. Batch processing of such systems supported the requirements of payroll and other such basic administrational business processing. The systems developed were lacking in data management facilities (even rudimentary database management systems were a rarity), and primarily geared at simple file processing.

These systems were centralised in their processing intelligence, connecting dumb transaction processing facilities at best. They were costly to develop, even more costly to maintain, and isolated in respect to other business processing that had potential interest in the data they held.

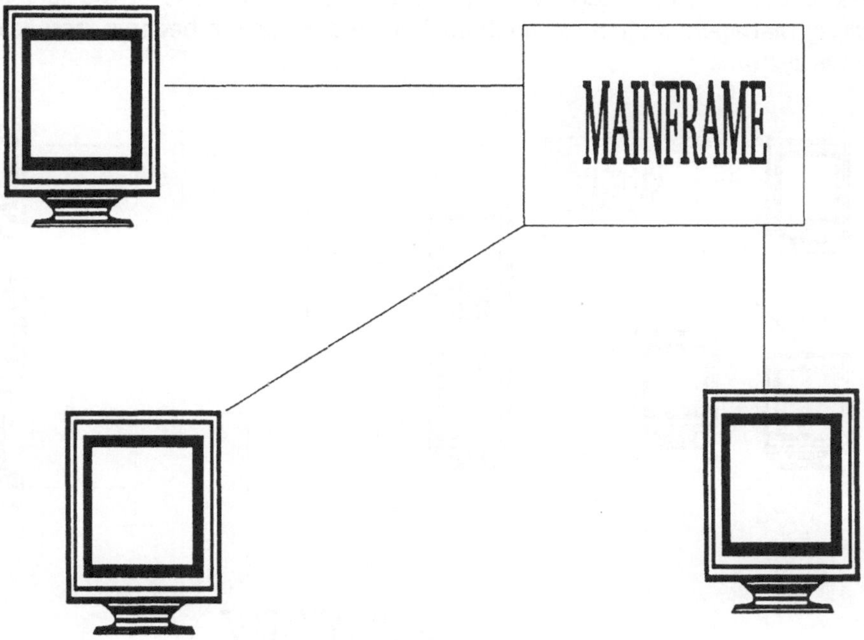

Figure 1 : The 1970s : Central Processing With Dumb Terminals

The early 1980s introduced database management systems to a wide commercial market, and at the same time the personal computer arrived. The two processing facilities (PC and mainframe) had the capability to talk to each other via LANs, although ease of access across the architectures was limited, and the capability to share the data they contained was significantly restricted.

The purposes that the two processing facilities were put to were often entirely different, with the large mainframes still undertaking batch processing activities and supporting administrative functions, whilst the PCs were used for estimating and forecasting and other such planning functions, as well as word processing type activities.

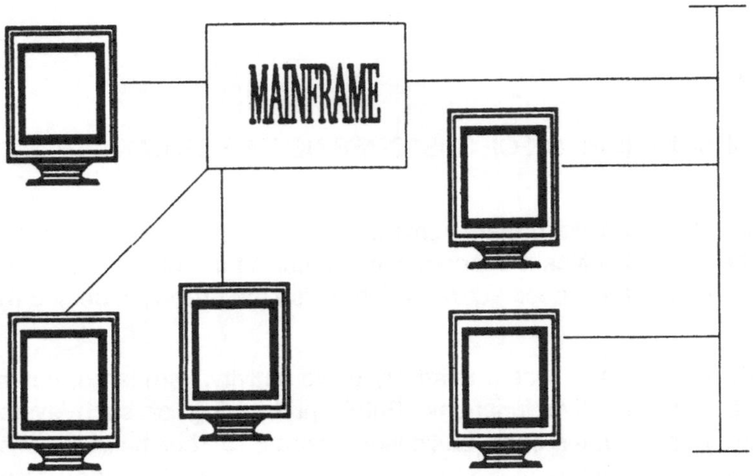

Figure 2 : The Early 1980s : PC LANs And Mainframe Connectivity

By the mid 1980s the PC world was able to come together via Wide Area Networks and started to share its data amongst larger communities of users. Functionality increased as processing capacities increased, and it was also possible to develop office systems in the environment, with the arrival of PC database packages. At the mainframe level processing activities became more powerful, and with the advent of a wider use of data dictionaries, and a growing awareness of the fact that data was a resource requiring management just as much as finance or people it became increasingly possible to share data across systems.

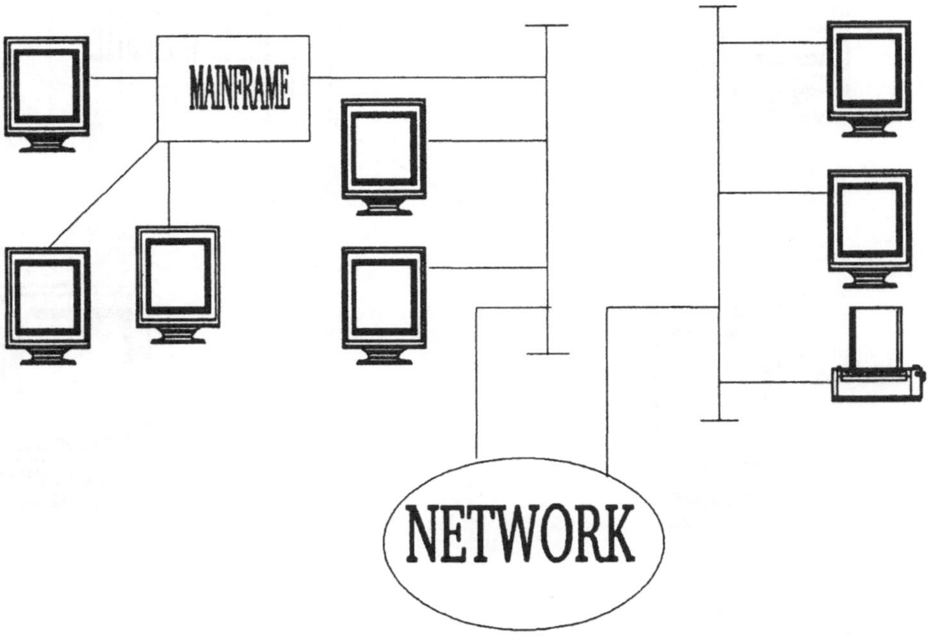

Figure 3 : The Mid 1980s : WANs And Mainframe Data Sharing

The end of the decade saw the arrival of corporate data centres, whose primary purpose was to make all data more widely available across an enterprise. Coupled with capabilities of local file sharing and local applications it is now possible for data to be distributed across the hitherto unassailable gulf between the PC and the mainframe.

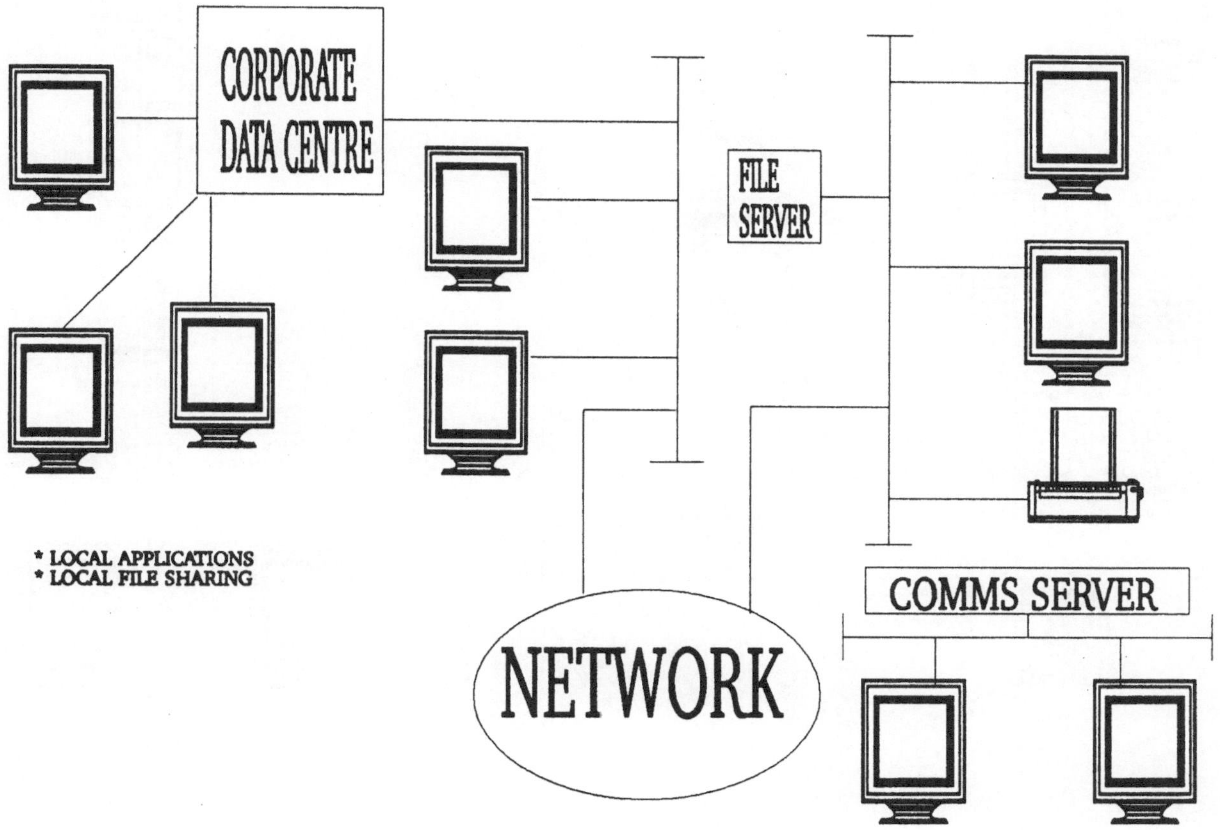

Figure 4 : The Late 1980s : Office Services And Local File Sharing

Stonebreaker [1] has argued that within a few years it will be possible to link a set of cheap PCs together, managed by a relational DBMS across a distributed network with the capabilities of large central processors in terms of MIPs. The days of the large central processor (such as the 100 MIP IBM Sierra) machines were numbered, he argued. At the same time Date [2] put forward his "12" rules of data distribution, and many people started planning for the day of the distributed system. To a large extent that day has already arrived. Technology (theoretically), already enables processor communities of PCs to emulate and exceed the capabilities of the large central processors. Intelligence, in terms of processing, is already on the desk top. The arrival of 486 and soon heralded 586 processors in PCs enables these prophecies to be realised.

Further developments in technology into the 1990s, object orientated programming, co-operative processing, interworking, complex WANs and other facilities are already being given realistic timescales for implementation, and many of the data management problems of distributed systems processing (notably two phase commit) are already being tested. In this respect the distributed data and processing time is already upon us.

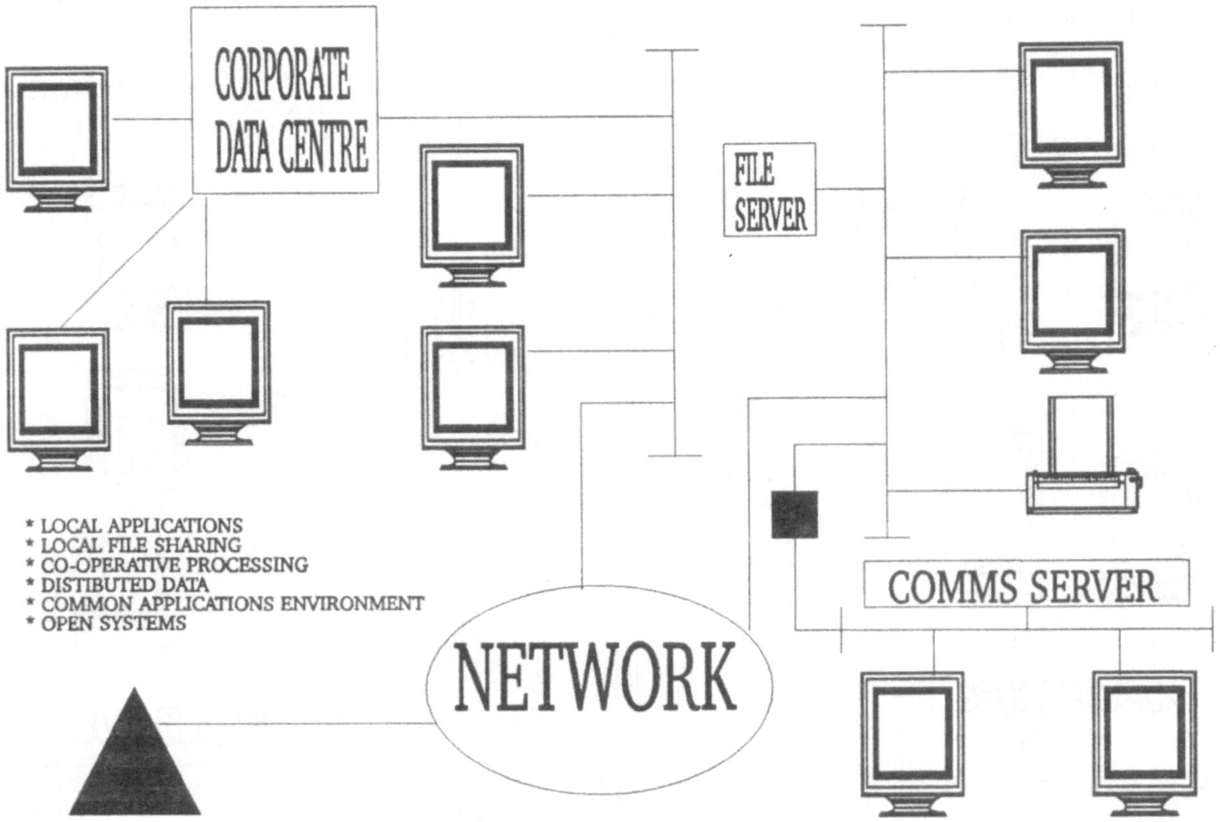

Figure 5 : The 1990s : Open Systems And "True Distributed Systems"

In terms of the business purposes for data processing, the goals have also changed equally rapidly. Instead of developing data processing systems to replace human administrative functions with automated ones, business personnel are looking for computers to give them the competitive advantage. Basic functionality considerations are taken as read, and the true purpose of systems developments in the 1990s is to increase organisations' market share whilst undercutting competitors. The systems produced are ever more complex, ever more expensive and ever more difficult to manage than was the case in the past, because of the business criticality of improvements in business performance offered by computerisation. In order for many companies to survive through the 1990's investment in the integration of systems for business gain, rather than administrative cost savings, is the name of the game.

The growing recognition that data is a significant and saleable asset for many organisations has lead many to consider its capacity for sharing across organisational boundaries in joint venture activities. The needs for such collaboration are based upon the premise that data is a valuable resource, and can be re-used, repackaged and resold.

In order to realise such business opportunities data processing personnel, and notably data management personnel, have to take on board new roles, address basic issues in new contexts, and acknowledge that wider ranging solutions to already existing problems within data management are necessary.

The business rationale for data processing is to improve business performance and create new business opportunities. Such requirements are already commonly stated within business communities, and data management personnel must be prepared to meet those challenges.

4.1.2 CURRENT DATA MANAGEMENT AND DISTRIBUTION ISSUES

Many data management personnel already clearly recognise the problems that exist in systems development in distributed contexts. Unnuk [3] made the fundamental observation that unless a system is analysed, developed and implemented by the same person, then all systems currently produced are, by their very nature, "distributed". Such a recognition forces developers to;

- address the major problem of project management in ensuring that all personnel on a project fulfil their roles effectively, and in co-ordination with each other;
- ensure that systems analysis and development standards are defined and understood;
- clearly define the architecture of support for the project (ie, CASE tool use and its linkage to the repository/dictionary);
- clearly define the likely architecture for design and development in the early stages of analysis, so as to ensure optimum support for business needs;

Even within a single geographical site this can be a problem, and one that is compounded where standards are non-existent, ill defined or not easily understood. The requirements for full and effective lifecycle support for all activities is well documented [4], and where CASE tools are used the requirements for and problems of data definition sharing and control are equally well known, [5], [6].

When one adds the problem of multiple geographical sites in which to undertake the development, the problems are instantly multiplied. The project manager must then recognise the added problems that;

- physical project management has to be devolved more comprehensively;
- electronic communications between the sites must be clearly defined and supported;
- quality and standards control must be even more rigorously supported;

Many such projects are undertaken within numerous organisations, and are completed as if they were located in one site. However, with the increasing business pressure to compete in a larger, if not global market, more wide ranging distributed developments are being initiated. It is already common for organisations to share data across their boundaries, and the Electronic Data Interchange communities are good examples of this. In the United States many large corporations make it a contractual necessity for all customers and traders/suppliers to exchange information only in EDI type formats. This is simply in response to the average cost of processing a paper invoice (c$10) and its equivalent electronic counterpart (c$2).

Such data distribution and use is effectively controlled in the UK also. EDI applications abound across many organisations, and have had a significant effect in reducing administrative costs. However, such applications really fall into our 1970s and 1980s mainframe application purposes of reducing existing administrative costs within organisations. The need of the businessman in the 1990s is for data processing to create new markets and give competitive advantage.

In such cases data is clearly an exploitable resource, capable of being shared and merged across a business community, that may be globally distributed in geographic terms, and required in many different natural languages. It may also be necessary for existing systems and data to be unified for the creation of the new business opportunity, requiring international co-operation in systems development terms. Such requirements already exist in the financial and tourism industries, and the next section of this paper examines how one such existing development in this context is coping with the technological capabilities available now.

4.2 International Data Management And Distribution Issues : The ATIS Project

4.2.1 DATA SHARING AND DISTRIBUTION REQUIREMENTS IN THE EUROPEAN TOURISM INDUSTRY

Many organisations are involved in tourist activities in varying contexts. These centre on the needs of travellers to be aware of facilities that are available in places that they wish to visit. All tourist travel is based on the availability of accurate information being provided on all relevant aspects of the places of interest. This includes the various options of travel type, accommodation and facility availability, and the required prices and times associated with them.

The information that is collected is done so by various parties. These are generally undertaken by organisations advertising locations to their best advantage. This is particularly true of national and regional tourist boards and tour operators, whose primary purpose is to attract visitors in large numbers to specific places.

However, in Western Europe there are a number of other information gatherers. They are both independent of the needs of national and regional economies, are not attempting to sell a definable product, and place the interests of the tourist at the top of their priority list. These information gatherers include touring clubs, who collect information to support the needs of their members. The members tend to be independent tourists, wishing to be flexible in terms of the places that they visit and stay at during any particular vacation. To support such requirements the clubs have collected information on all aspects of potential interest to the independent tourist. These vary from accommodation details and features to visit, to the legal and environmental details of the places to which the tourists tend to go. Information on the quality of many of these items (notably accommodation types) is included so that the members can have a degree of confidence on the facilities referenced.

Since many clubs in different Western European countries were undertaking similar activities for their respective members, senior touring managers felt that a degree of unification and standardisation in these matters would benefit all concerned. The member would have access to more detailed and wide ranging information over a geographically larger area, and the clubs could rationalise the costs of data collection and maintenance if it was undertaken in a concerted and centralised manner. It was also recognised that such unified tourist information could be sold and traded with other organisations and companies.

Three clubs became involved in such a unified initiative, known as The ATIS Project. The Alliance of international tourists Touring Information System, with partners from The Netherlands (The ANWB), The Federal Republic Of Germany (The ADAC), and The United Kingdom (The AA) made up the business consortia. Others were contacted to discuss their interest in the idea, and a number of positive responses to this approach were received. This extended the potential for co-ordinated touring information collection and provision in the future. The European Commission in Luxemburg also signalled its interest in the project, as one of its objectives is geared at attracting northern European capital, into southern European economies, resulting in EEC funding for the project under Directorate General 13 of the Community.

4.2.2 STRATEGIC BUSINESS REQUIREMENTS OF THE PROJECT

In strategic terms, the business requirements of the project were relatively easy to determine. This is because they had to reflect the expanding needs of the tourist industry and allow the concept of The Single European Market in 1992 to be reflected in the project. They can be classified as follows;

- that the results from the project provide a standard of agreement on international definitions for data of interest to tourists. This must include hotels, camp sites, national regulations, restaurants and travelling conditions within its scope;

- that both dynamic and static data must be catered for within the project. Static data is unlikely to require amendment more than twice per year, but the dynamic data, on items such as road information, is subject to change on a quarter hourly basis in some cases;

- that the standards of inspection of places and features must be uniform, allowing data quality to be guaranteed;

- that whilst the project would initially involve only three partners, it must have the flexibility and capacity to expand to include any number of further partners in the future, without significant technical difficulties;

4.2.3 THE DEVELOPMENT CONTEXT OF THE PROJECT : TECHNICAL ENVIRONMENTS

Whilst the strategic business requirements of the project were easy to determine, the development itself had to reference a number of other problems. These can best be described by examining the technical environments of the primary participants. Whilst all three clubs were significant mainframe computer users, the actual architecture of each was strikingly different;

- the German partner was a large IBM mainframe user, employing Adabas as its database management system, and Data Manager as its data dictionary;

- the Dutch partner, whilst also being primarily an IBM mainframe user, employed Datacomm as its database management system, and the ADR dictionary product Datadictionary to support it;

- the United Kingdom partner compounded these differences by being an ICL mainframe user, with IDMS-X as their database management system, and the ICL data dictionary DDS.

Hence, in machine hardware and software terms the clubs exhibited almost as much difference as they did similarity in political and business will. The mixture of the three types of newer (post hierarchic) database management systems were exhibited (inverted list (partly), relational and network), all running different dictionary environments.

It was immediately recognised that if ATIS was to be a success it would be necessary not only to have the capability to distribute tourist data via the solution, but to distribute the development and its controls. This would ensure total business relevance for the partners, but posed a number of distributed development questions for the personnel involved in producing the system solution. Not only would the commonly experienced problems of distributed systems development have to be addressed, but also;

- the problems of a development environment spread over different machine environments;
- the problems of a development environment spread over different organisations, with different development procedures and standards;
- the problems of a development environment spread over different countries, with different natural languages and with a target business environment containing even more such languages;
- an immature technical environment to work in in terms of distributed systems developments in such contexts;

To address these issues it was necessary to hold a strategic systems development conference, where all issues could be discussed, a policy agreed for their resolution, and a development plan produced.

4.3 A Strategy For Distributed Systems Development In An "Open" Environment

4.3.1 ANALYSIS STRATEGY

Even taking on board the technical problems discussed in the previous section it was fundamental for the successful development of the project that all work be undertaken in a business led environment. In this project these needs were even more clearly necessary;

- because of the potential risks of misinterpretation or understanding in respect to the different natural languages of the participants in the project;
- because the final solution and its implementation is required to be ported to other, different machine environments, and natural languages outside the three types exhibited by the initial participants.

These two primary requirements were hampered in technical terms by the lack of existing standards relating to the definitions of data dictionaries, into which the information was to be stored, and from which they were to be transferred to other such facilities. There are currently no recognised international standards for data dictionary content and connections existing. Although recommendations for standardising dictionary content and meaning are currently being worked upon, even these "standards" are subject to division. Work on the development of a set of Information Resource Dictionary Standards (IRDS) is being undertaken in Europe and Australasia, whilst in North America ANSI are undertaking separate work in the same field, which may not be directly compatible with the IRDS work in its outcomes. Coupled with the fact that it may take well into the 1990s to produce such a set of standards that suit the requirements of many users, dictionary standardisation is a major technical restriction to such developments.

4.3.2 DOCUMENTATION STRATEGY

It would be more effective in technical terms to wait for the production of a set of recommendations for dictionary standardisation in respect to at least one of the bodies currently working in the area. This was not possible given the fact that the business requirement for the system is current, and not a number of years away. It is also important to appreciate the very nature and environment of the project in terms of its geography, and its consequent political profile. To produce an achievable recommendation in this context was also a necessary requirement. In an attempt to categorise the likely problems associated with data distribution, the documentation of the analysis of the project was decided to be used as a prototype of the project's implementation.

The strategy that was produced to support this concept reflected both the political and physical aspects of the project, as well as its technical and logical needs. The outcome was as follows;

- the central physical location of the project was determined to be in West Germany, and consequently it was recognised that distributed working must be possible in the other two countries;

- that as a result of this decision on location, the central repository for the documentation produced was to be DataManager, which was the local, West German, dictionary. In this respect the other two dictionaries became its "slaves" for the duration of the analysis;

- that interfaces between the recognised "master" dictionary and its "slaves" needed to be produced internally within the project to allow distributed work on the business data definitions to be undertaken. As IRDS interface recommendations in this field do not yet exist, the resulting software developed to support the activity had to be produced and maintained by project personnel rather than the dictionary vendors;

- that only one natural language was to be used for the project, and that all work was to be undertaken in that language, which was determined to be English;

- that the analytical approach adopted was entity modelling and its associated activities, supported by a strict naming convention (IBM "OF");

- that communication between the dictionaries was to be via a unified network of PC interfaces, rather than by directly linking the dictionaries together in a truly distributed manner. This was because of the problems of the lack of vendor support and lack of standards in interface definition terms in this area.

These aspects of the strategy could be said to be sub-optimal in a number of ways in respect to a truly greenfield distributed development. This was accepted by both the business users and the technicians involved in the project, but it was felt to be the most simplistic strategy that could be developed which had the most effective chance of success. Its adoption would also enable a view on the implementation of the working system to be obtained. Consequently, the distribution of dictionary data in this manner could be used as a true "prototype" to identify any physical or logical difficulties, discrepancies or omissions in the strategy before it was placed before business users in a production context.

4.3.3 SYSTEMS DESIGN AND DEVELOPMENT STRATEGY

Given the fact that the investment in computerised infrastructure by the respective partners was significant prior to the initiation of the project, it was recognised that the resulting development must be transparent to each host environment, and thus truly "OPEN" in its form. This point is further emphasised when one considers the fact that potential target machine environments for the system to run on is not even restricted to the three current partners. Future partners must be catered for easily, and these may as easily be organisations with little or no IT investment, as organisations with large existing IT infrastructures, like the existing partners. The design and development of the system had to recognise;

- that the user presentation would be standardised and that communications would be based on international standards (X400, X500 etc);

- that the systems development must be modularised, thus allowing different users to "mix and match" functionality with their own requirements, but this would be achieved in a shared manner where common functionality was necessary;

- that the user view of the data would always reflect the ATIS "logical" view, regardless of where the data was actually stored;

- that the solution must be capable of running in a networked environment;

- that the solution must be able to be located on cheap IT facilities (PCs and/or minis);

- that users may not be DP literate, and therefore simplicity in operation must be achieved;

- that systems support must be possible in a distributed manner;

- that the design and implementation must be able to support many different needs, and therefore be flexible in its capacity to store and process data;

- that the design and implementation of the system must be able to easily interface with the partners' existing IT architectures and systems and thus protect, rather than threaten, their existing investment in IT and information systems;

- that the solution produced be forwards compatible with the partners' existing IT strategies and industry directions.

All of these points recognise the IT architectural variation of the 1990s discussed earlier. The target environment must enable co-operative processing to occur, that data be distributed in its structure and form, that there be a common applications environment, and that this is supportive of the Open Systems directives.

As some of these areas are not yet fully developed it was necessary to ensure that the ATIS solution be modularised and cheap. The capability to re-use aspects of the development as time passes and new facilities become available is essential (object oriented databases and programmimg, for example).

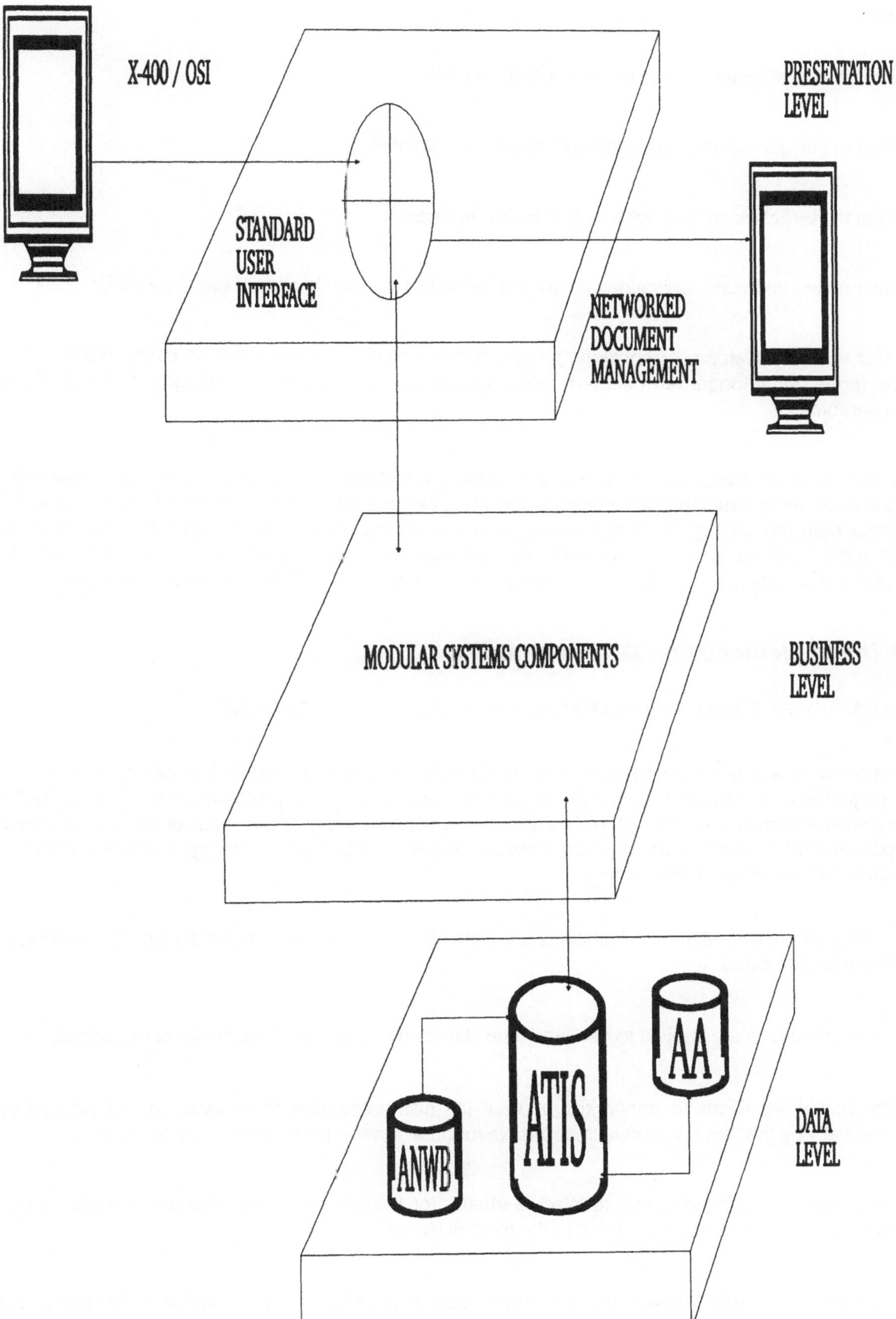

Figure 6 : The ATIS Systems Development Concept

Consequently, the design and development strategy proposed for ATIS consisted of the following points;

- that the target platform for the development is UNIX;
- that the target database management system is relational;
- that the target machine must be either PC or mini based;
- that networked communications be undertaken in UN standard manners (eg, EDIFACT);
- that tactical development solutions produced in the short term (pre 1993) be easily migrated from in terms of the longer term strategy and objectives as current gaps in international standards are overcome.

The current ATIS development is PC workstation orientated, allowing all users to undertake a fundamental set of functional requirements, including all necessary network communications as well as business data processing. The functional requirements specification that supports these objectives has been vetted and signed off, not only by the business users, as supporting current needs, but also assessed in its capacity to be a base investment in the achievement of the longer term strategy.

4.4 The Implementation Of The Strategy

4.4.1 DATA DEFINITION DEVELOPMENT IN A DISTRIBUTED ENVIRONMENT

The manner in which the process of international data definition development is being undertaken in this project in a distributed environment is quite representative of the problems currently exhibited by many such activities. Its very nature is truly open system in every sense, and as little or no vendor support exists for the activities, the most simplistic implementation of the strategy must be adopted. In this case the following activities occur;

- copies of the DataManager definitions are distributed over the PC network for parallel working on them to take place;
- all amendments are subject to date and time stamping to ensure the continuity of definitions;
- the actual definitions to be worked upon at the distributed sites are booked in and booked out manually by the three personnel responsible for data administration at the distributed sites;
- all amendments are returned to West Germany for inclusion in the central documentation on a weekly basis and uploaded back into the main dictionary;
- all distributed data transfer and communication is undertaken by the network, including data administration in terms of the authority for individual definitions to be worked upon at any of the relevant sites.

The administration of the distributed data definition development is undertaken in the most objective and controlled manner possible, given the lack of software support to actually achieve it automatically. In physical terms the PC interface ensures a degree of communication and access control to the data definitions. The relevant internal formatting and reformatting activities to load and unload the definitions into and out of the distributed dictionaries follow simplistic rules in terms of the times of the week at which they are allowed to happen.

4.4.2 CURRENT DATA DISTRIBUTION LIMITATIONS ON THE PROJECT

As can be seen from the strategy and its implementation, the distribution of data across the three sites is somewhat labour intensive and slow. Many significant limitations on the level of distributed activity that can occur currently exist, and these can be summarised as follows;

- the whole process is batch in its implementation, no real time data definition work sharing is possible;

- the interfaces between the dictionaries and the PC network are internally produced, and non-supported by the respective dictionary vendors;

- consequently the interfaces are passive in terms of their relationship with the dictionaries. Any changes to the interfaces require changing manually, as does the production of the code to achieve them;

- translation into Dutch and German is not catered for by the strategy or its implementation at all;

- the problems of administering the data definitions will be compounded by the addition of new partners into the project;

- the lack of standards direction, and consequently software vendor support for such data distribution activities, means the whole process is in its infancy, and will remain there until such time that international agreements upon standardisation can be achieved.

4.5 Conclusions

4.5.1 FUTURE DATA DISTRIBUTION SUPPORT REQUIREMENTS

It must be recognised that ATIS is an example of a current distributed systems development, operating in many cases at the front of, if not in advance of, the technical support requirements necessary for optimum distributed systems development. Tourist data is a current example of a new business opportunity in the information market. Just as in the past, data processing personnel must be able to react to and support business needs in the best manner possible at the time the business opportunity exists.

It is hoped that the business analysis and systems development strategies that have been proposed, developed and enhanced on the project are capable of more effective automated support in the future, and that the strategy options chosen are in line with current mainstream data processing thoughts, vendor developments and standards definition.

It is recognised, however, that if distributed systems developments are to be effectively undertaken in the future in the same way as single site developments are now, then a number of requirements must be supported, both by standards bodies and vendors, in an open, non-proprietory way. Components of such support are proposed to include;

- that Open System Interconnection (OSI) capabilities be widely implemented. This would allow easier communications between machines and software of different types to occur, regardless of the implemented data processing architectures that are existing within organisations;

- that IRDS standards (or ANSI equivalents) linked into an OSI environment would enable any interested user to share the common data definitions that have been produced within a business area or project;

- that the Portable Common Tools Environment (PCTE) will be in existence to enable any interested organisation to have the capability to maintain, alter or extend any existing data definitions of interest to them;

- that true distributed processing can be undertaken, following the rules and guidelines of objective data distribution as stated by Date [2]. This will allow real time distributed activities to occur and obey all of the integrity and consistency rules applicable within centralised database environments of the present.

It is the stated aim of software vendors to achieve the level of distributed processing, as it is recognised as being necessary to achieve a real time environment of relevance to commercial organisations. From the point of view of the project referenced in this paper, it is hoped that it will not take as long to achieve as is being estimated for the agreement of standards to support the concept of an IRDS. If it does, then business opportunities will be suboptimised, and some may never be developed at all.

4.5.2 DATA DISTRIBUTION, INTERNATIONALISATION AND THE FUTURE

As well as these widely stated support requirements that are defined as necessary for effective distributed systems developments, other issues will have to be addressed in the coming years. It can be stated that a number of initiatives are likely to be realised over the coming decade to assist in the implementation of internationally orientated systems developments using distributed principles.

The X/Open Corporation (1989) recognised the need for a wider capacity for systems and business unification across natural languages. The requirement for effective mixed language working, as referenced here, brings with it the need for standards that support a wider range of more complex natural languages than is accommodated by the ASCII 7-bit characters. For most European requirements an 8-bit system provides the correct balance.

The X/Open Native Language System, incorporated into the X/Open Portability Guide (Issue 3), enables a standard method of communicating in multiple languages. Work is also being undertaken in the ISO forum to develop a single 4-byte (32-bit) character set which will support all languages, and as the global market concept is an ever widening business concept, it is hoped that this work will be completed before the end of the decade.

4.5.3 DISTRIBUTION, INTRA-ORGANISATIONAL DATA MANAGEMENT AND THE FUTURE

The need for data access across organisational boundaries is ever increasing. The future will bring many more (numerically) and complex business requirements to access such data, and the management of that access is a major area for attention. If such requirements for "data interchange" across organisations, defined as;

The exchange of data between applications, by direct communication, by means of the user interface system, or by means of data access

are necessary, it is important to have a model upon which to focus attention. The Open Systems Directive [7] gives such a model (given below).

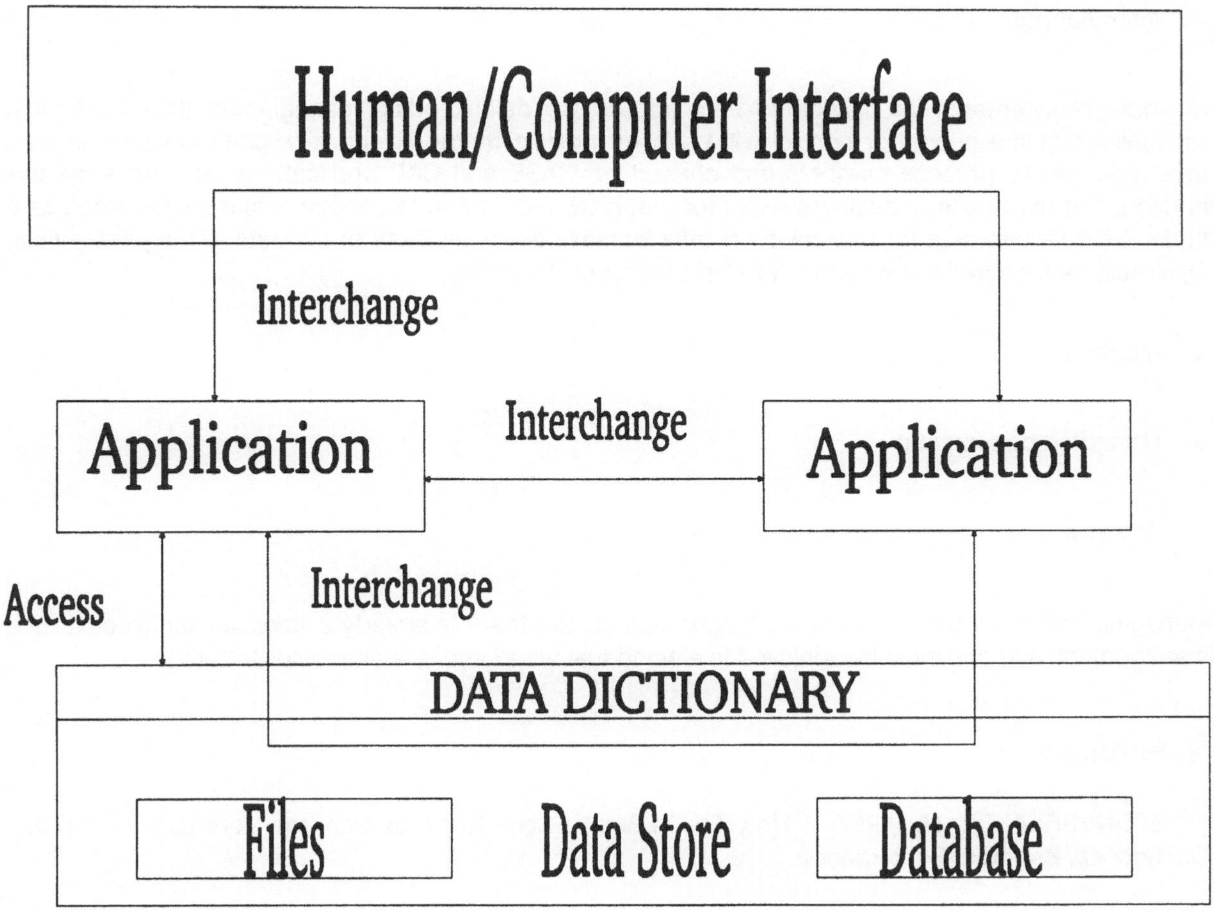

Figure 7 : A Model For Data Management

It must be recognised that;

- data can be contained in any data store;
- the human-computer interface is considered only as a means of interchanging data between applications;
- the components of the model can be distributed.

In this context data management will have impact in intra-organisational terms, as shown in Section 14.2 in both the fact that;

- highly flexible data access and interchange is needed;
- and this must be restricted to previously agreed transactions (such as Electronic Data Interchange);

As more requirements for distributed data access are defined, data management personnel must recognise that the needs for control will be in multimedia mode. Historically, computers have been used primarily to process numbers and characters. CASE and CAD applications have widened this horizon, and the needs of business users for graphical information (map data is already recorded as a future ATIS requirement for example) will only increase the complexity of the data management task. One must be prepared to manage extended data types, including;

- graphics;
- structured documents;
- images.

Managing individual data types is no longer acceptable: there is already a need for multimedia data management, and this must be achieved in a world that we all know, is already distributed.

References

[1] STONEBREAKER, M. (1987) : "How To De-Blue" : Seminar notes from the Very Large Database Conference, Brighton, September 2.

[2] DATE, C.J. (1987) : What is A Distributed Database System? Parts 1 and 2, The Relational Journal.

[3] UNNUK, A. (1990) : "Distribution : The Management Issues" : Data Management Bulletin Vol. 7 No. 2, pp 11-14.

[4] GIBSON, A.N. (1990) : "The Business Need For CASE, in Using CASE Tools For Systems Development", R.F.Williams (ed), Gower Technical Press, pp 9-14.

[5] HOLLOWAY, S. (1990) : "The Distributed Development Environment : CASE Tools And Data Dictionaries In Partnership, in Using CASE Tools For Systems Development", R.F.Williams (ed), Gower Technical Press, pp 25-40.

[6] WILLIAMS, R.F. (1990) : "CASE Tools And The Challenge Of The Post Implementation Phase, in Using CASE Tools For Systems Development", R.F.Williams (ed), Gower Technical Press, pp 79-92.

[7] X/OPEN LIMITED (1989) : The Open Systems Directive. Maple Press.

SECURITY IN A DISTRIBUTED ENVIRONMENT

Rodney Clarke
BIS Applied Systems

5.1 Introduction

Security is generally defined as the protection of an organisation's well being. Since information is vital to the success of many organisations the security of their information and of the technology used to support it is equally vital. In protecting this information three aspects, confidentiality, integrity and availability need to be considered. Confidentiality is the protection of the information such as to prevent its disclosure to persons unauthorised to access it. Integrity is ensuring that the data is accurate to within the degree sufficient to meet the purposes of the organisation. Availability means ensuring that the technology upon which the system depends makes the information available in a time frame consistent with the business objectives.

Distributed processing is not a defined term and as such may be interpreted in different ways. It will be sufficient for this paper to consider it as a system in which the processing is not centralised in one place. The classic image of a distributed system is one composed of several mini computers joined together in some fashion. However, we should note that systems such as local area networks (LANs) exhibit some if not all of the features that we associate with distributed systems. Clearly the security problems associated with such systems are likely to be similar.

5.2 The Issue Of Security

Why has security become such as issue today? There are a number of reasons that can be put forward but it may be useful to focus on two of these for the purposes of this paper. Firstly, because today we rely upon the information received that systems give us as being correct. There are no longer manual checks on the information before action is taken in many cases. An example of this is the familiar automated telling machine (ATM). In this system there is nothing between the machine and the customer, the customer reacts directly with the machine and any mistakes in the machine will be reflected directly to the customer. The customer assumes that the machine will give correct information on, for example, the balance of his or her account.

A second point is the importance of the information. The information may be financial transactions well in excess of a million pounds, it may be information which the organisation depends upon in order to make legal agreements, or it may be information which users depend upon for their own personal safety. In brief the information is critical to the organisation and to the user. In a situation where reliance is placed on something that is also critically important then it follows that we will want to be assured that such information is correct and will not fail us.

If this argument is accepted then much of the reasons for security are self evident; however, it could be argued that there are no threats to the security of the system. In this situation where is the need to take action against such supposed threats? It is difficult though to make this argument hold water when we all read in the press almost on a daily basis about the activities of hackers and the effects of viruses planted in systems. One of the major manufacturers of distributed systems, Digital Equipment Corporation, has been a particularly favoured target for hackers, and incidentally has also suffered from a much older threat, that of a major fire. Both of these different kinds of threats can result in heavy risks to the organisation.

It also pertinent to note at this point that deliberate threats are changing their nature as the ability of people to infiltrate the system improves radically. A case in point is the recent Aids virus which was clearly a well organised and well financed operation. Such threats are more likely to succeed if they take place. Another factor that may be noted is the increasing sophistication of devices intended for legitimate purposes such as protocol analysers which, nevertheless, place powerful tools in the hands of those who may be unscrupulous enough to use them for fraudulent or other purposes.

The one remaining argument may be that while the need for security is accepted and the evidence of threats admitted, such threats will not affect me personally, they will always happen to the other man, the other installation. The uncomfortable factor remains though that computer systems, distributed or otherwise, are today an attractive target. The chances are that your system will be affected.

To illustrate, mugging yields a relatively small reward typically under 100 and a relatively good chance of being apprehended and subsequently convicted. A major crime such as a bank robbery will yield increased rewards but the chances of being apprehended also increase considerably and the penalties on conviction will be substantial. By contrast, those people defrauding a computer system will know that the chances of being apprehended are very small, the rewards high and the prospects of conviction extremely low. Clearly on this basis computer systems rank as the "best buy" or perhaps we should say the "best steal"!

A further point worth noting here is that users of systems who deem them to be uninteresting to the hacker and who therefore feel they have no need for security may have to revise their opinions. Hackers are increasingly using low security systems as carriers for their data, as storage for their data, and as processing machines for their data. All of these activities will affect the availability of the system under consideration. All of these will cost your organisation money. Security is thus required to a greater or lesser extent on all distributed systems. The question remains of how best to go about achieving that security. Interestingly enough, the answer lies in taking a very similar approach to that taken in designing distributed systems. Owners of distributed systems have focused on the importance of data and data management, hence the title of the BCS specialist group. They have also been aware of the need for user involvement. While not peculiar to distributed systems, both of these aspects have been fundamental to them.

These aspects can be reflected in very much the same way so far as security is concerned. Systems function well if users understand their information needs and how to organise the data (possibly assisted by technicians) in such a way as to enable them to extract the required information from the data. The price of obtaining the information must also be understood, and the user will necessarily have to make decisions regarding the extent of the database he is prepared to support and the extent of the information which he wishes to extract from it. There will inevitably be "trade-offs", the user may only be able to obtain all the information he desires if he or she is prepared to pay for a complex data management system.

5.3 Managing Risk

In just the same way users must understand the risk to which they are exposed, and also make decisions on the security features they are prepared to pay for in order to reduce those risks to a justifiable and acceptable level. The risk of security breaches has to be considered in the light of the benefits obtained from the system, for example a competitive advantage. Only the user can evaluate this, and only the user therefore is in a position to be able to say whether or not the security feature is justified.

Just as data analysis and management is essential to the user so risk analysis and management is essential to the user. He may not necessarily need to understand all of the techniques that go into establishing the measure of risk but he needs to appreciate the risks that are arrived at as a result of that analysis and to appreciate what can be done in terms of managing them. Our own approach here has been to initially establish value by interviewing business users. This is achieved with the use of carefully constructed questionnaires which address the issues of confidentiality, integrity and availability. In fact we have extended this slightly by asking the user to consider the implications of :

- Disclosure of the data to unauthorised persons who may be within or outside of the organisation.

- The modification of data either accidentally or deliberately.

- A loss of data over a period of time.

- A total loss of data.

The value or significance of the data held on the system is then combined with the threat that there is to that data and the extent of the vulnerability which the organisation has to that threat to create a measure of risk. Experience has shown that there is a close correlation between threat and vulnerability, and we therefore address questionnaires at both these aspects on much the same basis. These threat and vulnerability questionnaires are normally directed at suppliers of the service rather than the users since they will be in the best position to ascertain the extent of these.

Our technique involves assessing the value of data in relation to a particular system. However, there is often no direct relationship between the value of the information and the technology used to bring it to the user. It follows that there is no reason why assessing the value of the data should not be carried out as a separate exercise and the data then classified in some form. This technique is used by the government for what is actually termed Classified Data. This is graded, according to its importance in the interests of national security, as Top Secret, Secret, Confidential or Restricted. However, in this case the technique has simply been used as it applies to a particular impact - that of disclosure. The different grades reflect the effect on the nation should the information be revealed to unauthorised sources.

Similar approaches have been used by commercial organisations, amongst them IBM. In this approach data is classified into four classes which have titles like "Restricted", "Registered Confidential", "Internal Use Only" and "Unclassified". These classifications apply to the data regardless of the system on which it is being used. The data may be classified according to its sensitivity or criticality so far as the organisation is concerned. Sensitive data is data which would impact the organisation if released to unauthorised people. Critical data is data that the organisation depends on in order to conduct its business and must therefore be made available on a timely basis.

The problem with data classification techniques so far is that they do not relate to the significance of the data to the effect on the organisation resulting from a threat. Our experience has been that an organisation's concern for data has to take into account the impact. Thus, one organisation may be very concerned about disclosure of data to outside parties while another will be far more concerned about changes being made to that data. Financial institutions are classic examples of organisations whose major concern is that the data should not be changed in some way for fraudulent purposes. Other organisations like airlines require availability of the data on a minute by minute basis. Their concern is to ensure the availability of the system. That concern will be shared by organisations running process control systems for example. Improved data classification techniques will help us to understand the extent of the protection which we need to apply to the data. The question remains of how we are to achieve the protection desired. In part this will have been assisted by the data classification process. The reason for this is that counter measures are not equally effective against all impacts. Contingency planning for example is concerned with making the data available within a set period of time. Encryption techniques are mainly concerned with the impact of disclosure, although they may also be effective against modification since a person attacking the system will not be in a position to judge which parts of the data he would like to change. Counter measures can, therefore, be applied which directly address the impacts which are of most concern to the user. Time and money will no longer be wasted on implementing security measures which, while they may make the security manager feel comfortable, do little to address the real needs of the users and may have operational implications which affect the user in carrying out the day to day business.

5.4 Security And Distributed Systems

If we now look at these aspects of confidentiality, integrity and availability in the context of distributed systems it becomes apparent that the distributed system has certain problems and certain advantages. Confidentiality, for example, is likely to be more of a problem in the distributed environment since it is inherent in such an environment that movement of data takes place freely within the network. Integrity may also be more of a problem since the data is quite likely to be processed in more than one location. There may therefore need to be some means of ascertaining that the processing that takes place in one processor is consistent with that which takes place in another. Availability, however, is likely to be improved over that of the mainframe system since we no longer have situations in which the loss of the hardware means a complete loss of all activities. Distributed systems enable other processors to process activities for the users. Typically, therefore, in a well organised distributed system the loss of a processor results only in degraded performance to remaining users. Contrast this with the mainframe situation where the loss of the processor results in all users having no facilities at all.

It can be seen therefore that there are advantages and disadvantages in the distributed processing approach so far as security is concerned. The popular view that it is more difficult to create a secure environment in a distributed processing system may simply be a reflection of the improved techniques that have become available within the longer established mainframe systems. Security is very often thought of as being synominous with access control and the sophistications of packages such as ACF2, Top Secret and RACF are well known. The industry, however, is now changing in three ways, each of which benefit the distributed processing manager wishing to create a secure environment.

Firstly, organisations are changing the manner in which they operate. Large and bureaucratic centralised organisations are being replaced by profit centres and business centres each of which enjoys a level of automony, and accordingly of responsibility by the manager. Managers responsible for many aspects of their business are not likely to be prepared to leave security to the security manager. They will also be better positioned to control security themselves. Secondly, improved techniques are now coming into play. For example, access control has previously been based upon the idea that a person is entitled to look at or update particular records or files. This is difficult enough to achieve in a single mainframe environment and may in practice be rarely achieved. Future access control systems are likely to be rule based. This will enable the system to establish whether or not a user is entitled to access particular pieces of data even when previously it was not aware of any connection between the user and the data. It will achieve this by comparing the attributes of the user with the attributes of the data to be accessed and, by following a series of rules, ascertain whether or not the user is entitled to access it. Other techniques that are hardly new but which are now becoming possible through the use of changes in technology are those such as surveillance and detection.

Surveillance is a common enough feature in other areas. We are all familiar with the closed circuit TV used to survey a building or factory in order to establish that no unauthorised persons are attempting to gain access. Clearly a similar approach can be taken to establish whether or not hackers are attempting to gain access to a system. Surveillance systems can have a strong deterrent effect as well as providing evidence should that be needed in order to complete criminal proceedings. To be effective, though, surveillance systems require a number of qualities. They must have low overheads since otherwise they will impinge on the operational efficiency of the system. At the same time they must record a large number of events. Equally, they must not be easily disabled by persons who would wish to switch them off. Similarly, it is better if intruders are not able to see whether or not the surveillance system is in operation. Finally, they will need to have analysis procedures available in order that the results obtained can be effectively analysed.

Expert systems offer an opportunity to considerably improve detection techniques. By comparing actions that take place in differing parts of the system and considering whether these actions are commensurate with normal business operations it is possible to distinguish activities more likely to be those associated with an intrusion into the system. This will enable management or security officers to focus their attention on the areas of business indicated.

The third aspect is that of improving technology. Encryption techniques, while by no means a new process, are now becoming much more widely available. Similarly, personal computers, once noted for their lack of security features, are now being built with hardware security built into them (an example is the recent range issued by Apricot).

5.5 Conclusion

Distributed processing has focused on the needs of the user and the management of the data required to fulfil those needs. If the analysis and management of risk is properly understood then the problems inherent from using a technology with limited security features becomes less difficult to manage. Managers are placed in a position where they have the information necessary to establish the security which should be exercised over their information. The fact that the techniques available within the hardware which they have chosen are not commensurate with the level of security required will not necessarily be a limiting factor. It will, however, in many cases require managers to take tough decisions regarding the relative merits of improved operational efficiency and competitive advantage against that of a loss of security.

CLIENT - SERVER ARCHITECTURES

THE CLIENT-SERVER ARCHITECTURE IN A MIXED DATABASE ENVIRONMENT

Nigel Geary Ph.D, MBCS
Henley Business Software Ltd

6.1. Introduction

In an ideal world all application products and languages on PCs, minicomputers and mainframes should have the ability to store and retrieve data from databases anywhere in the enterprise with minimal programming effort, provided only that data security and authorization procedures are in place and that systems are protected from unreasonable processing demands from users. If this could be achieved in a manner transparent to the user of the application and avoid the inconsistency and redundancy inevitable with file or database downloading mechanisms, the economic advantages would be irresistable. This could only be possible if;

- all computers and workstation/personal computers in the enterprise are fully networked;

- the software products selected are compatible to the extent that they have database connectivity.

During the 1970s and 1980s we have seen a rationalization of database architectures. The relational model, introduced by Dr E.F. Codd in 1969, has gained widespread acceptance and now enjoys the support of virtually all major database and hardware vendors. IBM introduced Structured Query Language (SQL) in 1974 to support the relational model, and the majority of relational database vendors have implemented SQL as an access method.

In the past database vendors have concentrated on trying to deliver a complete range of front-end tools and products to make their DBMS offering more competitive. However, it is now becoming imperative that all software vendors offer interoperability not only between front-end and back-end products from different vendors, but also that the back-end engines themselves can co-operate in distributed networks.

Fuelled by the dramatic increases in performance of personal computers and workstation hardware used on local area networks (LANs), multi-user SQL database servers for MSDOS, OS/2 and Unix are now available with Novell Netware versions under development. In turn the major PC software vendors have announced SQL versions of their products, but sadly few have been able to deliver working products to date. This chapter discusses portability, distribution and interoperability of SQL products and some of the efforts to standardize on remote data access.

6.2 Client-Server Database Systems

Client-Server database systems were pioneered by Gupta Technologies, Sybase, Britten-Lee and Metaphor Systems. The main reasons for adopting a client server architecture were:

- optimization of LAN based applications by reducing LAN traffic to a minimum;

- the ability to combine graphical user interface (GUI) based workstations with powerful database back-ends;

- better PC-to-mainframe integration (SAA Cooperative Processing).

The technology has been proven in the field and has been boosted by widespread endorsement from vendors such as IBM, with System Application Architecture (SAA) Remote Data Services (RDS), Digital Equipment Corp with SQL Services under PCSA, and Microsoft with SQL Server (a derivative of Sybase) under LAN Manager and Named Pipes.

In nearly all cases SQL is the standard which has been adopted to handle the data access because:

- it is a readily available standard (ANSI/ISO);

- it has the potential of providing application development independent of the back-end database engine;

- it provides unified access to micro-, mini- and mainframe-resident database servers.

6.3 Connectivity Versus Portability

In the time since the first commercial SQL products came to market (Oracle 1979) great store has been placed in the need to make software portable across hardware and software platforms. For example, by using ANSI standard C and writing code which is over 95% independent of the target hardware, companies like Oracle have been able to port their products to some 70+ different hardware/software platforms.

While there has been a wide range of proprietary operating systems this approach has paid high dividends and vendors have been able to offer portability of applications as well as rudimentary distribution in an homogeneous network of databases. Two factors now make this portable/ homogeneous approach less attractive:

- Open Systems (OSI) standards and the widespread adoption of the IBM PC as an industry standard have reduced the number of proprietary systems;

- the larger proprietary vendors of hardware such IBM, DEC, Tandem and Hewlett-Packard are now offering their own SQL database products directly which over time will become optimized within the operating system environments.

It is now very common, therefore, to find medium to large companies using multiple database products within their operational and information systems.

In the remainder of the 1990s the market will demand greater connectivity between products from different vendors. The number of diverse platforms will reduce, and hence the focus will move from portability to heterogeneous networking of databases. It is unlikely that large independent suppliers like Oracle will be quick to provide connectivity to their competitors although they have delivered gateways to IBM DB2 through Oracle residing on the host.

6.4 SQL Compatibilty

6.4.1 SQL SYNTAX

From SQL's introduction in 1974 it took some 12 years for a standard to emerge for the SQL language in the form ANSI/ISO SQL'86. The next standard is already being prepared by ISO which is currently known as SQL2. All vendors comply to a lesser or greater extent to the SQL'86 standard, but each vendor has provided extensions in a number of functional areas such as outer joins, result sets and various concurrency schemes. Provided that the user sticks to the SQL'86 standard it is relatively easy to port the SQL portion of an application from one product to another.

6.4.2 APPLICATIONS PROGRAMMING INTERFACES

Portability of the application code of the host language, such as COBOL or C, is restricted because each DBMS product has a different Applications Programming Interface (API). The API defines how the program submits an SQL query for execution and how to retrieve the results of a query. IBM has different APIs for each of its SAA database products, DB2, SQL/DS, SQL400 and OS/2 Database Manager. In order to overcome these differences SAA defines a method of embedding SQL in host lanaguages, and precompilers are required to strip out this embedded SQL and to replace it by API calls to the target engine. Independent vendors, such as Oracle and Gupta, have implemented precompilers to allow SAA compatible programs to be written for their DBMS. However, in order to gain maximum control programmers will generally want access to the API.

6.4.3 MESSAGE FORMATS AND PROTOCOLS

In a distributed environment SQL statements and the results of queries have to be moved across networks. The way this is done requires the definition of message formats and a protocol for handling messages (FAP). The formats and protocols of all vendors are currently proprietary. The only way in which two vendors can interwork is if one vendor, or a third party, provides a gateway. Gateways are quite common in the world of LAN internetworking and for mainframe terminal access from LAN based workstations where one protocol, Netbios or TCP/IP, is used across the LAN but another is used outside the LAN, IBM LU6.2 or ICL CO3. The SQL FAPs are independent of the network protocols and sit above them.

6.5 Efforts at Standardization

Both the standards bodies and vendor groupings are attempting to define standards which can provide a workable platform for heterogeneous interoperability. These include the International Standards Organization Remote Data Access committee (ISO/RDA) and associated committees, the Open Software Foundation, SQL Access and OpenSQL, which are consortia of software and hardware vendors.

6.5.1 INTERNATIONAL STANDARDS ORGANIZATION

ISO have defined a number of standards related to database management:

- Commitment, Concurrency, and Recovery (CCR) which defines a two phase commit protocol similar to IBM's LU6.2;

- Transaction Processing which defines transaction management;

- Remote Operations Services Element (ROSE) which defines Remote Procedure Calls (RPC);

- Abstract Syntax Notation (ASN.1) which defines data representation within messages.

These together provide the platform for ISO/RDA which is nearing draft international standard status. While RDA is not specific to SQL databases there is an SQL sub-committee of RDA. Many vendors and user organizations are represented on the RDA committee. Vendors individually and in groups are taking the recommendations of RDA and are likely to fill in any blanks left by submitting their own recommendations or implementing working products with their own solutions.

6.5.2 OPENSQL /SQL ACCESS / OSF

In 1989 Tandem Computers with Digital Equipment Corporation sponsored a multi-vendor consortium which led to SQL Access group later that year. Meanwhile some participants in OpenSQL, Sybase for example, have also forged ties with the Open Software Foundation.

6.6 Available Products

While we wait for RDA/SQL products to appear many user organizations and application builders will want connectivity between database products sooner rather than later. In the client-server market PC SQL front-end products are starting to appear which could be used as clients to large corporate databases. These front-ends include forms tools, spreadsheets and word processor packages both under MSDOS (character-based) Microsoft Windows and OS/2 Presentation Manager. The best way forward for such organisations is to use gateway-based SQL networks which will meet most of the users' connectivity needs. Such a system has been developed by Gupta Technologies (Menlo Park, California) and is known as SQLNetwork.

6.6.1 SQLNETWORK

Gupta Technologies was the first company to provide a database server for use on MSDOS LANs. Basing the engine on an IBM DB2 compatible version of SQL and the system catalogue, SQLBase first appeared in October 1986. SQLBase relied on the NetBIOS LAN protocol and hence was compatible with the vast majority of networks.

6.6.2 IBM DB2 CONNECTIVITY

By July 1987 the same company provided an Advanced-Program-to-Program-Communications product, SQLGateway/APPC, which used LU6.2 to communicate with SQLHost on an IBM MVS mainframe running DB2. SQLGateway makes the connection to DB2 from with PC products such as Lotus 1-2-3, dBase (Clipper) and MS Windows applications totally transparent to the user and developer.

6.6.3 ORACLE SQL*NET GATEWAYS

Recently, SQLNetwork has been extended with the addition of SQLGateway/Oracle to provide a gateway into Oracle's SQL*Net running under OS/2. It is now possible, therefore, to connect simultaneous to SQLBase on MSDOS or OS/2, Oracle on OS/2, DEC VAX under VMS or Unix host and DB2 on an IBM MVS mainframe within a single application session.

6.6.4 SQL/DS and OS/2 DATABASE MANAGER

Work is currently underway to provide further SQLGateways for IBM OS/2 Database Manager and SQLHost for SQL/DS on VM and DOS/VSE systems.

Future products will support other database engines such as SQL400, SQL Server(Sybase) and Ingres 6.

6.6.5 ENHANCED FRONT-END FUNCTIONALITY

SQLNetwork was designed with PC applications in mind. Certain functions within the API of a PC oriented database server such as SQLBase may not be present in a host product such as DB2. An example is the concept of result sets and scrollable cursors. Many PC applications, particularly under Windows and Presentation Manager, provide ease of use by presenting list boxes and item selection lists rather than command or function key choices. This method of selection requires database cursors which can scroll backwards as well as forwards through a query result. This is not available in DB2 but is provided in SQLNetwork through what are called front-end result sets. As queries are fetched from the host database they are cached so that the user can scroll back to a previous row or rows.

6.7 Conclusion

It is likely to be a year or two before a solid set of products based on the ISO/RDA standards emerges for client-server APIs and FAPs although many vendors will want to offer or publish their own implementations as open standards. Client-server database architectures are the first step to interoperability between front-ends from one vendor and back-ends from another. With IBM failing to deliver a common API across its range of hardware and new major players such as Microsoft entering the SQL database market it is unlikely that any one vendor will dominate the field. SQL gateways between heterogeneous database systems will become more common especially at the LAN-to-mainframe level. This will give users and developers what they want in terms of simple connectivity in the short term while products migrate to open systems standards over time.

THE CLIENT-SERVER ARCHITECTURE IN LARGE DISTRIBUTED BUSINESS PROCESSING ACTIVITIES

Colin Calder
Automobile Association

7.1 Introduction

The primary rationale for information technology use within organisations is to provide business activities with added power and value in the discharge of their operational functions. Organisations have invested large amounts of money in information systems and technology to improve business performance, with the result that many large data processing functions have been created to support the businesses use of such facilities.

In some large corporations these data processing functions are now the size of individual companies, employing hundreds of people and spending millions of pounds per annum. The Automobile Association is in that position, with a data processing function, entitled the Management Service Group, employing over 550 people directly, and spending millions of pounds on information technology every year. The AA has a total of over 14000 employees, with business focus upon member services (such as breakdown assistance and touring information), commercial services (including publishing and retailing) and financial services (insurance and general finance). The AA is a household institution within the UK, with over 7,000,000 members and 2,000,000 motor insurance policy holders. The AA is in fact the largest motor broker in the UK, and has retail and service outlets nationwide.

All of these business service functions rely heavily on information technology support, not only for reducing direct cost for the businesses, but also providing added value facilities and new business opportunities, thus creating competitive advantage. In the support of these activities the Management Services Group has a defined goal, in terms of its mission statement;

To assist the AA's businesses to better compete, control cost and maximise their profits and services through the exploitation of Information Technology.

In achieving effective discharge of this mission statement MSG has to ensure not only that businesses receive the best possible service from the Group, but also that new technologies are fully exploited, and that the approach to the exploitation of these is achieved in the lowest risk environment possible.

7.2 The Forces Of Change

The dynamic nature of data processing, coupled with the continual needs of ever more wide ranging business support requirements results in the continual examination of any large computing function's positioning. The businesses are continually, and quite justifiably, demanding a variety of new improvements for their business from IT. These business demands can be stated to include:

- reduced training costs for IT facilities;

- improved management information;

- greater flexibility in the use and functionality of IT;

- higher quality services;
- access to lower cost technologies;
- improvements in value for money.

Yet the environment of change is not only coming as a result of new business demands, it is also resulting from market pressures on IT functions within the business environments that are being supported. Key features to recognise in this context include:

- speed of response to market demand;
- changing marketing mixes;
- the requirements of access to shared data;
- the need for IT services to become customer orientated;
- the fact that many IT services have to be marketing driven.

When one adds in a consideration of the IT world and the developments that have occurred within it over the past decade a number of other issues have to be included in the IT support strategy for business demands that is reflective of market pressures. These include:

- international standards;
- the recognition of the use of widely used "de facto" standards;
- commodity products;
- distributed processing power;
- new, lower cost IT architectures;
- the convergence of intelligent workstations and personal computers.

All of these issues converge on Management Services Groups and have to be addressed in the context of a global IT investment environment for the businesses and the organisation as a whole. The pressures placed upon data processing from both business demands and industry advances are increasing all the time. Consequently, many management services functions have had to face up to the issues in a clearly defined and objective manner. The issues must be crystallised into a strategy from data processing departments capable of taking account of all of these points in a business relevant manner.

7.3 The Changing World Of Technology

The simplistic period in the development of data processing and information technology solutions, based upon the belief that the mainframe has all the answers' is long gone. The business demands referenced in the previous section cannot be met by this approach any longer if the mission statements of management services functions are to be truly supported. These needs, as has been indicated, must be met by a mix of technology. This often dims the influence of the central processing facilities in business terms. The costs of such architectures, their inherent problems of linkage and the way in which they treat their users, not allowing them to do work of their own, has heralded the arrival of new architectural profiles for data processing.

The best example of this new direction in data processing can perhaps be given in reference to the CLIENT-SERVER DESIGN. The concept states that;

"At the point of execution, each business process should have the minimum dependence on wide area networks for access to computer power and transport of data."

Based upon the capability to link data together, logically and physically, regardless of its geographic location or storage format, the Client-Server Concept harnesses the three existing pillars of Information Technology. It enables the central processor and its associated data to be tied into both departmental servers and intelligent workstations. Thus reducing the dependence that front office business processing systems used to have on mainframes, enabling multiple types of work to be transacted with a significantly higher degree of processing availability.

The profile of the IT architectures available to businesses has changed so significantly over the past three years that one can confidently predict a continual change in emphasis in the mix of processing capacity increasing during the remainder of the decade. The pre-eminence of dumb terminals has already been eclipsed. With the increasing capability of the intelligent workstations to support:

- local applications;
- user presentation;
- word processing;
- spread sheets;
- data download;
- electronic mail;
- desktop publishing;
- data entry.

It can easily be seen that the computer industry is now going through a "fourth wave" of development. Initially there were mainframes, then came minicomputers, which were then overtaken by the intelligent workstations and personal computers, which is now superseded by the capabilities of distributed computing and networking. The issue for all data processing departments is how to harness the power of these waves together.

7.4 Investing In IT For The Business

When an organisation is addressing the strategic issues of data processing support for business processing a number of factors have to be taken into consideration. These can be represented as the four dimensions of IT investments, categorised as:

- cost containment;
- managerial effectiveness;
- added value products and services;
- competitive positioning.

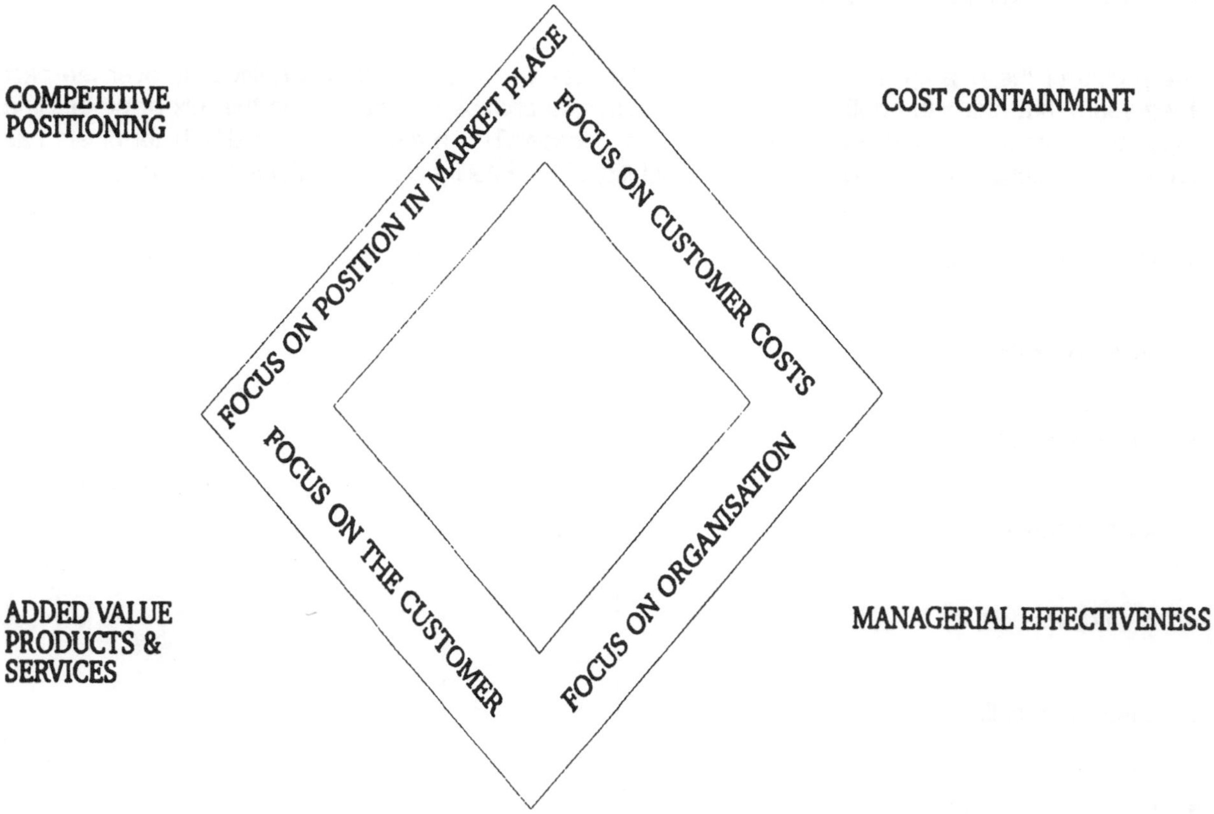

Figure 1 : The Four Dimensions Of Information Technology Investments

In the past decade, many organisations have been able to take on board the first two of these issues, as they focus attention upon the costs borne by the organisation and the structure of the organisation itself. In essence these are easy targets as clearly defined boundaries and metrics can be used to assess them. However, times have changed in IT, and this change has to be recognised and responded to by the data processing managers. Attention must be shifted to the needs of the customer and the position of the organisation in the marketplace. In essence, a change from focusing away from internal data processing department issues to external business issues. This point has been clearly stated by the London Business School [1];

The business demand is to progress from using isolated applications that are 'necessary to run the business' to harnessing a complex, often incompatible mix of technologies, into an integrated web of information systems.

It is simply no longer acceptable for data processing managers to say to their customers that the mainframe will answer your needs because it will not. The costs are too high (in both financial and risk terms) in investing significant amounts of money in proprietary solutions to business problems. No one vendor has all the answers, and no one vendor has all the best answers to the issues that they do address. It is necessary to develop IT structures to support the necessary mix of technologies best suited to the customer rather than to the supplier.

7.5 The Use Of The Client-Server Concept In The AA

AA Insurance Services is the largest motor broker in the country. There are over 200 high street shops broking insurance for the customers of the AA with a policy holder base of over 2,000,000 customers. To most effectively support the processing of such a large business in IT terms it was essential that the proposed solution met the needs of the customer in all contexts. It was essential that:

- the IT solution provided was the most cost effective one available;
- that the IT solution should enhance the capabilities of the business to compete within its marketplace rather than be a hindrance to it;
- that the solution provided would be able to integrate all business requirements together in one information systems and technology environment.

To provide such a total customer support service a strategy that de-risked the implementation of the support for the business was necessary. It had to make use of the already existing investment in technology by the business (in large central processors), whilst at the same time extending the functionality offered in that environment to meet the newer needs of the business (word processing, document management, etc). It also had to reduce the impact of data communications failure on the capacity of the business to transact its activities, ensuring maximum "up time" for the system. One of the key issues to be resolved by the new system was a way to improve the availability of the systems to the front office customer to over 99%. A significant limitation of the existing mainframe/dumb terminal system was its availability (averaging 93% - 95%). When one recognises that AAIS gives over one million motor quotations per year, and that this is growing at a compound rate of over 10% per annum an improvement of 5% in up time is a significant competitive benefit.

The global solution chosen was a combination of the existing ICL mainframe processing facilities as the back end server to wide and local area networks capable of interworking with the mainframe using open systems standards, commodity products with an emphasis on supplier independence delivering an architecture of local, file, print, communications and database servers to the business via a workstation front end user service.

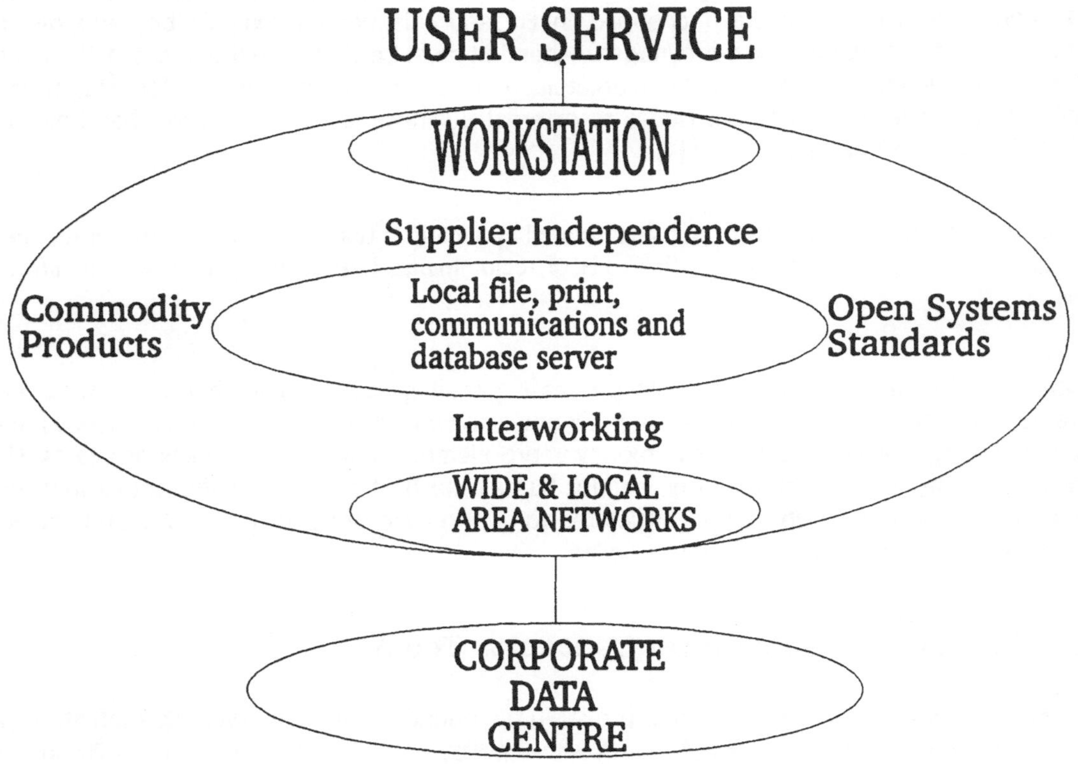

Figure 2 : The Client-Server Concept Architecture For AAIS

The benefits that this accrues to the business can be stated to focus upon:

- greater flexibility and choice in IT options for the business;
- lower costs to the business;
- a quicker delivery time to the market;
- a solution based upon international standards for networking;
- the creation of new business opportunities by its availability.

7.6 Integrated Business Services Using The Client-Server Approach

In the past, the entire emphasis and reliance on the central processors to transact all AAIS business meant significant restrictions to business growth. By using the Client-Server approach the benefits of the mainframe can be harnessed without having to pay all of the costs. The functionality benefits of the mainframe, linked to wide area networks enables AAIS to undertake effective management of the corporate customer file, central accounting, global marketing and renewals processing, all linked in an EDI context. It enables other job functionality to be distributed to the more local areas where they are of most immediate benefit at cheapest cost.

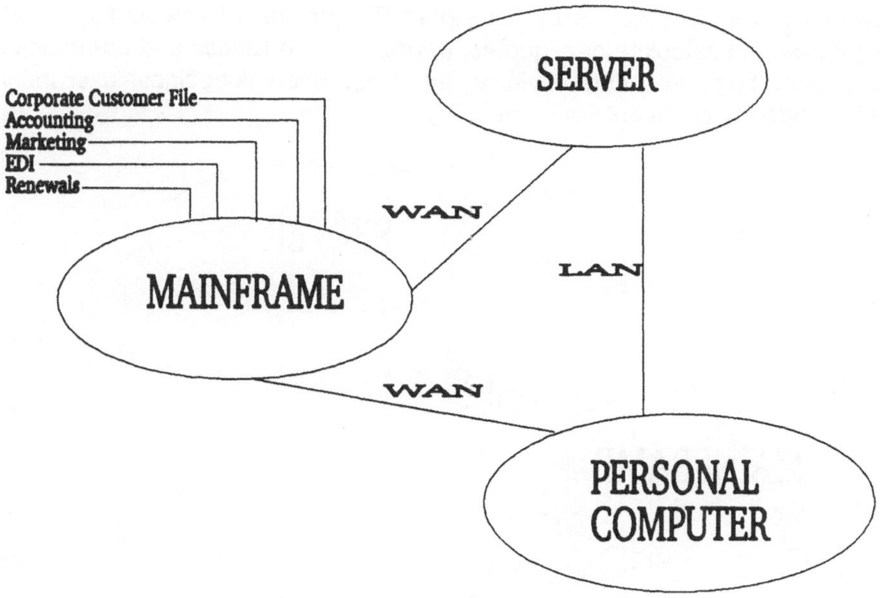

Figure 3 : Mainframe Functionality Within The Client-Server Architecture

At server level effective control of relevant coordinating processing can be achieved. This focuses upon the production of local management information in a more readable format faster. Communications in store and forward terms are managed by the servers as a go-between from front office to back office in the architecture. The communications protocols are also handled in this environment, where processing costs are cheaper. Local files are collated and held and local direct input is also possible. Ring backs and telesales are coordinated and the diarying of activities is also handled. All printing requirements are undertaken at this node, again reducing processing costs whilst at the same time increasing delivery service levels to the business personnel requiring the information.

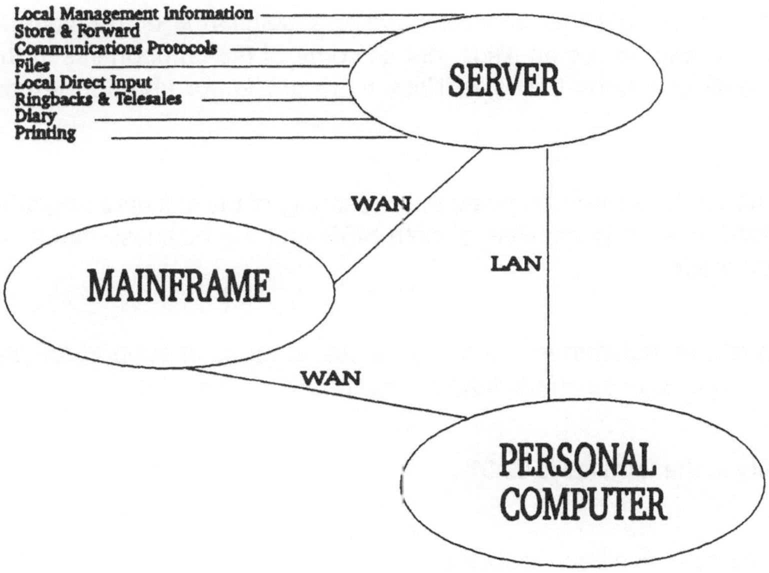

Figure 4 : Server Functionality Within The Client-Server Architecture

At the front office end of the architecture the intelligent PCs are able to issue documentation to the customers. Adjust cases and calculate new quotes, transact new business and communicate between the users. This is all undertaken in secure environment. It also enables business user training to occur on site rather than outside the office environment.

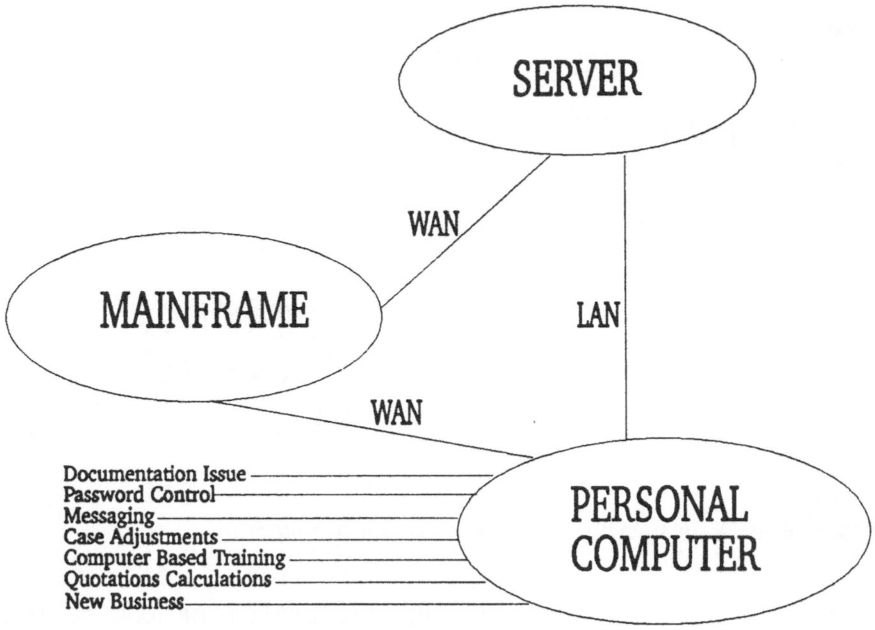

Figure 5 : Client Functionality Within The Client-Server Architecture

7.7 IT Issues In The Client-Server Implementation

The production of the total client-server architecture implemented within AAIS has many different components within it. When the system went live (in March 1989) the total configuration incorporated different proprietary and de facto standard architectures at each level of the structure.

The communications architecture that underpins the total solution is both unique and complex. The complexity on its own would not be an issue, but as some of the components in the architecture are non-OSI or international standards based facilities there are future upgrade issues to a totally OSI conformant structure.

Other areas of attention to be addressed relate to the security of the software upgrades and the manner in which they are distributed. It is the view of both MSG and the business that this is an area where improvements can be made.

However, in respect to the requirements of the business, in terms of support for processing activities the following positive conclusions can be drawn:

- service availability at the terminal is 99.3%;
- the mainframe charges have been reduced;
- service location is the customer's choice;

- there is now timely presentation of customer documentation;
- first time business closures have increased;
- cash flow for the business has improved;
- there is greater staff satisfaction with the new solution;
- trade up opportunities have increased;
- the business has increased marketing flexibility.

These are significant business benefits from the development of the client-server approach, many of which could not have been provided by the older, or "traditional" approach to business processing support. They do show, it is felt, that new solutions to business problems are both achievable and beneficial.

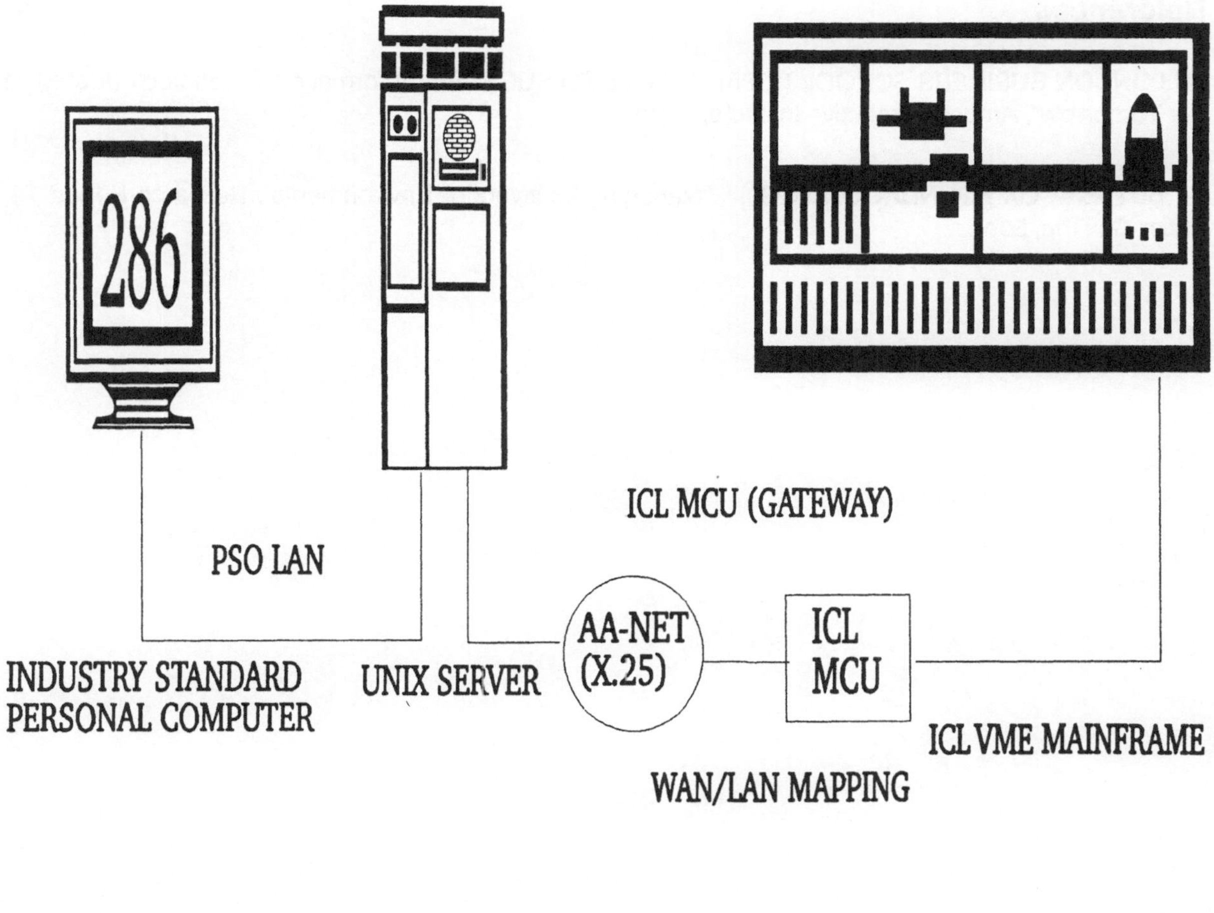

Figure 6 : Client-Server Communications Architecture AAIS March 1989

This opinion is not just one held by the data processing personnel within the organisation, but by the businesses themselves, and is independently confirmed by Butler-Cox [2].

7.8 Conclusions

The client-server issues in data and processing distribution have already provided huge benefits to businesses that have adopted them in a strategic and planned manner. Investment decisions based upon corporate objectives and needs will necessitate more and more organisation to look outside their existing proprietary environments into the open systems arena.

The purpose of all management services and data processing functions is to provide a bridge between the defined business objectives and the developments within the computing industry. By providing such a bridge the business is given an architecture to support its goals which includes the essential component of customer choice linked to added value where the data processing personnel have been able to put together a cohesive and relevant IT strategy.

New technologies, new concepts and new needs require different approaches to the resolution of business needs. The growing recognition of the fact that information is an asset to be managed, and data is a resource that can be re-used in different contexts means the significant investment made by organisations in areas such as data and processing distribution really creates a significant power behind any business.

References

[1] LONDON BUSINESS SCHOOL (1988) : "CLUES TO SUCCESS : Information Technology Strategies For Tomorrow", Amdahl Executive Institute, 86pp.

[2] BUTLER-COX FOUNDATION (1989) : "Managing Multivendor Environments", Research Report 72, Butler Cox Plc, 50pp.

DICTIONARIES AND DISTRIBUTION

THE ROLE OF DICTIONARIES IN OPEN DISTRIBUTED SYSTEMS

William Olle Ph.D.
William Olle Associates Ltd

8.1 Introduction

The ISO activity on database standardisation has been assigned to one of the largest technical subcommittees, namely ISO/IEC JTC1, which has the all embracing title of "Information Systems." It has many sub-committees and the one which has had responsibility for database standards since 1984 is SC21 which has the title "Information Retrieval, Transfer and Management for OSI".

SC21 has six working groups, four of which are developing standards for the upper layers of the OSI Reference Model, one for the new Reference Model for Open Distributed Processing and one for database. The work of the database working group, JTC1 SC21/WG3, is the focus of this article.

SC21/WG3 is concerned with several projects related to the management of data in computerised databases. Such databases are typically those found in commercial applications of computers. This excludes bibliographic databases and the kind of public databases disseminated using television as a means of communication.

In 1984, SC21/WG3 inherited three projects from ISO TC97/SC5 (Programming Languages), where each project had previously been handled by a different SC5 working group. Two of the three projects inherited from SC5 have been partitioned and, together with one new project, can now be identified as follows:

1.21.3	Database Languages
1.21.3.1	NDL Network Database Language
1.21.3.2	SQL Relational Database Language
1.21.6	Information Resource Dictionary Systems
1.21.6.1	IRIS Framework
1.21.6.2	IRDS Services Interface
1.21.6.3	IRDS Command Language and Panel Interface (work suspended)
1.21.6.4	IRDS Support for SQL Applications
1.21.30	Reference Model of Data Management
1.21.31	Remote Database Access

SC21/WG3 has four so-called Rapporteur Groups, each of which is responsible for one of the four main project headings in the above list.

Each project will be reviewed in turn. It should be noted that standards work is very dynamic. Each of the Rapporteur Groups meets approximately every six months. The status of the projects is very much "time of going to press".

8.2 Database Languages

8.2.1 NETWORK DATABASE LANGUAGE, NDL

The Network Data Base Language standard (ISO 8907:1986) was 20 years in the making. The work was started in the USA in the mid 1960s under the auspices of the CODASYL organisation. It was nurtured there for over a decade until ANSI initiated a committee in 1978 to develop a formal standard.

There was considerable controversy surrounding the ISO NDL work. Many argue that it is based on an obsolescent technology, while others feel that there has been a heavy investment in commercial products and in application systems based on these products and hence a standard is needed for that reason alone.

When drafting the standard, ANSI made a number of changes to the original base document which they took over from CODASYL in 1978, which at the time were made in good faith with the objective of making the standard more in line with widely accepted thinking. The result of these changes was that the NDL standard and the commercially available products are some way apart.

Some of the changes made represent the removal of functionality which is felt to be obsolete, and other changes represent the addition of new functionality which is felt to be needed in a 1980s DBMS. Yet other changes are syntactic rather than functional, and the interface with host programming languages has been considerably improved.

8.2.2 RELATIONAL DATABASE LANGUAGES, SQL

This first relational database language standard (ISO 9075:1986) is based on IBM's SQL, which was developed in their research laboratories during the 1970s. A document drafted by IBM was accepted by ANSI and subsequently by ISO as the base document for the first version of the standard. Many European member bodies complained bitterly about the lack of inter-table referential integrity in the 1986 version of the standard.

Referential integrity means that the definition of a column or set of two or more columns in a table can include an integrity constraint which refers to "matchable" columns in another table. Such a constraint needs to be checked when either the referencing or referenced table is updated. This problem has been resolved by issuing a revised ISO 9075:1989 which is formally entitled SQL Database Base Language with Integrity Enhancements.

Other shortcomings in SQL are being overcome in the version which is currently going through the approval process and is informally identified as SQL2. It is intended to replace the ISO 9075:1989 and contains considerably more functionality. SQL2 was subject to a first Draft Proposal letter ballot during 1989, and the major national bodies working on the standard voted against it because they felt that it contained too many inconsistencies. A revised version will be subject to a second letter ballot during the second quarter of 1990.

Two interesting pieces of new functionality in SQL2 are the Information Schema and the Schema Manipulation statements. The Information Schema consists of a definition of (among other things) a set of SQL tables in which may be recorded the results from translating a schema definition. The Schema Manipulation statements may be used for such purposes as destroying a schema, altering a table definition, dropping a domain, dropping a table or a view and for revoking the privileges which allow an authorised user to perform certain functions. It should be noted that the statements used to define schemas, tables, views and so forth are classified as Schema Definition statements.

SQL2 is not regarded as the last word in Database Language standards, and the ISO Rapporteur Group responsible for the development of Database Languages is already working on an SQL3 for which considerable extra functionality is already agreed.

A few general comments on SQL are in order. Those who were hoping for a nice, friendly, easy to use language may well be disappointed. The Data Definition Language in the 1986 version is very simple but, without the integrity enhancements included in the 1989 version, it must be regarded as extremely limited. The main disadvantage is that the validation rules which the data is required to satisfy have to be programmed into the application programs updating the data in the database.

The Data Manipulation Language is designed by programmers for programmers and will do little in itself to reduce the high cost of implementing large complex information systems. The language is intended to be used to build languages which are easier to use by non-programmers.

The Data Definition Language and the Data Manipulation Language are the subject of separate conformance requirements. This means that an implementor can implement the DDL with his own easy to use, necessarily non-standard, user manipulation interface.

8.3 Information Resource Dictionary Systems

The standards work on IRDS also started in ANSI in about 1981. ANSI coined the term "Information Resource Dictionary" to reflect what was hoped would be an outgrowth of the data dictionary system concept (referred to in various products as either a data catalogue, a repository, an encyclopaedia, or a directory).

The term "Information Resource Dictionary" is intended to imply that the dictionary may contain information about other things than just data. The term "information resource" is one which appears to have acceptance in North America and one hears frequent reference to large companies attempting to "manage their information resource". The approach is intended to represent an advance on the more established concept of "management information systems".

8.3.1 ANSI IRDS WORK

The proposal for an IRDS standard which ANSI X3H4 submitted to ISO SC21/WG3 for the first time in 1983 was an overwhelming document. The fact that it consisted of around 1000 pages of single space typing was only the beginning of the problem.

A careful study of the voluminous ANSI document first submitted to ISO in 1983 (prior to the ISO reorganisation) showed that ANSI X3H4 had fallen over backwards to avoid using any existing DBMS, and in so doing had created a third Database Language, which they saw as necessary to define the content and functionality of the proposed IRDS. Definition of this new definition formalism represented a significant part of the 1000 pages.

The technical approach chosen sparked off strong reaction from ISO national bodies, not least from BSI, who felt that a third facility for modelling data, in addition to that in NDL and SQL, was the last thing needed in ISO standardisation. The modelling approach chosen by ANSI was identified as a Entity Relationship approach, but was in fact an extremely weak variant of that family.

It was based on one kind of relationship, namely an asymmetric many to many. An example is shown in Figure 1. An asymmetric many to many relationship between two entity types A and B would mean, for example, that an A could exist without B but a B could not exist without an A. In Figure 1, a SUPPLIER could exist only if it had one or more PRODUCTS, whereas a PRODUCT could exist with zero, one or more SUPPLIERS. No other kinds of relationship were possible.

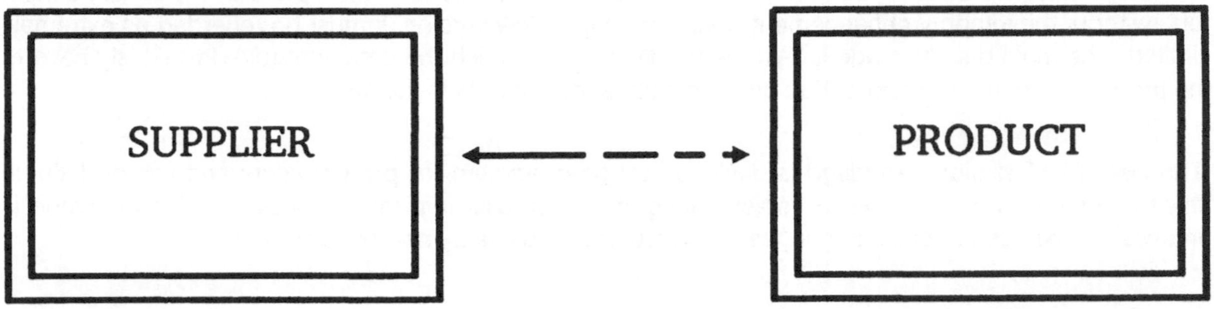

Figure 1 : Example of a "Zero, One or More" to "One or More" Relationship

The effect of using such a weak modelling approach was that the semantics of the data had to be defined in a plethora of rules expressed in narrative form - hence the length of the document.

8.3.2 ISO IRDS FRAMEWORK

It has been recognised and accepted in ISO that several IRDS standards will be needed and that these must be coordinated to ensure that they fit into a standard framework. An IRDS Framework standard (DIS10027) is currently awaiting final approval from the ISO council. This standard shows how the other IRDS standards should be related to each other.

8.3.3 ISO IRDS SERVICES INTERFACE

The IRDS Services Interface is an internal interface at which all IRDS services are to be provided. The term "internal" here is intended to distinguish the interface from a human "language" interface for use by a user at a terminal.

The interface recognises two levels of data definition. These are referred to as the IRD Definition level and the IR Dictionary Level. (The practice of prefixing every name with the two letters "IR" is one of the more tedious aspects of the ISO IRDS standards.)The dictionary definition level is defined in the Services Interface standard using SQL data definition statements. It consists of a set of 33 inter-related SQL tables. The content of these tables represents the permitted structure of an information resource dictionary.

The data modelling facility to be used to model the content of a dictionary is, after much anguished debate within ISO, also accepted as being SQL. For some time, the data modelling facility used was an evolution from that used by ANSI. While it was certainly considerably improved version over that used by ANSI, it was sufficiently different from SQL (both in terminology and in its way of handling constraints) to cause unnecessary extra problems for implementors and for users.

The structure of a dictionary is defined using the SQL2 Data Definition statements, with extensive use made of referential integrity constraints to prescribe how the defined tables are inter-related. The effect of using SQL to define the dictionary definition level (the structure of each dictionary) and also of using

SQL to model the content of the dictionary means that many of the dictionary definition level tables can comfortably correspond to those in the SQL Information Schema. However, the IRDS standard is concerned with functionality over and above that provided for the SQL Database Language. Such functionality may be informally referred to as "added value functionality" in the sense that it is additional to that provided in the SQL standards.

One of the major pieces of such functionality is that for version control. While specifications are being developed in a dictionary, they go through several iterations. It is necessary to exercise control over this development process.

The approach to be used when defining the services to be provided at the services interface has also been a subject of intense debate. Perhaps one of the major questions to be asked is the extent to which the approach used should deviate from that used in SQL.

The services available at the interface are currently defined using Pascal language bindings. However, this is intended merely as a convenient definition technique and is not intended to limit use of the dictionary to programs written using Pascal.

Although the SQL Schema Data Definition Language has been used in defining the standard, it is not the intention to constrain implementors to the use of SQL. An implementor can use any construction tool he wishes, including an SQL implementation. As indicated above, the content of a dictionary can be accessed using any programming language.

8.3.4 IRDS SUPPORT FOR SQL

The remaining standards project in the ISO IRDS family of standards is that for a module to define the structure of the content of a dictionary. This is intended for use by designers who are developing a schema for an SQL application. This development process will usually be an iterative one and frequently subject to version control.

8.4 Reference Model Of Data Management Standardisation

This standards work was initiated within ISO and had its first meeting under SC5 in September 1981. It had been started as a result of a French initiative.

Some of the more important objectives of the Reference Model of Data Management Standardisation are to identify the interfaces for standardisation, position these relative to each other, and to identify the facilities provided at each interface.

The scope of the model was initially restricted to scope of the current standards work in SC21/WG3. This standard was the subject of a Draft Proposal letter ballot in the latter half of 1988. The proposal was rejected and the reasons for the negative ballots took four meetings to reconcile. One major change is that the Reference Model now addresses the question of distributed databases. This aspect of data management was excluded from the first Draft Proposal (DP 10032).

The Reference Model positions a data management system in an information system relative to the OSI layers as shown in Figures 2 and 3.

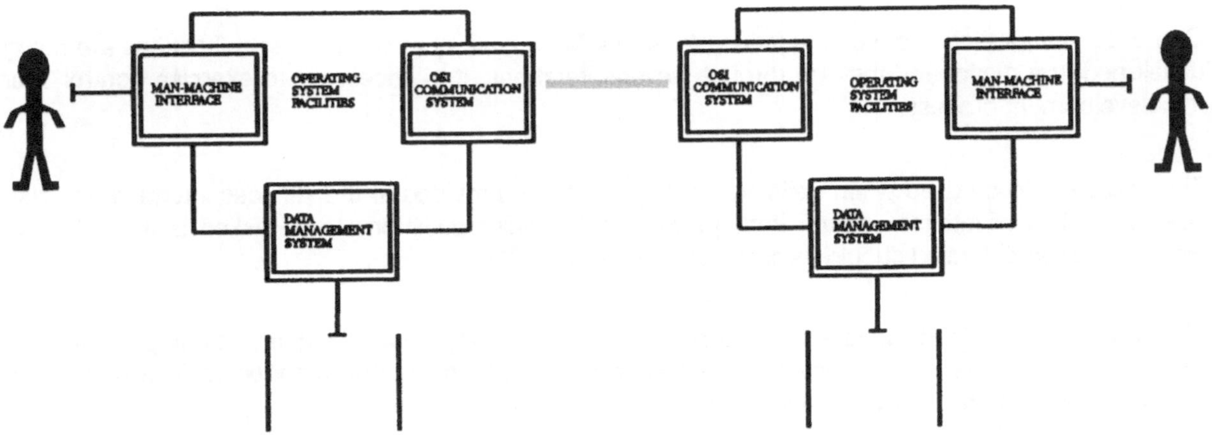

Figure 2 : Position of Data Management System Within an Information System

Figure 2 shows the following:

- in a real system, a data management system provides an interface to a collection of persistent data;
- the interface to human users is provided by a man-machine interface;
- the interface to other real systems is provided by what is in this standard called an OSI communication system;
- each interaction between any pair of the three - data management system, OSI communications system and man-machine interface - is handled by what in this standard is referred to as operating system facilities.

The layered architecture defined in the OSI Reference Model (IS 7498) has been the basis for the development of a family of OSI standards. A similar but separate layered architecture would be appropriate for a data management system. Figure 3 depicts the use of a layered architecture in separate stacks for OSI, data management, and man-machine interface in one real system. This multi-stack approach is not necessarily limited to the three stacks shown overleaf in Figure 3.

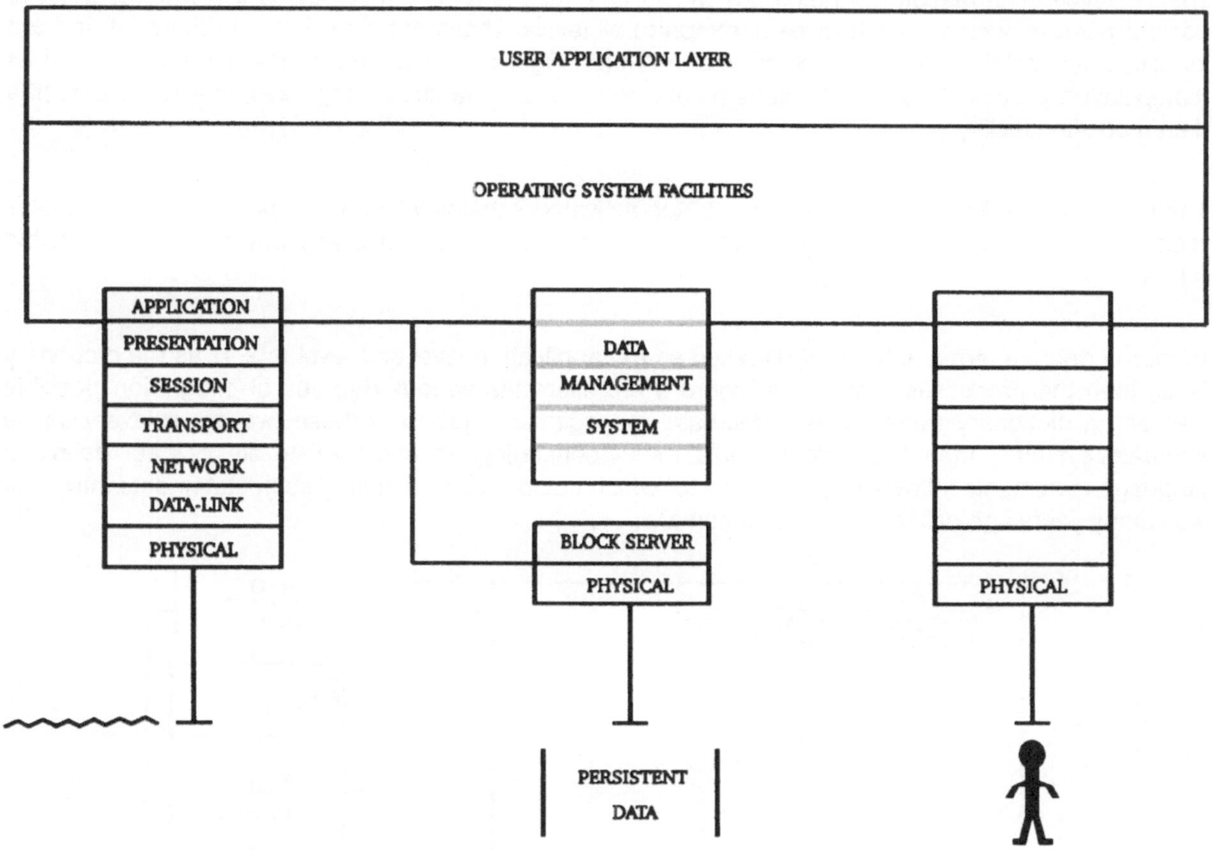

Figure 3 : Multi-Stack Layered Architecture

8.4.1 DATA MODELLING FACILITIES

The Reference Model introduces the concept of a "data modelling facility". The term is used to replace "data model" which has often caused confusion because many people use it to refer to a specific application area such as order entry or hotel reservation. The Reference Model suggest that this kind of data model be called an "application data model".

A data modelling facility is defined as a set of data structuring rules and an associated set of data manipulation rules. The Reference Model does not propose any specific data modelling facility. On the one hand it was recognised that there are different data modelling facilities in use, such as those implicit in SQL, NDL and the one used in the ANSI IRDS standard (as mentioned above).

8.4.2 INTERLOCKING LEVEL PAIRS

Another major aspect of the Reference Model is the concept of interlocking level pairs. The level pair concept comes from the IRDS standards work. As indicated above, the IRDS Services Interface recognises two levels - the dictionary definition level and the dictionary level. Below the dictionary is what is called the application level which is the level typically recognised by a database management system. The first Draft Proposal for the Reference Model referred to specific level pairs in specific terms. The problem was that much of the functionality can be seen to be common across all level pairs. The second Draft Proposal will treat level pairs in abstract terms rather than specific terms.

Figure 4 (taken from the most recent draft of the Reference Model) indicates the Reference Models view of interlocking level pairs in abstract terms - namely in terms of levels (N) and (N+1) rather than specific levels. The reason the Reference Model emphasises an abstract view is that there is a set of basic processes which are felt to be common to all levels. These are also shown in Figure 4 and are identified as install, populate, select and activate. Figure 4 also shows the binding of a data manipulation process to a specific schema and to a set of data structuring rules, which are part of a data modelling facility.

The figure shows the distinction between a non-activated schema which is simply a set of data tables recorded in the level above and an activated schema which may have any one of several possible forms.

In more concrete terms, if level (N) is taken as the application level and level (N+1) as the dictionary level, then the processes 3 and 4 in Figure 4 represent the various degrees of integration possible between a dictionary system and a database management system. If these two are in every sense separate systems, then the "select" could mean generating an intermediate file of data definition language statements followed by an "activate" which could mean compiling such statements into what was many years ago called an "object schema".

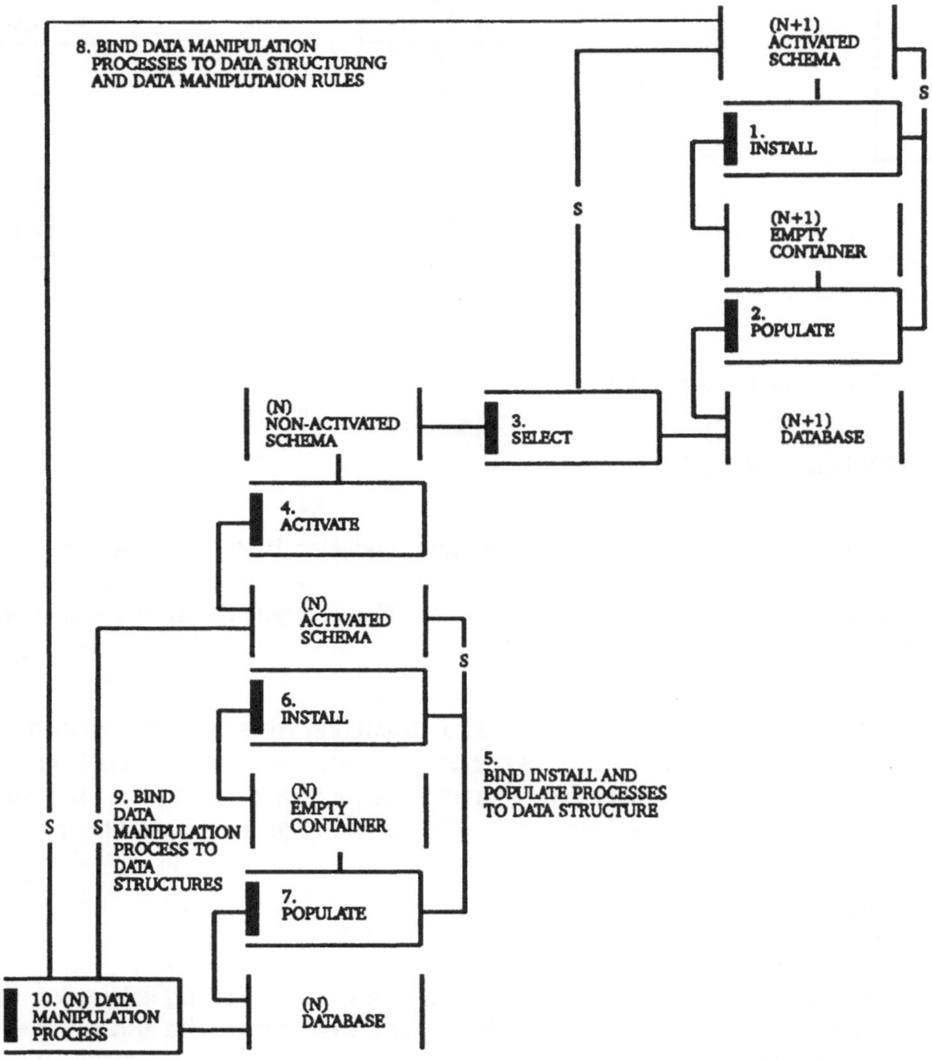

Figure 4 : Interlocking Level Pairs, Basic Processes, Binding and Data Manipulation Processes

8.4.3 LEVEL PAIRS AND DATA MODELLING FACILITIES

The relationship between level pairs and data modelling facilities is another concern addressed in both the Reference Model of Data Management and the IRDS Framework. Figure 5 (not taken from the draft of the Reference Model) attempts to display this relationship diagrammatically in terms of concrete level pairs.

One of the major thrusts behind the Reference Model work has been to make it possible to achieve a maximum degree of integration between a DBMS and a dictionary system within what the Reference Model calls a data management environment. This is one of the reasons put forward for using the same data modelling facility on different level pairs. The Reference Model addresses this question of the coexistence of data modelling facilities in a data management system.

8.4.4 COEXISTING DATA MODELLING FACILITIES

The principles for the coexistence of two or more data modelling facilities established in both the Reference Model and in the IRDS Framework can be explained in terms of Figure 5. At the Application Level more than one data modelling facility may coexist. For example, one might have two NDL application databases and two SQL application databases. Each of the four databases has its own schema (in the old NDL sense rather than the SQL sense).

Each of these schema must have been prepared using a set of data structuring rules belonging to a data modelling facility. Each schema is represented (in the form of data rather than in the form of concrete syntax statements) in a dictionary database. Each dictionary database itself has a schema (here called a dictionary schema) which must also have been prepared using a set of data structuring rules belonging to a data modelling facility. This data modelling facility may be the same as one of those used at the application level. After considerable debate, the IRDS Services Interface standard is now using the SQL data modelling facility.

To permit a dictionary schema to be extended, in other words to provide dictionary extensibility, it is necessary to go up yet another level and to consider the dictionary schema as being represented in a dictionary definition database. Again the IRDS Services Interface standard regards this database as an SQL database. Figure 5 shows the same data modelling facility (DMF0) for the dictionary definition schema as for a dictionary schema.

Regarding the multiplicity of schemas and associated databases for each level pair the IRDS Framework is necessarily more specific and hence more constraining than the Reference Model. Figure 5 overleaf shows only one database for each schema. It also shows two application schemas in a dictionary database and two dictionary schemas in a dictionary definition database. This picture should be regarded as a tutorial illustration of the abstract concepts in the Reference Model using specific level pairs than as a representation of the IRDS Framework.

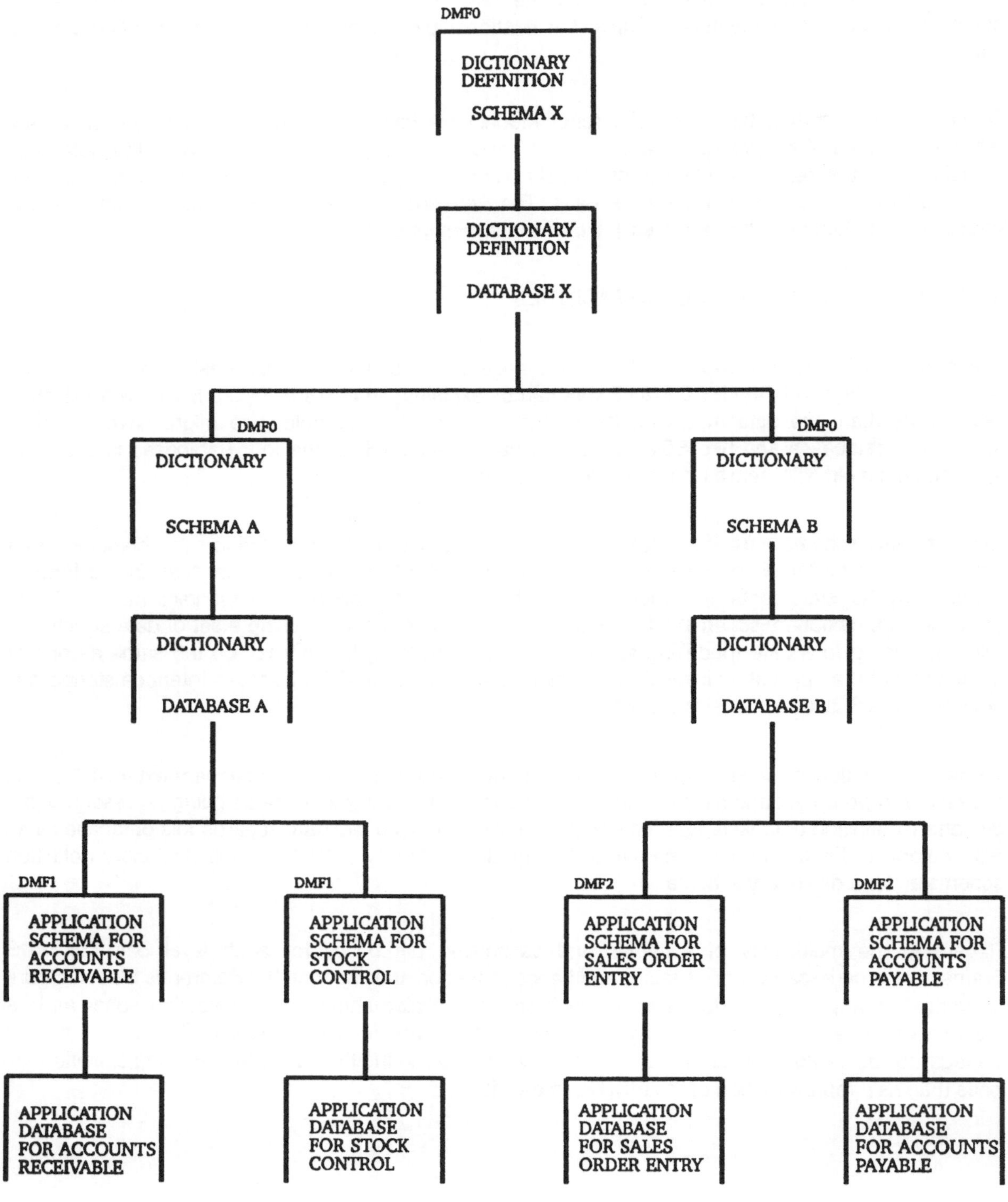

Figure 5 : Vertical and Horizontal Co-existence of Data Modelling Facilities

8.4.5 POSITIONING OF ABSTRACT PROCESSORS

The final aspect of the Reference Model is the positioning of a number of so-called abstract processors. The three major processors are identified as follows.

1. User Processor.
2. Distributed Database Controller.
3. Generic Database Controller.

Each of these three may be decomposed and replaced by two or more abstract processors on a lower abstraction level and by the interactions between them.

The basic relationship between any two processors is regarded as a simpler client-server relationship. The two processors are typically in the same real system, although the possibility that they are in different real systems is not specifically excluded.

Figure 6 (taken from the most recent draft of the Reference Model) shows the positioning of two of the three processors. In order to indicate the boundary around the data management system, a fourth abstract processor is included in Figure 6. This is a File Server which is between the Generic Database Controller and the data.

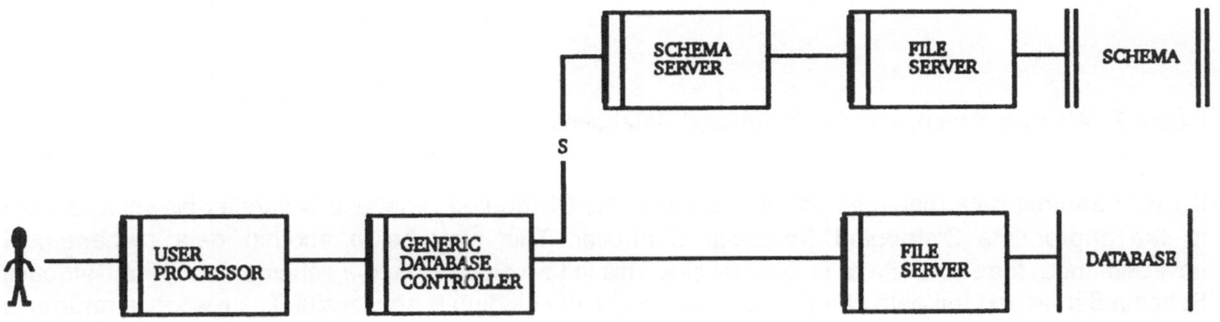

Figure 6 : Placement of Abstract Processors

Other diagrams are presented in the Reference Model showing the positioning of more specific processors, such as an RDA Server and an RDA Client, relative to the above three abstract processors. Figure 7 is an example of such a diagram in which, the processor which in Figure 6 is called the Generic Database Controller is decomposed into two processors, which in Figure 7 are called a Distributed Database Controller and a Local Database Controller.

The Distributed Database Controller receives requests from a User Processor in the same data management environment or possibly from a data management environment at a different site. The loop containing the communications underneath the Distributed Database Controller is intended to illustrate the second alternative graphically.

The Distributed Database Controller determines from a Distribution Schema whether the data to be accessed is at the same data management environment or at another one. If it is at the same environment, the Distributed Database Controller issues a request to the Local Database Controller. This binds to a schema through a Database Schema Server (as in Figure 6) and the data can then be accessed if the binding is successful.

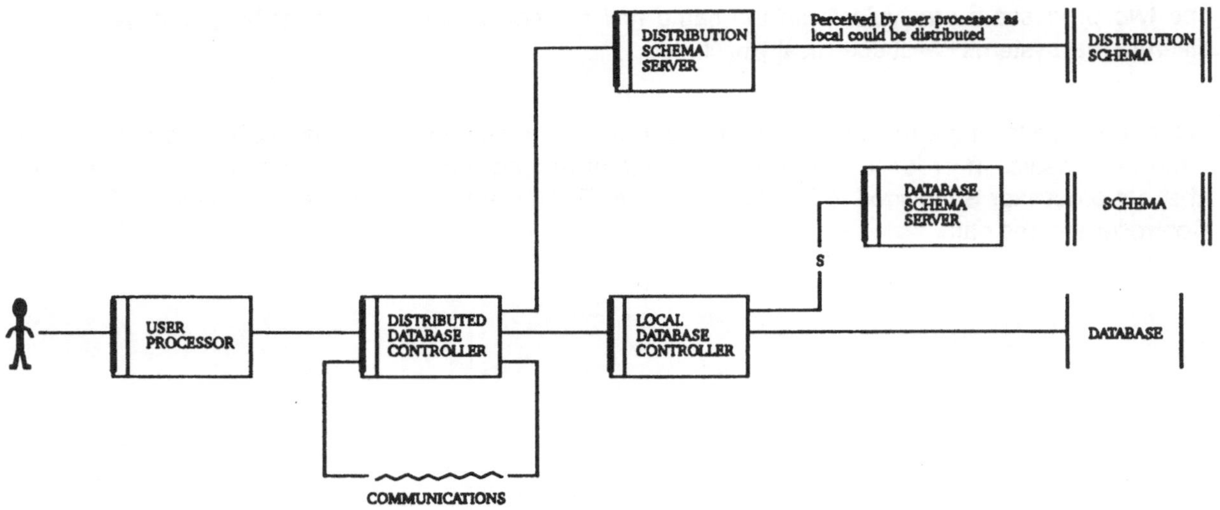

Figure 7 : Abstract Processors for Distributed Databases

If it is at another data management environment, the Distributed Database Controller issues a request to the appropriate Distributed Database Controller. This may be in another data management environment at the same site or at another site. This in turn also binds to a schema through a Database Schema Server and the data can then be accessed if the binding is successful. The response returns to the originating Database Controller.

8.4.6 POSITIONING OF DICTIONARY PROCESSORS

Figure 8 is a further decomposition of Figure 7 showing the positioning of the IRDS Services processor between the User Processor and the Distributed Database Controller.

It is important to note the tie-in between Figure 5 and each of Figures 6, 7 and 8. Figure 5 refers to different levels of a database, such as application database, dictionary database and dictionary definition database. Figures 6, 7 and 8 are intended to apply to databases on each and every level. The implication is that a database on any of these levels could in theory be distributed across several data management environments.

Figure 8, however, shows a specific processor for IRDS Services, and this processor would have cognisance of two level pairs, specifically the dictionary definition level pair and the dictionary level pair but not the application level pair.

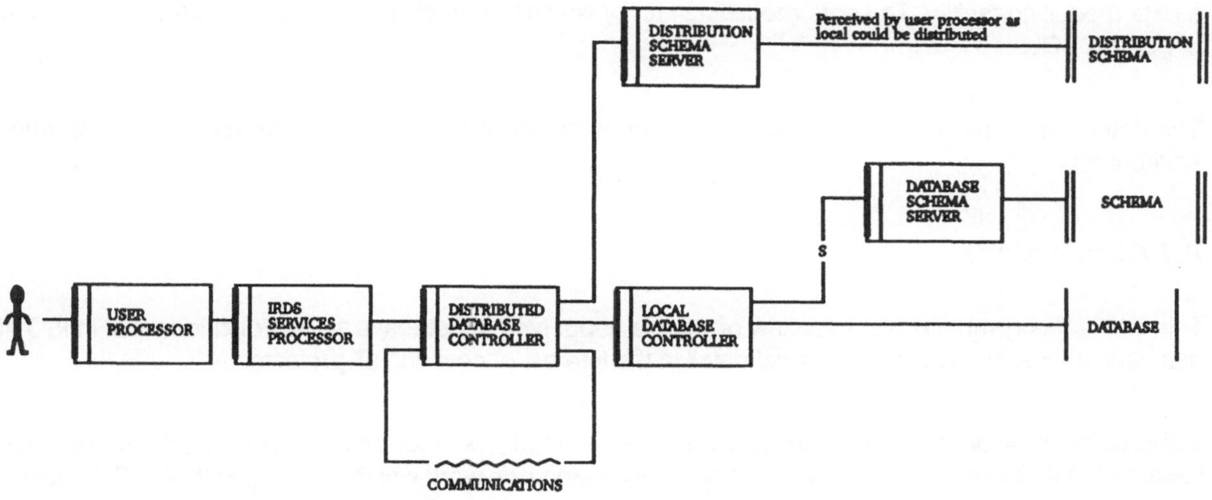

Figure 8 : Abstract Processors for Distributed Databases Showing Position of Dictionary Services

8.5 Remote Database Access

This project has been initiated within ISO since database standards work became part of the Open Systems activity. Early work on the base document was performed in an ECMA subgroup. The project clearly requires the combination of database and OSI expertise and interfaces with standards of both kinds.

In general terms, the standard being developed is concerned with the accessing of a database in a distributed environment, but it should not be considered as a standard for a distributed database system.

If a client processor at one open system knows that it needs some data which is located at another open system, then that processor can use the service provided at the RDA interface to access the data. It is important to note that the facility is intended for interactive use and not for bulk transfer of large volumes of data from one open system to another.

Two standards are being prepared: the OSI Generic Remote Database Access Service and Protocol has been the subject of a Draft Proposal letter ballot (DP9579); the other standard is directed to the use of the semantics of the SQL Data Manipulation Language as a means of specifying the access to the remote database.

8.6 Export/Import

One other project was recently the subject of a new work item letter ballot. This is a standard for exporting and/or importing all or part of a database from one data management environment to another. The two data management environments involved may or may not be at the same physical location.

It is intended that this standard can be used for a database which is structured according to the rules of a data modelling facility. The data modelling facility which will receive first consideration (as in the case of RDA) is SQL.

The definition of the data in the importing environment must be consistent with that in the exporting environment.

8.7 Conclusions

This article has given a broad overview of what is happening in database standardisation work in ISO. It has been necessary to avoid technical detail in the interest of covering all projects.

It should be mentioned that the resources of most, if not all, member bodies, such as BSI, are directed towards the ISO work. In BSI, there is no database standards work which is not specifically ISO related.

CENTRAL REPOSITORY CONTROL OF A DISTRIBUTED DEVELOPMENT ENVIRONMENT

Philippe Turner-Loisel
Manager Software Products Ltd

9.1 What Is A Distributed Development Environment?

The word distributed is more and more frequently used when talking about processing and about databases. But what does it mean and why are distributed databases, distributed processing and a distributed development environment needed?

9.1.1 THE DISTRIBUTED DATABASE(S)

We have today the possibility to quickly and precisely process data. Does this give us the right information to make the appropriate decisions for our business? The right information can be qualified as accurate, timely and concise.

How do we achieve the accuracy? If the sources of data to be processed are the right ones, the data to be processed will be reliable and if the processing is correct, the information obtained will be accurate. This means manipulating data which is real, exact now, and therefore which is collected from where it is used.

Here is our requirement for a distributed database, no duplication but shared access to data stored in various locations - various DBMSs, various formats, various sites and even various operating systems and processors. Each item of data should be ideally stored close to the location where it will be used the most frequently and where it is crucial for it to be available without unnecessary delay. Centralisation of all the data in one location would result in intolerable communication delays when accessing the data from a - or a set of - remote site(s) for transaction processing.

This means that the other systems which need to access that data might have to gather it from many different locations. For ease of programming, the access to the data will be achieved through a "userview" which might be made up of many data items coming from many files and databases which are likely to be on various machines and in many locations. The distributed database can be as complex as this. This concept is a headache today. Is the solution to use many copies of a unique DBMS right across the world? Does the solution lie in the way we access the data, ie. is SQL the common language to be used? What steps are taken by the major players in the Data Base Management System arena? (Model 204, IDMS/R, ADABAS, ORACLE, SUPRA, DB2, TERADATA,)

Certainly, most of us agree that distributed databases will not affect every business. Only those sites which have multiple vendors' hardware, multiple sites or multiple DBMSs need to be concerned. Already, a large number of companies are trying to implement the use of a single DBMS across the whole enterprise.

9.1.2 DISTRIBUTED PROCESSING

Some machines are better than others for dealing with specific tasks. The cost of processing grows with the size of the machine used. Some tasks are definitely PC/PS tasks whilst some others are more suited to the mainframe. It is difficult within the same job to switch from one level of processor to another. Ideally, each machine should be used to its maximum potential and if there is a choice of machine size and make, at equivalent performance or more exactly to obtain an acceptable performance, the cheaper is obviously the better. In other words, don't monopolise the mainframe when you could use a PC/PS.

Currently, when one is at a terminal or a workstation one might have the choice of one or two alternatives as far as the environment one accesses is concerned, ie. the operator is using a PC/PS or he/she is using the machine as a terminal accessing a network. This is a conscious decision and the two environments in most cases are kept well apart. Communication between various machines for sharing data between environments is still too often a one-off batch transfer of data from one environment to the other. This explains that some processing which could be done adequately and cheaply in a PC/PS environment is sometimes performed more expensively on the mainframe to the detriment of other applications running at the same time.

Distributed processing addresses just that problem which is very common. The operator should be able to get on with his/her job without having to know which is the best way of dealing with it. Today, it is possible for our end-users to have a menu-driven system which allows them to do just that. However, there are few companies which have invested in the development of such systems. Such a task requires expertise and time, two factors which are very much in demand. In these isolated enterprises, the decision of what should be done where has been taken by the programmer or the analyst, based on a static set of values. The ideal situation would be when the machine itself could decide on where to perform the required processing based on its own knowledge of the network, ie. which processor is free, which processor is best for this, what is the amount of data to be processed, etc. Today, there are machines which have a "processor manager" which distributes the tasks to a set of similar processors within a single box (DEC/VAX approach for example); nothing as sophisticated as distributed processing in its wider sense.

Distributed processing can be thought of in a different way. On a Wide Area Network, the processing could be shared between processors (of varied size and shape) which are at different nodes of the network.

Certainly, most of us agree that such distributed processing will not concern every business. Only companies with many sites which all have their own processing power might be tempted to invest in such advanced technology now. Only those single site companies which have a need for saving CPU time need to consider it otherwise.

9.1.3 THE DISTRIBUTED DEVELOPMENT ENVIRONMENT

Who believes they belong to a distributed development environment? I should think that most of us come from a distributed development environment. But how many of us are aware of it and, more importantly, how many of us are happy that the development environment is properly managed and controlled?

A development environment becomes distributed as soon as one of the following premises are true:

- development is carried out in more than one location;
- applications are developed to be run on different machines types;
- applications are developed using more than one language;

- applications are developed using more than one database;
- the packages used in the company have been supplied from various unrelated suppliers;
- the computer department is accommodated in two or more distinct buildings;
- more than one machine is used and these machines are not connected;
- many projects are running in parallel;
- more than one person is working at developing applications.

I therefore believe that most of us belong to a distributed development environment. Unlike distributed databases and distributed processing, the distributed development environment is not a new concept and it is real for most of us today. Very few companies can afford to ignore its problems because most companies - if not all of them - suffer today from the mis-management or even the total lack of management of it.

9.2 The Areas Which Have To Be Monitored In A Distributed Development Environment

The first problem is the poor communication mechanism which exists between the parties. The end-user's needs are gathered, not reflected accurately in the business analysis phase, modified at the design stage and disfigured at the construction stage. This explains why the systems developed using traditional approaches seldom respond to business needs.

The second headache might be one of the causes of the first problem mentioned above. It is already experienced by most of you. This is the definition and the implementation of naming conventions also called naming standards. This is an area which should have been addressed and solved from Day One in any enterprise. Unfortunately, the first person involved had his/her own undefined standards and believed in everybody's inventiveness and common sense. This does not work! As early as possible, rules should be defined for better communication. There are a lot of publications - books and articles - covering this topic and I refer to these publications the people who have a particular interest in it. We believe that less than one in ten mainframe installations have a completely defined and used set of naming standards.

As a result of this weakness, time is wasted in communication between users and DP/IS professionals, also multiple definitions - often incompatible - of the same item exist. The same item of data is stored many times, under different names, with different values. This uses more storage space than necessary and even sometimes introduces more I/Os than should be necessary during the execution of certain routines, therefore slowing down the performance of vital applications.

The third problem is the lack of usage of what has already been done (no reusability). The same model is drawn over and over again, the same functionality is provided by many different modules, the same validation test is performed several times on the same item of data, all things which are expensive to develop, expensive to maintain.

In the last few years, this problem has been heightened by the multitude of workbenches which are PC based and which do not offer a corporate approach. Data is entered once at the planning stage, entered again at the analysis stage and then retyped on the mainframe in a catalogue, a dictionary, etc. There are far too many chances of mistyping, misinterpreting and losing the genuine information. They do not permit the use of the information already present in the current systems (no possibility for retrofitting). The refined information obtained in the final stages of development cannot be passed down to the planning phase for further planning work. They are offering support for a sequential, linear development life but not for the development lifecycle.

Often, the management structure has been established to take care of the technical aspect of the jobs involved (project support) but hardly any consideration has been given to the management of the most valuable asset, the data. Some personnel must be allocated to look after the data. A well defined data administration function must be established. There is no central corporate pool of information and data maintained. Different views - individuals, users, programmers, analysts, projects, management or others - exist. Companies should work now - and without delay - at normalising definitions. This is what MSP has been saying for years, this is what IBM has recommended to their users whilst waiting for its repository.

In most companies, a few people are aware of these needs but everybody is too busy keeping their heads above water, ie. writing new applications, not addressing business needs.

Now that we have defined the problems which are inherent to a distributed development environment, we need to concentrate on how a company can take a decisive advantage over its competitors by providing on time the right systems to respond to constantly changing business needs.

9.3 The Repository Solution

The repository allows a company to monitor its distributed development environment and offers a large degree of automation to tasks dealing with administration and control.

Looking at the various points highlighted in the above chapter: The naming standards must be defined and accepted at company level. The repository then allows a controller to validate any new entry on the repository. Three tasks are involved:

- Identification and selection of the recent entries;

This can be based on a date and time stamp, a log file or in the structure of the repository itself (versioning facility and its management). Whichever means of obtaining the requested list of entries you choose, it should be obtained easily.

- Validation of the entry name;

For each of the new entries listed, the repository can extract the names which do not follow the standards defined, ie. which are using terms or abbreviations which are not allowed. It will offer an alternative name in most cases. This can be provided to the originators as a report (daily, weekly) showing the invalid name given, followed by the alternative valid names proposed.

- Comparison of new entries with selected existing entries for elimination of synonyms and homonyms.

When satisfied that the name is given in accordance with the standards in force in your organisation, the repository can also offer a list of objects documented on the repository which could possibly be one and the same object as the one newly added. A brief description of the objects in the list provided will help in tracking down the homonyms. This brief description itself could be governed by very strict guidelines with regard to its size and contents.

This name validation process can be actioned on-line if thought desirable, but most of the time we shall assume that, for efficiency reasons, a batch routine is more likely to be used on a periodical basis. The event triggering the run of such a routine can itself be documented in the repository and an automatic recognition of the event can be implemented.

The implementation of such a naming control facilitates reusability. Indeed, when adding a new member, if it is found that the member already exists, the user does not need to define it again. At most, he/she will complement the existing documentation. If the object under consideration is a new module which needs writing, one might find that such functionality is already provided by an existing module.

To take the most advantage of the use of a repository, the facility must be available to everybody (of course with various levels of authority). The corporate approach must be enforced, explained and accepted. No project - however small - should be allowed to be developed independently from the repository.

The metamodel supported by the repository should be of an open architecture type in order to allow import and export from other tools. Some sophisticated repositiories available today even provide you with an import/export facility which gives you a basic data manipulation facility to palliate the incompatibility of the definitions across tools. The rules used for the translation of the member definitions for communication with various outside tools are also stored on the repository.

The repository is to the data administrator what the electric sander is to the joiner. Without it, the worker can do the job but it is much more time consuming and very much skill related. The major benefit of the repository resides in the automation of the control and administration of the environment. This is achieved through versioning, user profiles, file protection, restricted use of certain commands, generation from the repository.

9.3.1 VERSIONING

- The structure of the repository should reflect the various states of a system: one or more development statuses based on one or more test statuses based on a live status which itself comprises the modifications implemented to a previous structure (historical status);

- The structure of the repository should also reflect the project approach of the development project status within departmental status;

- The structure of the repository should be supported by strict control of the various access levels given to users. Access must vary from one person to another and for one given person, authority might vary from one project to another. The data available, the functions available can even be restricted depending on the stage reached by a given project.

This versioning capability is the key factor for the control and the promotion of information and definitions during the development life cycle.

9.3.2 USER PROFILES

Each user should be linked to a single or a set of profiles defining which area of the repository he/she can access, which he/she can update or delete or populate.

Another desirable level of security consists of the protection by password of selected objects which therefore could be accessed only by special authority requested there and then, just before allowing access to the protected object.

The passwords used in the logon command can be recorded in a LOG file, on which every access or, more importantly, update is recorded.

The versioning facility and profiles give the administrator the possibility of checking completeness at user level, project level and departmental level. In the same way, the consistency checks can be run against information held at project, department and corporate level.

9.3.3 RESTRICTED USE OF CERTAIN COMMANDS

Some functions cannot be made available to all users. A limited set of tailored commands should be available to the users. This series of commands should be accessed by the end-users through a menu-driven system.

9.3.4 GENERATION OF COPYBOOKS AND DBMS DEFINITIONS

Since the information held on the repository is checked for accuracy, the database definitions should be automatically generated from it. For consistency purposes, the copybooks for all languages should also be extracted from there. It is possible to forbid native database management facilities (creation, maintenance on the DBMS) therefore enforcing their usage through the repository.

9.3.5 CONTINUOUS MONITORING OF THE ENVIRONMENT

For quality assurance purposes, routines can be established to compare the definition of objects as they are defined in the repository with their counterparts in the live environment.

9.3.6 INCORPORATION OF EXISTING DOCUMENTATION AND SYSTEMS

The repository owes its name to the fact that it is the privileged place where all information reposes. If existing systems bear any value, they should be retrofitted, as any information which needs recording should be stored on the repository.

9.3.7 IMPACT ANALYSIS AND INTERROGATION FACILITIES

The repository allows you not only to document everything but, more importantly, it offers endless possibilities for extracting information. Certain types of access are more efficient than others, but there is no restriction on how to access information stored in the repository. The format and layout of the reports generated are free and definable to satisfy individual needs, likes and dislikes.

9.3.8 AUTOMATIC DOCUMENTATION

Interfaces between precompilers and the repository can be written to disallow compilation of any module which uses an object not defined in the repository.

There are hundreds of other tasks which can be automated in conjunction with the use of a repository. We believe that the repository is the right approach and that without it you will always be kept busy keeping your head above water, you will be constantly fire-fighting and you will provide less and less of a service to your enterprise.

9.4 Why The Repository Approach Is Correct

The cost of purchasing and implementing a repository is not cheap. We therefore have to look at the benefits of using such a tool. The time devoted to set up an adequate set of naming standards will be recovered by a saving in the amount of maintenance required by the new systems as they better serve the business needs thanks to better communication.

The automation of the enforcement of naming standards is easily justified as, in a sizeable environment, the manual enforcement of such a standard will require many man hours per week, without any hope for this requirement fading away.

The computerised repository will save effort which would otherwise be spent redefining objects already defined, writing modules which already exist,

The automatic generation of copybooks and database definitions will speed up the programming time and save the database administrator's time. Its major benefit is also an assurance that the definitions are accurate and match each other. This will be reflected by a reduction in testing time needed and in maintenance effort needed for error solving. This also facilitates impact analysis when any change to data definitions is requested.

Any information can be obtained within minutes and is accurate. This obviously allows management to react faster and therefore gives a competitive edge to your business.

The repository is not a goal on its own. The goal is to obtain the right information at the right time. The establishment of a repository allows you to monitor the usage of data and the development of systems. It is also an ideal starting point for the successful implementation of a CASE environment.

With a repository, information management is no longer a world of fear and of unknowns. It becomes a world of knowledge and of calculated decisions.

With a repository you are in a position where the applications developed more closely support your business because they are responding to business's requirements. The presence of the repository allows faster development of better quality applications, which gives your business a competitive edge.

When looking at what changes will be imposed on us in the next few years, investment in a repository solution today will reap significant returns in the future. To list but a few of these possible changes:

9.4.1 TAX CHANGES

New rates are introduced based on the family cell, introduction of a European tax on salary, new taxation for countries outside the EEC, new deductions at source, new option for salary payment through bankers'cards.

9.4.2 CURRENCY CHANGES

New European Monetary system, salary now linked to the exchange rate.

9.4.3 INCREASE IN THE NUMBER OF CUSTOMERS

Handling of more different currencies, increase of the size of the customer number field, a customer's address must now include the country, telephone numbers can now be up to 15 figures,

9.4.4 PRODUCTION OF NEW REPORTS TO MEET EEC REQUIREMENTS

New standards will be introduceld for a number of central data processing outputs, including:

- letter and reports layouts;
- invoices;
- reminders;
- pay slips.

Also, it must be remembered that letters should now be issued in one (or more) of the EEC languages when trading in the community. New forms are introduced to allow for the analysis of population movements and migrations within the EEC. Employers must now offer an investment plan to their employees as part of their pay package.

In summary, it is essential that the distributed impact of data processing be considered as an integral part of any business. In terms of the use of repositories in this environment the following points must be actioned:

<u>Review your environment now</u>

<u>Postion yourself for the future</u>

<u>Think strategic : invest in a repository now !</u>

VENDOR DEVELOPMENTS

DEVELOPING PRODUCTS TO SUPPORT DISTRIBUTED DATA PROCESSING

Carlos Miguens
Independent Consultant

10.1 Introduction

The client-server architecture is readily adaptable to distributed processing by placing the client and server processes on two different machines. Separating the client and server processes should be transparent to both end users and application programmers. To achieve this transparency the Relational Database Management System (RDBMS) must cope with different hardware architectures which may have different character sets, different representations for floating point numbers, and other hardware dependant differences. The RDBMS must also cope with many different networking protocols, adhere to industry standards and have performance which allows it to be used in core production applications.

Historically databases have been built using a two process architecture, for various reasons such as security and modularity. This two process structure has been called a Frontend-Backend architecture. More recently this has developed to become more sophisticated and become known as a Client-Server architecture.

In this chapter we shall look at the development of a client-server architecture and at an implementation of an architecture designed to cope with a complex distributed heterogeneous environment.

10.2 Remote Data Access

The client and server need to be able to communicate with each other without regard to the underlying communications mechanism. Whether the two processes are on the same machine - the simplest case - or on two machines on different continents. The communications facility must allow the client to communicate with the server in all of these situations without change in the application code. The facility must intercept all communications between client and server and hide the details of the underlying communications mechanism.

The client extracts and manipulates data in the database using a query language; in most cases today that query languauge is SQL. To aid applications portability the ANSI SQL standard was developed, which defined some syntactic and semantic conventions to which vendors should adhere. Given two servers which both understand ANSI SQL to a given level, say INGRES and DB2 at ANSI level 1, then one could be forgiven for assuming that a client could run unchanged against either server. There are two problems which become apparent when one tries this out in practice:

- the protocol between the client and server are different;

- the two implementations of SQL, whilst both conforming to ANSI, are different.

To cope with the first problem a sub-committee was set up by ANSI (X3H2.1). This committee has developed the Remote Data Access (RDA) standard which was originally proposed by ISO and driven by the Europeans. This standard is not yet ratified. RDA defines message formats and communications protocols that allow heterogeneous SQL systems to interoperate, exchanging queries and data.

The importance of RDA is that it isolates both client and server from the details of communication allowing the communications mechanisms to be changed and enhanced over time without a change in either the client or server code. It allows RDA to fit in well with the OSI seven layer model as these protocols mature, and gives vendor transparency in the Client-Server model.

RDA gives a standardised protocol based on native relational database constructs, these include:

- commands;
- queries;
- tuple descriptors;
- tuples;
- status messages.

An application or client would send a query to the RDA facility, this facility then packages the query in a standard packet and dispatchs the query to the server, which may be a communications server. When the query reaches the data server the RDA facility presents the query for processing. The server uses the same mechanism for returning data or status messages.

10.3 A General Communications Architecture

INGRES has such a facility called the General Communications Facility (GCF) encompassed by the INGRES General Communications Architecture (GCA). This GCA is based on the ISO RDA standard but is a tried and tested implementation, used successfully throughout INGRES Release 6 products.

An example of how GCA works in practice is provided here for the INGRES environment. Firstly an INGRES application as a client must connect to a database server. This is done using the standard SQL statement CONNECT. The connect request is sent to a named server, which provides transparency of database server locations by keeping a list of available database servers locally and throughout the network. The name server also knows where in a network a database can be found. Once the name server finds the database to which the application has requested a connection it passes back the address of the server to GCF. The GCF can then establish the connection directly with the relevant server. There are five types of server;

- Name Server;
- Database Server;
- Communications Server;
- Star Server;
- Gateway Server.

Once the link is established the application can start to send queries to the server, as shown in Figure 1.

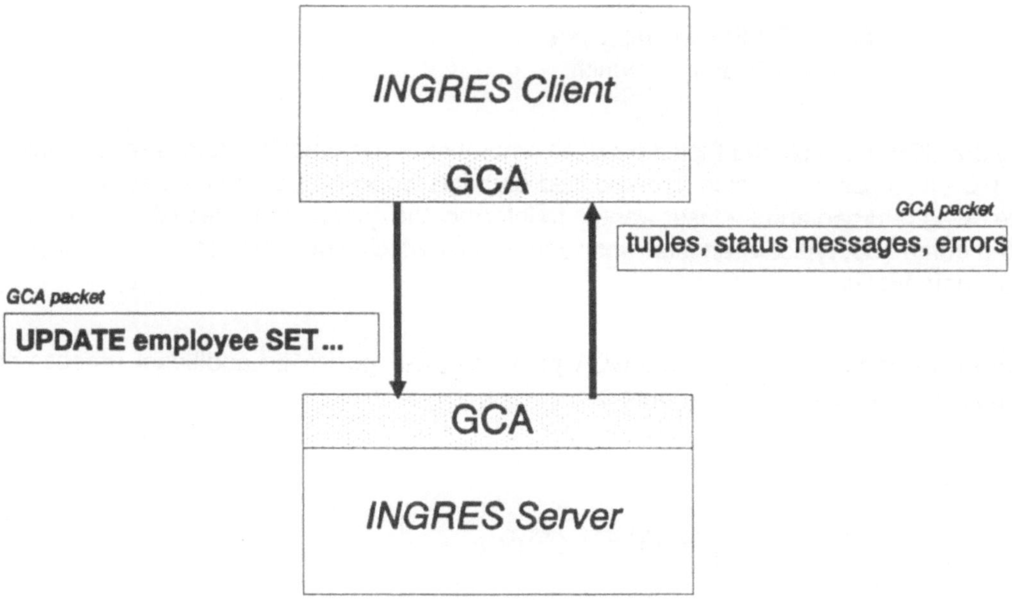

Figure 1 : Global Communications Architecture

Assume we are operating on a local machine which is not networked, therefore both client and database server reside on the same node. Using the following query as an example:

UPDATE employee SET (salary = salary*1.01)
WHERE name = 'Miguens';

The application would send this query as text to GCA, GCA is part of the application process. The query is usually a textual SQL query separated into query text and query data. A typical query such as the UPDATE will be made up of the text of the update statement, mixed with data values associated with the target list. Some queries have no textual SQL associated with them, only a special message type (such as a COMMIT). This is done so that the parser can be bypassed in certain circumstances for performance reasons. The SQL is packaged into a standard GCA packet. This packet or envelope is then sent to the server. When the server receives the packet is does not know what the packet contains or where it is from. It is only by reading the packet that the server can determine the user that sent the request and what the request is, in this case an SQL query.

Next the server will remove the SQL query from the GCA packet and will send it to the part of the server which will execute the query. When the query has been successfully executed the server first sends a tuple descriptor in a standard GCA packet to the client. The tuple descriptor describes the format of the tuples which will be returned so that the client can build buffers of the correct format. The tuple descriptor contains the following information to describe tuples:

- name of the columns (attributes);
- data type;
- length of attribute.

Then the server will send the tuples, once again in a standard GCA packet. There may be many tuples as in the case of the following query:

```
SELECT * FROM employee
  WHERE name = "Smith";
```

In this case the GCA may split the tuples between a number of packets. The data is reassembled at the client end. GCA also has a provision for expedited data this would be useful in the above case if many tuples were being returned and the user wanted to interrupt the query. In this case the client could send an expedited command, typically an interrupt, to the server which would process this command before sending any more tuples.

In the case of a remote site access the GCA packets would go via an additional process called a communications server, as shown in Figure 2.

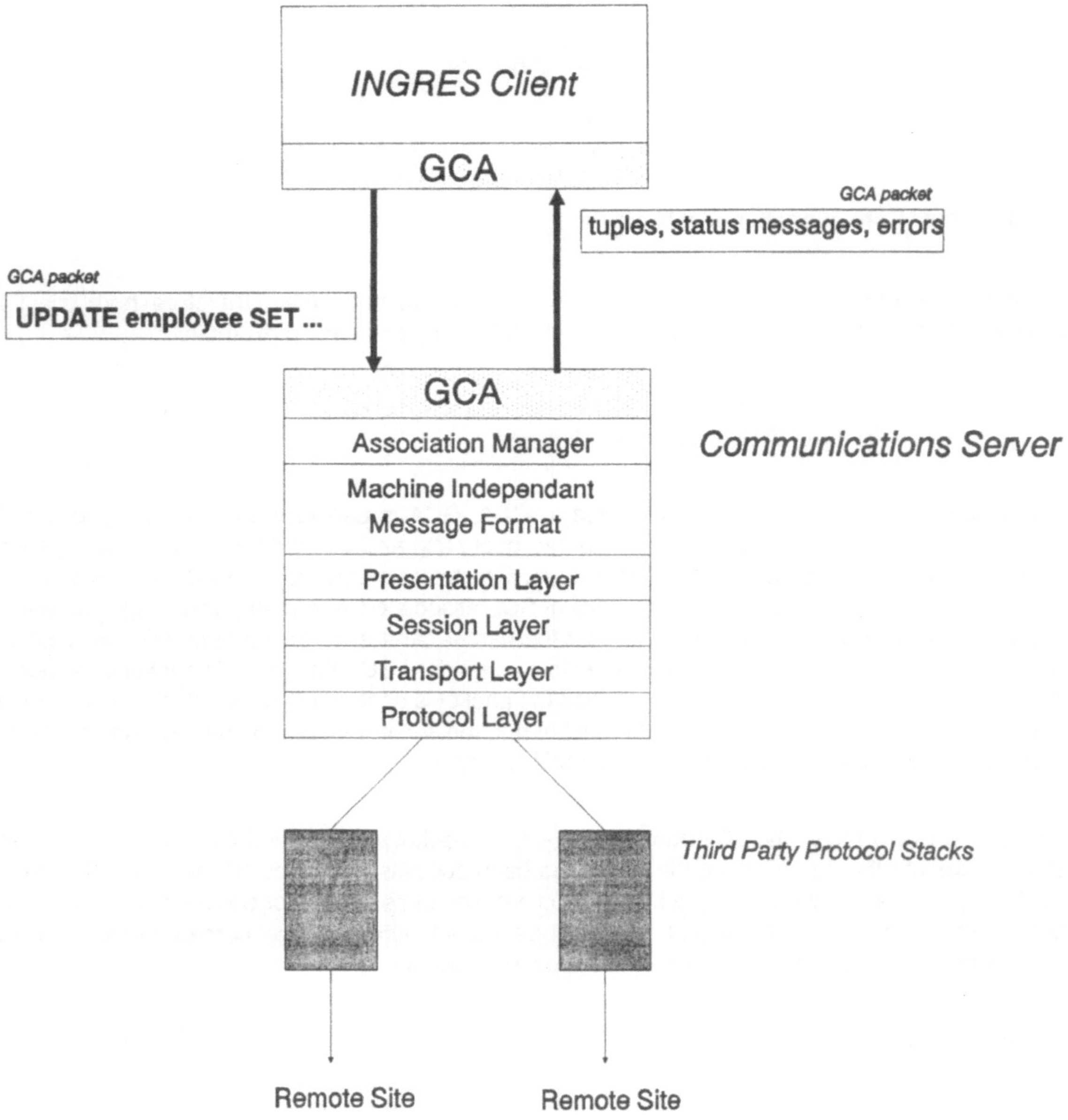

Figure 2 : Communications Server

There will be a communications server at both local and remote sites. The communications server takes GCA packets and sends them over a network using the available protocols, such as TCP/IP or SNA. The communications server is multi-threaded and is thus capable of receiving GCA packets from many clients. It is also capable of handling multiple protocols, this means that it is only necessary to add additional communications servers when the GCA traffic reaches saturation. GCF consists of the upper four layers of the OSI basic reference model: Application, Presentation, Session and Transport. The Application layer, ie. GCA, is part of all processes, and provides the mechanisms for local interprocess communication. The Presentation, Session and Transport layers, along with Network protocol specific code are contained in the communications server process.

10.4 Do You Speak Open SQL?

Lets us assume now that two vendors have an implementation of GCA, and assume too that we can connect a client from one vendor to the database server of another vendor. As an example try to connect an INGRES application to a DB2 database. Whilst both systems implement ANSI SQL, there are differences, which mean that the connection would fail. These differences arise because:

- the standard is incomplete, it has no provisions for dropping tables, removing grants, standard error messages, copying data from files into tables and so on. These are operational requirements which must be implemented by vendors;

- in addition to the extensions to SQL mentioned above, each vendor implements their own particular extensions: Rdb for instance has a facility to create a table from the DEC CDD dictionary. In the best cases all vendors implement an extension in the same way: such an example is the REVOKE statement. In the worst case each vendor will have their own implementation of a particular extension;

- the standard falls short too on the semantics of database operations such as the way in which cursors work and how transaction semantics should be defined. In practice these things are left as "implementation defined".

There is only one way to address these problems and that is to have a standard which encompasses all these issues. As a vendor trying to solve some of these problems we could not wait for ANSI to catch up so we had to devise a standard of our own: we called this Open SQL.

We examined the various prevalent implementations of SQL, about 10 in all, and from these extracted commands which all implementations possessed in a similar form: this we called Common SQL, and it formed the basis of Open SQL. In addition to these commands there were some obvious omissions, such as the ability to use compiled queries because some systems do not have such a feature. So a series of extensions were also defined, this formed the second part of Open SQL. The final part of Open SQL is a set of generic error messages, numbers and a standard catalogue interface. We implemented Open SQL as part of the INGRES system and re-wrote the INGRES toolset using Open SQL, so that it could work across multiple database systems. User applications too can use Open SQL, and are thus guaranteed portable applications across a divergence of database systems.

10.5 Plug And Play Revisited

Going back to our premise but now assuming that the two vendors have implemented both GCA and Open SQL, could we now connect a client and server from two different vendors and make them work?

Could one, for instance, run the INGRES tools against a foreign database such as DB2? In theory this would work: in practice we can't tell, since no other vendor has yet implemented Open SQL or GCA. Once again we had to take up the challenge. This we did with INTELLIGENT GATEWAYS

10.6 The Intelligent Gateway

An INGRES gateway is responsible for providing a GCA interface and for translating Open SQL to the local dialect. Let us examine this in more detail.

A gateway does the following things:

- accepts messages in GCA format;
- accepts Open SQL and modifies to the local dialect;
- interfaces to the target system to execute a query;
- translates all data returned to Open SQL data types;
- translates all error messages returned to Generic Open SQL error messages;
- provides an interrupt mechanism to interrupt running queries on the target system;
- showing the native system catalogues as Open SQL standard catalogue interface - this is required primarily for the INGRES tools to work.

The gateway is not a two way mechanism: there is no provision for DB2 applications, for example, to access INGRES servers, as shown in Figure 3.

More importantly, there are certain areas that the gateway is not responsible for. The gateway does not try to add to the functionality of the target system, for example if the target system does not provide referential integrity the gateway does not add that capability. The gateway does not and must not subvert any of the host database's inherent mechanisms. For example, it must use the local query optimiser, it must honour local security restrictions and so on. The gateway must, however, gracefully reject requests which the target system cannot handle.

The gateway just described is one type of INGRES gateway known as a relational gateway. There is a less common type of gateway called a non-relational gateway. As its name suggests, this type of gateway is used for database and file systems which cannot be queried using relational techniques, such systems as IMS, VSAM and RMS. The design for a non-relational gateway is consistent for all implementations. The design objective is to make the data available to the client as if the client were accessing an INGRES server.

This involves providing a relational interface to a non-relational database. The client passes the SQL request to GCA in the normal way. The gateway parses the inbound SQL requests, utilizing the INGRES catalogues it evaluates the query, optimizes the request and utilizes the local data manager to obtain the non-relational data. GCA is then used to pass the data back to the requesting client, with a relational "look".

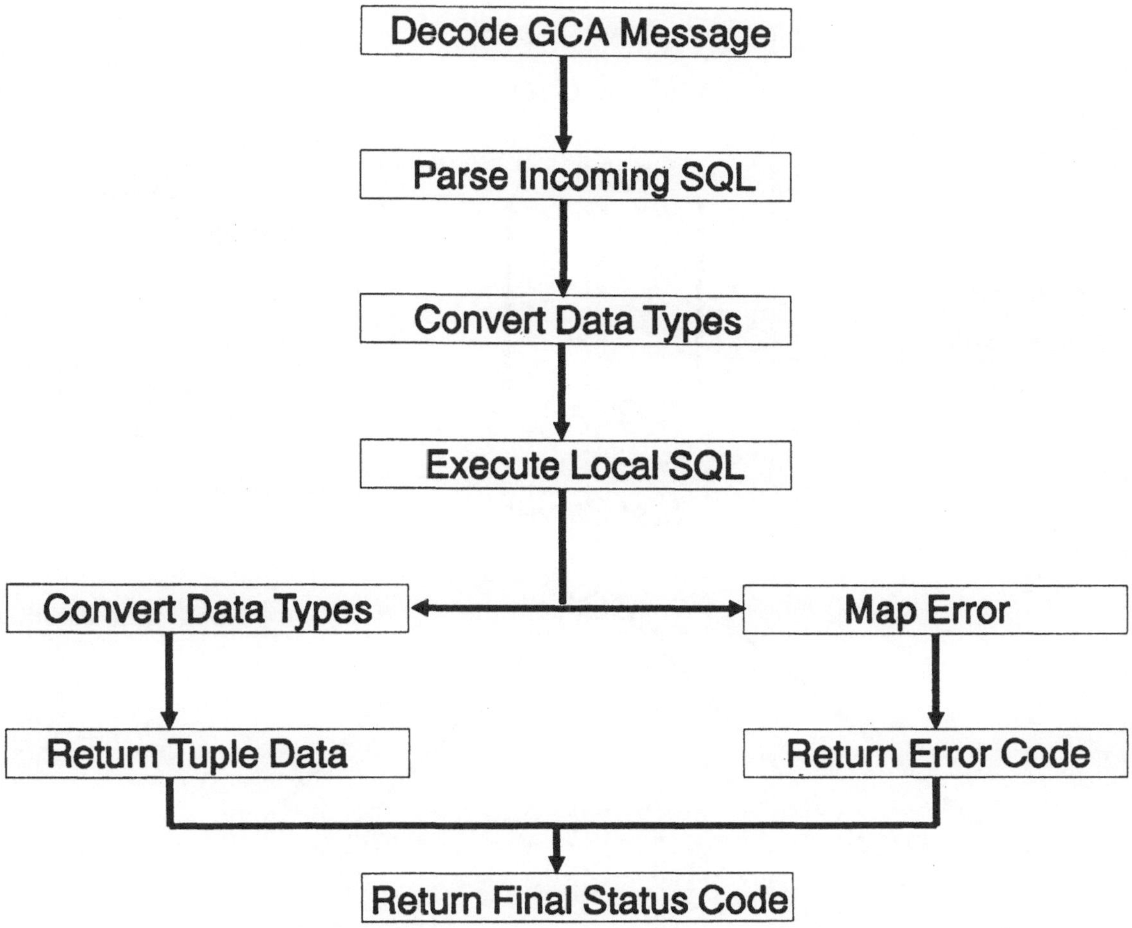

Figure 3 : Gateway Processing

10.7 Bringing It All Together

Having built a Global Communications Architecture and having used that throughout the INGRES product range we are in a position to add a final element to give us full distributed database capabilities.

A distributed database can be thought of as a collection of data which belongs to the same system. This data, however, may be spread over the sites of a computer network. To enable the transparent integration of the data a Star server architecture should be adopted. Figure 4 overleaf shows an example of this architecture with a distributed database made up of DB2 and INGRES data.

At the top level is the global schema. This defines all of the data which is contained in the distributed database as if the data were not distributed at all. Therefore the global schema can be defined in exactly the same way as in a non-distributed database.

Each global relation maps transparently to a relation at local level. This architecture is required to enable a client to treat the distributed database as if it were centralised. He need not concern himself about the distribution of data. For example, the client makes no reference to the location of the data, instead he just uses the global schema. This property is called distribution transparency.

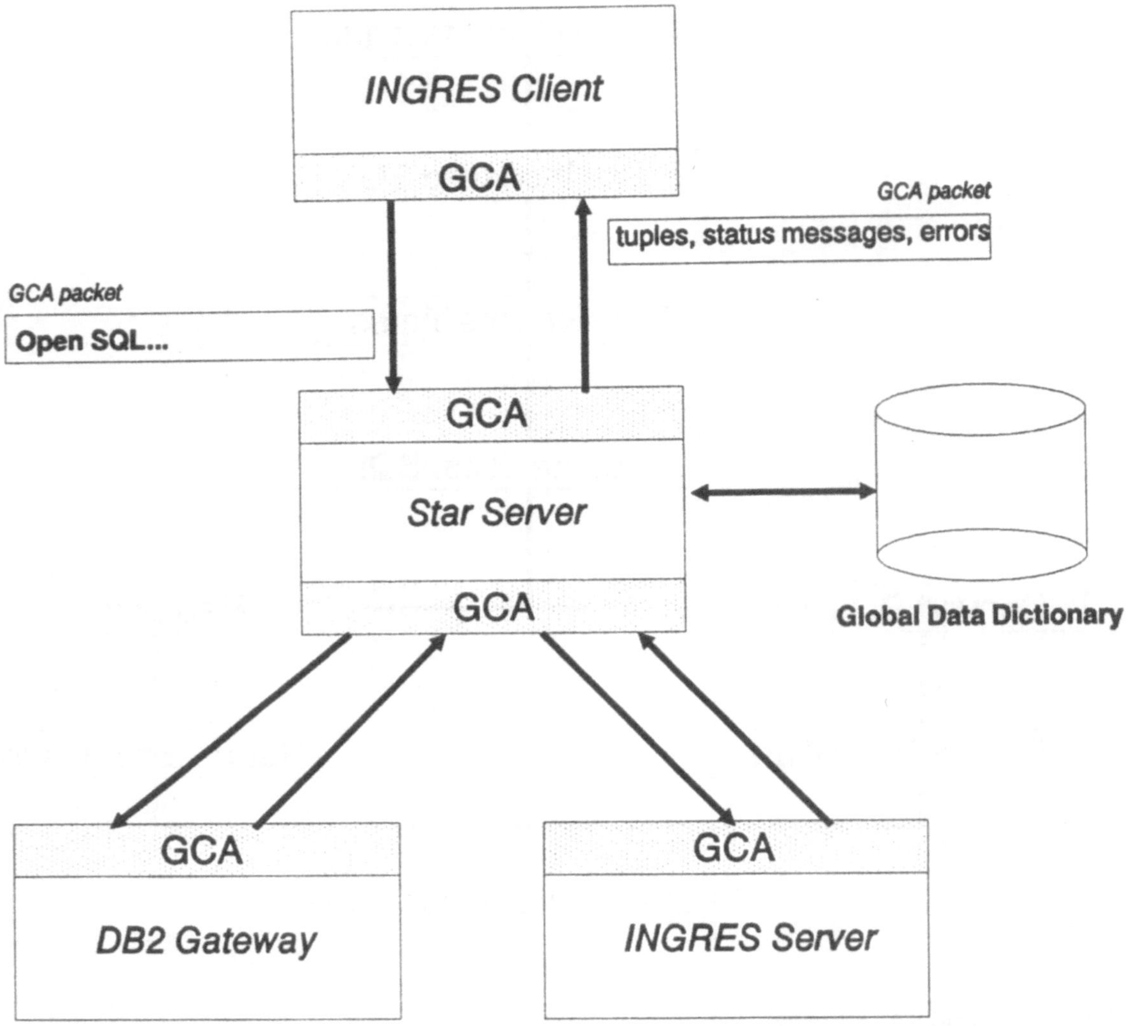

Figure 4 : Distributed Architecture

Distribution transparency is important so that the client need not specify where the data is located and thus should the location of the data change at some future point in time the client application would have to be changed. The GLOBAL DATA DICTIONARY is accessed by all clients and so gives a consistent view of the distributed database, whilst easing system maintenance.

Under this architecture, and because of the Global Communications Architecture, we can replace the standard INGRES DBMS server with an INGRES/Star server. This process provides all of the functionality required for a distributed database system without having to write any specialist code. The Star server handles the global data dictionary and all aspects of transparency.

The Star server is responsible for connecting to the relevant local databases, once again using the GCA protocol, optimizing distributed queries, handling distributed fragmentation, transaction recovery and all other distributed operations transparently. Because the Star server isolates all other parts of the system from knowing about distribution and uses these standard interfaces, a distributed database can be as complex as required, just by incorporating the relevant components - much like a house is built using standard bricks, roofing tiles, doors and so on.

10.8 Conclusion

The INGRES vision is one of a future where all databases will converse in a standard form of SQL and use a standard Remote Data Access protocol. Because of our leadership and experience we are pushing various standards bodies towards Open SQL and GCA, ANSI and Access/SQL amongst them.

The realisation of this vision would make "plug and play" between different vendors software a reality.

DISTRIBUTING DATA ACROSS AN ENTERPRISE

Lilian Hobbs Ph.D.
Digital Equipment Co Ltd

11.1 The Business World

Companies today have moved a long way from the small factory in a town, serving local industry. A typical company today will often have many branches or offices or warehouses scattered around the country or even around the world. The data that was once held manually in ledgers has now moved into many different types of computer systems, ranging from PCs to powerful mainframes. This has resulted in many people possessing some degree of computer literacy, from the secretary who is an expert in word processing, to the Senior Manager who is an expert with spreadsheets. Typically they all share one common goal: to read, update or create company data. This boom in computer awareness and the reliance by companies in using IT as a key component in their overall business strategy has resulted in an explosion of the demands now placed upon computer systems. As a result, businesses are making heavy technical demands on their systems, requesting many new systems, or enhancements to existing ones. This has resulted in a tremendous backlog of requirements, but this is still not stopping the advancement of computing. In fact, if anything, it is probably stimulating it.

What we have today are organisations who demand an IT strategy that allows them to create a distributed environment which can be easily managed. It also has to be flexible, to cope with change, the business expanding and markets changing, yet still retaining its compliance with standards and providing the company with the financial incentive to install it initially.

11.2 What Is Distributed Data?

Few organisations today would deny that their business is not distributed in some fashion, but many might argue that their data naturally belongs in one place. The problem here is that Distributed Data means different things to different people. So first we must ask ourselves, what do we mean when we say our data is distributed across the enterprise?

Basically we can categorise approaches to data distribution into:

- Local;
- Global;
- Extraction and Replication.

Depending on the hardware architecture and software available, we will see that, within each of these categories, there are many different styles of data distribution that are possible, many of which are probably adequate for the needs of most businesses today. The remainder of this paper will concentrate on describing how data can be distributed using Digital's VAX Architecture.

11.3 The VAX Architecture

One of the main reasons for the rapid growth and success of the Digital Equipment Corporation has been the VAX Architecture, which has enabled the company to become an industry leader in providing distributed computing and integrating computing resources throughout an enterprise. The philosophy behind the architecture is simple; a VAX is a VAX is a VAX. Therefore irrespective of whether you purchase a low-end 1 vax unit processor (vup) micro-vax, a VAXstation or a 100 vup aggregate throughput on a VAX 9000 model 400 mainframe, they all run the same Operating System, VMS, which therefore means that they will run the same software. The expansion of this architecture over many years has enabled many organisations to start small and they grow into building very powerful distributed systems, using a whole variety of different VAX machines.

11.4 Network Application Support (NAS)

As we move into the 1990s, Digital's Information Technology strategy is aimed at creating an open, unified environment, where access to information is allowed from a wide variety of desktop devices and allows new and existing applications to share information and resources, regardless of the operating platform. Digital's implementation of this strategy is Network Application Support (NAS).

11.5 Distributed Functionality In The Operating System

Before we even consider the database management systems and the distributed capabilities that they offer, we must first look at the capabilities provided in the VMS Operating System. Let us consider the example of a company that is driven by the orders it receives. The volume of those orders will determine whether the marketing department feel that a new sales campaign is required, whether the manufacturing division require extra supplies or staff, and will enable the Board of Directors to see how effectively the company is performing. The company has its own style of working and does not want to be turned upside down in order to implement a computer system to assist them in managing their business.

What is required here is for the data to be held in one central place, but for it to be accessed by a number of different users who process the data locally on their own systems. This can be achieved under VMS by creating a VAX Cluster.

A VAX cluster can be thought of as a form of Local Area Network. It can be implemented in several ways, but one of the most common is to have a number of VAXes linked together as the cluster, but sharing the same disks. For instance, the booking system is using several large powerful VAXes to take the orders, the Accounts department are using workstations and the marketing group have their own PCs which can talk to a small VAX, enabling them to become members of the cluster. In one fell swoop we have distributed the data amongst the organisations in the Enterprise, yet still enabled them to maintain their own familiar environment.

11.5.1 LOCAL DISTRIBUTION

Once we have set up this environment, then it becomes easy to set up local forms of data distribution. For example, we can create:

- Client/Server Environment;
- Data Partitioning;
- Distributed Lock Management;
- Distributed Data Dictionaries.

The VMS Operating System automatically manages the locking issues via its own distributed lock manager. Therefore products such as Digital's premier relational system Rdb/VMS use the lock manager very effectively to enable all these users to access this central pool of data, without contention, and very importantly, still maintaining the integrity of the database.

A typical problem faced today is that holding the data in one large database would be acceptable, provided everyone had timely access to it. One simple method that can be used to provide fast access to the data, is to employ the technique in the database system of Local Data Partitioning. If we take the example of the bookings system, instead of storing the bookings all in one physical table, the bookings are split by, say, surname across a number of disks, with the database system seeing this as one logical table. Rdb/VMS users have found that by using this technique they can achieve far greater throughput in their database systems.

TP monitors can also provide a mechanism for distributing the system in a local environment. When based upon the client-server model, the processing can then be split between the front-end, which is handling the forms presentation, character I/O, field validation and error handling, and the back-end which comprises of the application and is responsible for coordinating the resource manager. The use of TP monitors such as Digital's ACMS, which is tightly integrated with the languages, forms and database management systems used to create applications, is yet another example of how distributed systems can be created.

11.5.2 ACCESS TO CORPORATE DATA FROM THE PC

No office today is complete without its PCs. While these friendly devices provide cheap, easy to use software, we tend not to think of using them for accessing the main corporate database. Yet if we stop and think, they provide us with a golden opportunity to perform distributed data access and also distribute some of our data locally.

Let us consider the department within the Enterprise that has many PCs, using say spreadsheet software. Rather than having to learn a new spreadsheet software, they would prefer to extract the data from the corporate database, bring it across to their PC and then use it there to generate standard management reports. Using this approach, each machine is then being used to perform the tasks it is most suited for ie, the mainframe for fast searches of large volumes of data, and the PC for easy, smart presentation of the small subset of data selected from the corporate database.

Products such as SQL/Services that are a standard component of Rdb/VMS provide just such functionality. Using this product the user can sit at their PC, using familiar MS-DOS spreadsheet software enhanced to include SQL/Services, thereby enabling it to communicate with the VAX using the network. The VAX will then execute the query, find the data, and then transfer across the network only the data that has been requested. Hence the query executes very quickly on the much faster processor, and network traffic is kept to an absolute minimum. Why tie up the small PC with intensive searching when the mainframe can do it much faster? SQL/Services is not restricted to accessing databases on the VAX; it can also access databases on an IBM machine such as DB2.

11.6 Data Dictionaries - Managing The Distributed Data

Once we start to move data away from all being held in one place, we really need some mechanism for identifying where all the data in the Enterprise is used, and how. When you consider that we tend to spend more and more time maintaining systems, what can we do to make this process far more cost effective and efficient? The key to success is the Data Dictionary or Repository. If you want to know where something is used, ask the dictionary. Let us look at the typical set-up for developing applications. There is a Corporate Data Dictionary that contains all the standard data items that are used across the Enterprise. Each project team has its own collection of data items that are specific to that application. The requirement is to share all this data, but still provide each project team with autonomy over their data.

11.7 The Requirements Of A Distributed Data Dictionary System

It is essential that the ability to define the Dictionary as distributed in the form of a number of physical files located either locally or on the WAN is provided by the software. This will include being able to support the following features:

- Tracking and Impact Analysis;
- Two Phase Co-ordinated Commit Protocol to Maintain Integrity;
- Multiple User Access;
- Integration with all development tools, eg. forms, TP monitors, languages.

VAX CDD/Plus provides all this capability and more. Its real strength lies in its ability to distribute a dictionary anywhere on the WAN, with the dictionary software maintaining the integrity of all these discrete dictionaries. How long did it take, the last time you had to work out what the impact of changing a field in your system would be? In a distributed environment the Data Dictionary must be able to produce a list of everything that has to be changed, including forms, TP systems, databases, programs and 4GL applications.

Hopefully, it is now apparent that distributing data does not necessarily mean creating a wide area network. As we have seen, we can solve many problems just doing it locally.

11.8 Global Data Distribution

Global Data Distribution is probably the first thought people have when they think about distributing data, and they will without doubt consider the most difficult aspects of this form of distribution.

Today, with so many companies distributed around the country or even the world, they invariably need access to the data held at those remote sites. The questions we should ask ourselves is what form of access do they require, why is the data distributed?

It could be that all we require is the ability to access remote data. For example, a customer can visit the office of a major company, the data they will hold locally will be for customers of that branch, but using the network they can access the customers records at their local branch. This can be achieved today with the standard remote database capability provided in Rdb/VMS, so all we need to know is the location of where the data is stored.

11.9 Distributed Database Management Systems

Ultimately to distribute segments of data across the Enterprise while viewing this as a single database, then a truly distributed database system is needed. However, due to the complexities involved and the limitations of some of the associated technologies such as networking, it will be many years before we see a distributed database system that can resolve all of these problems, whatever the scenario.

What is it that makes a distributed database system inherently different from a conventional database system? Just some of the functionality that is required is:

- Horizontal Partitioning;
- Vertical Partitioning;
- Global Query Optimiser;
- Metadata Managers;
- Backup/Recover All or Part of the Database;
- Very Robust Two Phase Co-ordinated Commit Protocol;
- Concurrency Control.

Consideration has to be given to managing the situation when the data structure in say the Basingstoke part of the database has to be changed, but the database must stay up, since without it, the business will grind to a halt. Then once the changes have been implemented, all local applications must be updated to see the new structures.

Although this may be considered a rather extreme example, once we start to break the data up and distribute it around the enterprise, the procedures involved in maintaining its integrity become far more complex. Do not underestimate the demands that will be placed upon a distributed system.

11.10 Replicated Data

Do not be discouraged by thinking that the news on distributed databases is not good. Wait, it could just be that a Replicated Database satisfies the business need.

A replicated database is a form of distributed database that is often totally ignored. Yet it provides a capability that for many organisations meets most of their requirements.

Consider the company with 100 branches or depots. Head Office decides on the pricing policy for the hundreds, maybe thousands of stock items that they carry. How does the company ensure that every outlet is charging the same, and also keep track of the sales at each location?

Head Office manages the main corporate database, which contains the master pricing table. Using the distributed database software this master price list would be sent down to each of the company's outlets. Whenever the prices change, these would be sent automatically to the local outlets. Therefore they would only receive the changes, not the whole price list. Thus making very cost-effective use of the company network and without the local outlet having to manage its own database.

Alternatively, this configuration could be used to perform a multi-site rollup. This would involve taking all the details from each local database and transferring this information automatically to the main database. This is another form of distributed capability that is useful to many organisations but is rarely offered.

VAX Data Distributor is a product layered on top of Rdb/VMS which provides this functionality. The software runs automatically and is responsible for establishing the network links, transferring the data as specified and maintaining the integrity of the databases involved in the transfer.

11.1 Conclusions

We have seen that it is possible today, using a set of products based upon strategic industry standards, to easily distribute data around the enterprise. Information can be shared with all users, have a consistent look and feel across a multi-vendor environment, yet still utilise to the full the architecture on each of the vendor platforms.

Distributed data is here to stay, and the future holds even more exciting possibilities to support the growing needs of todays complex business processes and structures.

RESEARCH IN DISTRIBUTION

SSADM AND DISTRIBUTION : SO WHAT'S THE PROBLEM?

A. Jenkins and G.R. Hidderley
BIS Applied Systems & The SSADM Research Centre

12.1 SSADM

SSADM (Structure System Analysis and Design Method) is a structured set of procedural technical and documentation standards, designed specifically for analysing business needs and undertaking software development. It consists of a two-part framework - covering business requirements analysis and design - which is sectioned into stages. Taken together these stages provide a complete set of techniques for data modelling, requirements analysis and software design. SSADM is inherently flexible and is the most effective method available for organisations requiring one standard approach to deal with a wide variety of development issues.

A formal description of SSADM can be found in the Reference Manual, published by the National Computing Centre Ltd.

12.1.1 THE HISTORY OF SSADM

The Government is the largest user of information systems in the UK. In the early 1980s it recognised that major savings could be achieved by adopting a standard for software development. A fundamental requirement was that the standard should provide a rigorous and unambiguous mechanism for analysing business needs and for undertaking design, but other needs included the ability to implement it in support tools, to use it on projects built either in-house or turnkey (or through facility management), and to be usable by a wide range of IT staff, both naive and experienced.

12.1.2 HOW IS SSADM DEVELOPED?

CCTA recognised that the information needs of the private and public sectors are similar. So it shares the policy task with those in industry who are best placed to help.

Future product strategy is determined by the Design Authority Board. This is chaired and supported by CCTA, which represents government computer users and ensures that the most important criterion determining the future of any management method - the needs of the users - is fully taken into account. In this way SSADM is the only truly user-oriented major method. It is developed by users for users. The parallel needs of private-sector users are input by the representative from the Computing Services Association, and by The National Computing Centre. The British Computer Society is also fully represented at the Board to ensure that professional, academic and longer-term research interests are fully taken into account. The Board now also has representatives of users via the SSADM User Group. The Design Authority Board takes a five to ten-year view of software development, schedules the introduction of new features and controls release strategy. CCTA then undertakes the necessary planning, development and trials to ensure that these releases are delivered on time.

The removal of barriers to trade across the European Community in 1992 is expected to reinforce the need for open standards, and the Board is keen to ensure that SSADM relates effectively to this. To achieve this it may be necessary to align the SSADM approach more closely with other publicly available open standards - for example MERISE, which is well established in France - or to extend it with new features which may be required by developers in other member states. CCTA is not progressing this subject with appropriate authorities in other EC countries.

12.1.3 SSADM RELEASE STRATEGY

Since its inception, SSADM has been placed under rigorous change control. But with the diversity of users and the number of companies providing commercial services this was extended during 1987 to include a fully planned and public release strategy.

The broad content of each new release is now published approximately nine months in advance of the release itself. Three months later - about six months in advance of the release - a detailed description is published for the benefit of users, consultants, trainers and tool builders. The changes themselves will then be published as revisions to the reference manual.

12.2 The SSADM Research Centre

12.2.1 CURRENT POSITION

The first SSADM Research Centre is now well established within the Department of Computing at Birmingham Polytechnic. The Centre, which has been endorsed by CCTA, involves six academic staff and four Research Assistants. Funding for the Centre consists of a grant of £150,000 (over the three years from April 1988) from the National Advisory Board Special Initiative, a donation of £50,000 (in equipment) from Apollo Computer UK and approximately £100,000 worth of software from the software suppliers PSI, P.A., Metron and Logica. Additional DTI and CCTA funding has also been obtained for specific CASE projects.

The major areas of study are:

- "Knowledge based" (AI) techniques within SSADM; both in the form of "advisors" and as a component of computer-based support tools;

- flexible multi-user CASE tools based on developing standards such as POSIX, "Windows", PCTE and IRDS;

- interfacing Capacity Planning tools to SSADM, firstly via bespoke interfaces from the "physical design" stage to existing PC-based packages, and secondly through PCTE or IRDS based CASE tool interfaces. The use of AI techniques is also being pursued to help form a fully integrated tool set;

- development of additional SSADM techniques for the design of distributed systems with particular emphasis on distributed databases and network design.

12.2.2 RELATED DEVELOPMENTS

The Centre's expertise has been recognised by:

- the selection by the BCS of the Head of the Centre as its representative on the SSADM Design Authority Board;

- the election to the Executive Committee on the SSADM User Group of another team member;

- the establishment of a BCS Working Party on SSADM under the aegis of the Data Management Specialist Group of the BCS, with the Head of the Centre as its first Chairman.

12.2.3 THE SRC AND DISTRIBUTED SYSTEMS - EARLY WORK

Initial work in the area of this paper has concentrated on interfacing capacity planning with SSADM. The emphasis in this research is in the area of forecasting future demand for IT capacity with the objective of ensuring that service requirements are met, in particular capacity planning of future application development workloads. The challenge here is to obtain, at the earliesr opportunity, sufficiently detailed information about the nature of the workload to estimate its likely usage of IT capacity in order to meet service requirements. What is also important is to ensure that service-level agreements of existing workloads will not be violated. In summary, the principal aims of this research are to:

- develop a framework for closer interworking between capacity planning and application development functions;

- force application developers to become pro-active in ensuring that new applications are modelled and that adequate IT capacity will be available to meet agreed service levels;

- develop prototype computer-aided support for the framework by interfacing application development (CASE) and capacity modelling tools.

A number of key developments have taken place and significant progress has been made in the following contexts:

- a close collaborative link with CCTA has been established. This will be an important source of information on areas relating to this study;

- contacts with a number of suppliers of capacity modelling tools have been made. The following companies have donated their tools to the research project:

    - Metron Technology (the "ATHENE" and "PERSEUS" packages)

    - Logica Financial Systema (the CAPACITY/Q package)

    - Performance Systems Incorporated (the SCERTII package);

- work is in progress on defining the interface between capacity modelling tools and tools which support the physical design process within SSADM. In particular, an IDMSX optimising tool has been enhanced to link with an SSADM CASE tool and capacity modelling tool;

- the development of a model showing the interactions between Capacity Planners, Application Developer and Service Level Manager, and the data required to support these interactions, has been initiated. This model will be used as the basis for investigating how SSADM should be enhanced to promote these interactions:

- an investigation of the mapping between modelling tool input requirements and SSADM outputs has been initiated. The aim is to identify deficiencies and to develop a rule-based approach to modelling capacity requirements as the application development moves from Stage 2 to Stage 6;

- network design packages are also being evaluated in order that they can also be interfaced with the framework discussed in the above.

12.2.4 CURRENT DISTRIBUTED DATA AND PROCESSING SYSTEMS RESEARCH

It is our view that the work on capacity planning and network design has direct links into the design of distributed systems. In particular, the crucial issue of performance of distributed database systems is directly related to the network design and to the "sizing" of processing nodes within the network.

12.2 The Motivation For Developing Distributed Database Applications

12.2.1 PERFORMANCE

The most important factor in motivating designers to examine distributed database solutions is that of performance. An intuitive examination of problem/solution leads people to believe that the advantages of:

- local processing

- and parallel processing.

will lead to an improved response time from the overall system. Whilst this is true if almost all the processing is "local" it becomes less true when the number of "remote" accesses becomes significant or the proportion of "update" accesses vs read accesses becomes important. The performance of a distributed database application will degrade in proportion to these two factors. With little practical experience of distributed database applications it is not possible to say with certainty where the "break even point" lies. The reasons for the performance degradation include:

- concurrency control required to lock copies of data so updates do not violate the data integrity of the database;

- extra system management involved in ensuring that transactions are passed to the appropriate nodes for execution;

- inter-node communication overheads;

- database management overhead at each site.

This performance degradation will increase in proportion to the number of copies of the data held in the system.

12.2.2 RELIABILITY

The concept of "graceful degradation" is attractive. That is, if a node fails (hardware or software) other nodes will only be minimally affected. However, the design of the system can seriously affect the reliability of the system. When a node fails users may experience problems because:

- transactions which update data at the failed node cannot continue. The reason for this is that maintenance of the data integrity at that node and over the whole database becomes difficult to guarantee. Database recovery may become uncertain;

- users cannot read data only held at that node;

- any isolated parts of the network will appear to have failed, thus compounding# (a) and (b) type problems.

There is a balance to be found between reliability (for read access) and performance. Reliability in terms of update availability is certainly not a function of more copies of data, whereas read reliability and performance is.

12.2.3 ECONOMY

A distributed system can be tailored to fit a systems performance requirement and size more closely than a centralised system. This is particularly true for dedicated systems. As an application grows and shrinks (that is the number of users, the volume of data, etc.) so the network can have additional nodes added or nodes taken away. Similarly, a node can be expanded or reduced in view of the changing requirements at that node. Storage and processing capacity can be closely matched to local processing needs, which should constitute the bulk of the work. However, most practical experience to date suggests that costs increase in proportion to the level of distribution.

12.2.4 LOCAL CONTROL

The ability of employees to control their own processing while not being a product of distributed systems per se is seen to be an advantage. This may take the form of the provision of customised interfaces at local sites. However, a distributed database system requires as much, if not more coordination and control as a centralised system.

12.2.5 LINKING REMOTE DATA

An advantage which is stated by many Data Base Management System (DBMS) suppliers is the ability to link together databases stored on connected machines. Often this assertion is qualified by the statement that the DBMS need not be the same (eg. Oracle, Ingres, DB2, IMS, IDMS, etc). Usually this interface is via a so-called "gateway" which may be an SQL interface or it may be a file.

While it is undoubtedly an advantage to be able to share data stored in databases in separate geographical locations and different DBMSs, there are a number of problems with this type of system:

- the data model used at each "site" (names and structures) may well be different. Whose responsibility is the conversion between one definition and another?

- updates, if at all possible, may not have the 2-phase commit protocol;

- SQL dialects vary.

It is doubtful if this type of system would be described as a Distributed DBMS (DDBMS). This type of solution demonstrates a lack of coordination. While this function may be useful to solve practical problems, no one would see the development of new applications using this type of system as beneficial.

12.3 Experience With Distributed Design

There is little practical experience of implementing distributed database applications mainly because there is no commercially available DDBMS. Most commercial experience is in the field of distributed systems and files.

Practical experience of building distributed systems has produced some general "rules":

- Associate processes with the data they use.

- Reduce data transmission.

- Associate data with the clerical actions.

SSADM Stages 1-4 are followed by systems developers in practice, but generally without the emphasis on mathematical techniques. For example, "Function/Data/Time Analysis" (BIS) is a method by which developers can examine the requirements which a distributed system is trying to fulfil. This approach examines the way that data is used and the limits on the response time and concurrency of the data.

12.4 Theoretical Approaches To Distribruted Database Design

Distributed database application design is in its infancy. However, considerable academic interest has been shown in the physical implementation of databases over computer networks [1]. This work has evolved out of work on the "File Allocation Problem" [2].

Broadly speaking, the steps (SSADM Version 3.0) which a design must pass through are as follows:

1. Conceptual database design (SSADM stage 2).

2. Table design (RDA, TNF) (SSADM stage 4).

3. Logical fragmentation.

4. Fragment allocation.

Steps 1 and 2 are the same for a centralised database design. Steps 3 and 4 are specific to distributed database design and are not yet incorporated into SSADM, but may become part of stage 6.

Fragment allocation can be varied depending on some basic assumptions. The simplest application design is to assume "completely connected" network of nodes. For example, a PSS based system could be considered to be completely connected. The data which has to be collected to perform fragment allocation includes the number of reads and the number of updates to each logical fragment at each node in the network. It is possible to vary the allocation method to consider replicated and non-replicated fragments and to take into account the number of copies of fragments [3].

The major assumption that the network is completely connected is often not true in practice. Hence the allocation of fragments will not be appropriate for the network. Distributed database design can be extended to encompass:

- network reliability;
- file availability;
- delay constraints within the network.

The steps outlined above have been extended [4] at step 4 to include:

4. Evaluate network constraints.

5. Evaluate file availability constraints.

6. (Iterated).

6a. Channel allocation.

6b. Fragment allocation and capacity allocation.

However, the steps outlined above are not appropriate for existing networks.

Theoretical design techniques fall into two categories, those which are based on heuristics (those that will produce a solution but not necessarily the best one, and those which will produce an optimum design for a set of constraints.

Some observations of design techniques:

- The quality of the results are dependent on the quality of the data input. These are usually estimates (number of reads and writes to a fragment from a site).
- Any change in usage or application constraints may have a significant impact on the model, that is the resultant design may be radically different from that produced from the original constraints.
- Optimal models and design techniques can take large amounts of time to produce an answer and may therefore be an impractical method for application design.

12.5 Pragmatic Approaches To Distributed Database Design

In the absence of any practical experience in the design and use of distributed database applications, it may be difficult to produce design tools to assist in the application design process.

The first design decision has to be at the feasibility stage.

> Is the design likely to be centralised or distributed?
>
> The answer to this question may be centralised, distributed or a mixture. The answer will be based on the application profile (logical divisions, update frequency vs access frequency, node activity, etc). This information is not likely to be detailed statistical data, rather general statements about the operational characteristics of the system.

Design can proceed as for a centralised design with the addition of identifying what may be known as "Logical Application Groups" [5]. That is a partition of the application which is logically separable from the remainder of the application and which communicates through a relatively narrow interface. This is the smallest area of an application which could be a candidate for distribution.

Once a logical design has been produced, the LAGs which are to be distributed can be entered into stages 3 onwards of the design process.

The allocation of fragments around the network could, in the first instance, be fairly rough using a basic formula like "All Beneficial Sites" [3] and any changes to the number or location of copies would occur during the operation of the system.

Therefore the ability of the DDBMS to cater for dynamic changes in the number and location of fragments can be seen to be important.

12.6 Tackling Distribution In Methodologies

Of the major available general methodologies, only Information Engineering makes any reference to a process for distributing data. However, the process is poorly documented, not fully supported by associated CASE tools, and because only a "core" standard of IE exists it is not fully implemented by some purveyors of the method. ORACLE's SDD product also claims to support distribution (specifically ORACLE "Star"), but again support is not complete.

SAD ("Yourdon"), JSD and SSADM Version 3 currently make no provision for this type of solution.

It may be that a lack of implementation of distributed databases is related to the inability to document the design process using the "standard" methodologies.

12.7 SSADM And Distribution

12.7.1 STRUCTURE

SSADM consists of six "stages" covering the majority of the systems development lifecycle (implementation and business analysis are not covered). Within these stages a variety of techniques for systems modelling are used; some of these techniques can be said to be data oriented, while others are process oriented. The major data driven techniques are Logical Data Structures (akin to Bachman diagrams), Relational Data Analysis and Physical Data Base Design.

Processes and the events which cause them to be triggered are described by Data Flow Diagrams, Entity Life Histories, Process Outlines and Physical Process Specifications.

Much effort is expended on separating out the development of the "logical requirement", ie. what the business/organisation wants to achieve, from processes of deciding how this is to be achieved using hardware and software ("physical" design).

In Version 3.0 five of the stages of SSADM are concerned with development of the logical system design, while only Stage 6 handles physical design. This issue is remedied to a reasonable degree in Version 4.0.

12.7.2 HOW SSADM FAILS TO HELP IN DISTRIBUTED SYSTEM DESIGN

SSADM (Version 3.0) has no techniques to help model network designs, or to model user service times for computerised tasks. It has no techniques to help with performance modelling, other than that of tuning the database against defined transactions (Physical Design Control). This means that no account is taken of the general capacity planning requirements where various parameters, including processor speed, line speed, screen design and channel to disc allocation can be adjusted within a model to develop an optimal design. While it can be argued that these are merely required extensions to physical design, it should be remembered that both at feasibility study and at the end of outline design stages, decisions have to be made about future costs and hence viability of a project. Without some design techniques to "complete the system picture", this decision making process will be fatally flawed. Hence even for the minimal level of distribution, a centralised machine with a network of dumb(ish) terminals, some crucial modelling techniques are missing. This weakness is reflected in the late addition (in Version 3.0) of any form of dialogue design techniques reflecting much of the batch focus of the method in its early incarnation. However, improvements have been made in Version 4.0, but further work still requires to be done.

The position is even more serious when more complete forms of distribution are considered. Neither the logical specification of programs nor their physical process specification have any mechanism for describing partitioning of code. Hence the common type of approach where input validation and output formatting are done at an intelligent user terminal cannot be mapped onto the design documents. The more interesting cases of the SQL server and distributed transaction processing (as in ICL's TPMS product) clearly cannot be documented in SSADM terms.

(Note: such systems are implemented in projects using SSADM, but without any standard design principles or documentation.)

The classical form of distributed database systems, as discussed in an earlier part of the paper, needs mechanisms to describe both distributed processing and distributed data partitions/fragments. The current data modelling techniques in SSADM do not allow for the description of non-centralised data, neither are there any rules for the conversion of a final logical data model to a distributed database solution. The problem is therefore twofold:

- no diagrammatic conventions to show distribution;

- no design method to achieve "sensible" distributed designs.

Problem 1 also has repercussions in the analysis stages of SSADM, for it makes it very difficult to describe systems which are already distributed to some degree.

It is perhaps possible in this case to represent distribution using the "location" field in the Data Flow Diagram process boxes, but this is normally used to describe a functional section within an organisation, eg. Accounts. Furthermore, no mechanisms exist to show distributed data stores or to show the location of "in-company" external entities. It is a subject of some debate as to whether logical data models during analysis should be able to show current location of the entities. The argument is rather academic, as no diagrammatic construct exists to show distribution, even if this was considered desirable!

The second problem area covers two issues:

- How to achieve a "good" design for distribution.

- What new diagrammatic (or matrix based) techniques and additions to current techniques are needed within SSADM to help with the "good" design process.

Both these areas are the subject of current work within the SRC.

12.8 Status Of SSADM Work In This Area

Version 4 of SSADM, officially launched in 1990, is provided as a core method with a series of interface guides. These interface guides are meant to provide guidance on how to extend the core techniques into certain specialist areas. For example, an interface guide for turnkey systems is to be provided. In this paper's area of work, an interface guide for distributed systems is at an early stage of definition. The content, however, is not yet fixed, and neither is the availability date. As with many of the proposed interface guides authors have to be found to produce the work, which will then have to be ratified. This may take a number of years to complete.

Within the SRC we are actively continuing to evaluate current pragmatic and theoretical techniques in order to make our own contribution to this work. Current work is focusing on two major areas:

- network design integrated with earlier work on capacity planning;

- evaluation of proprietary techniques (such as Function/Data/Time Analysis from BIS) for their value as possible SSADM extensions.

Perhaps of more long term importance in this area will be the influence of the convergence of structured methods across the EEC, with the Euro Method Initiative. Convergence between IE and SSADM Version 4.0 can already be seen in terms of LDS modelling, and with the incorporation of the other European methods (such as those from France, etc), a consistent approach to the distributed nature of systems developments may be developed. As with other chapters in this text, the role of Europe in terms of business, data processing and systems integration is a key issue for the 1990s. By its very nature, Europe is a distributed system in its own right. With new markets for data and data processing services opening up in Eastern, as well as Western Europe distrbuted data processing will become an ever more important aspect of business development.

12.9 Conclusions

An opportunity exists to influence the development of the UK de facto standard for systems development in such a way that designing distributed systems becomes a standard task for the analyst, using a structured set of available techniques.

Finally, it is now highly likely that SSADM will be a major influence on the development of techniques within the proposed Euro Method framework. Any work done now on distributed systems will have great influence, as other European "standards" such as MERISE do not offer any solutions in this area.

References

[1] LARSON & RAHMI (1985) : Tutorial - "Distributed Database Management", IEEE Computer Soc.

[2] DOWDY & FOSTER, (1982) : "Comparative methods of the file assignment problem", ACM Computing Surveys, 14,2, pp 288-313.

[3] CERI & PELAGATTI (1985) :"Distributed Databases Principles and Systems", McGraw-Hill, 0-07-010829-3 .

[4] IRANI & KHABBAZ (1979) : "A model for a combined communication network design and file allocation for distributed databases", Proc. 1st Int. Conf. on Distributed Computer Systems, pp 15-21.

[5] ROCKART, J. & LEVENTNER, J. (1977) : 'Centralisation vs Decentralisation of Information Systems", Sloan School, MIT.

DISTRIBUTED DATA RESEARCH

Anthony Law, Morris Sloman and Jonathan Moffett,
BP Research and Imperial College, London

13.1 The Technical And Business Environment

Today, large centralised computer services are becoming the exception rather than the rule. The preference for decentralised business management is echoed in the provision of decentralised IT services, with coherence being provided by corporate networks. The role of the centre is increasingly to provide essentially central services such as corporate databases and accounting, or expensive specialised services such as high powered numerical processing.

Increasing autonomy of individual users is supported by personal computer technology and, for more powerful requirements, by personal workstations. The overall picture is at once fragmented, as computing power is distributed increasingly towards end users, and more coordinated as these corporate islands - or, perhaps, archipelagos - become linked by networks and exchange data electronically.

Distributed processing systems and communications services are increasingly moving from a supportive role to a central one in many commercial, industrial, educational and research organisations. They are becoming essential to the core objectives of the organisation. If the system fails to meet its requirements, the effect can be catastrophic - particularly in areas such as process control, Just-in-Time manufacturing (JIT), or financial trading.

13.2 An Example - Electronic Data Interchange

Electronic Data Interchange (EDI) began simply as a means for trading partners to exchange electronically the documents they formerly exchanged by paper - orders, confirmations, delivery notes, invoices and so on. EDI is legally based on bilateral agreements between trading partners. Most EDI exchanges are mailbox based: users do not have direct access to each other's systems.

With its increasing acceptance, EDI began to change business practices. For example, in a conventional purchase, whether paper- or EDI-based, the customer sends an order; delivery is accompanied by a delivery note; and an invoice is sent following which payment is made and acknowledged. New development in EDI enable a customer to have direct access to the supplier's stock and pricing database: this is used not only for direct electronic placing of orders but also to generate lists to check delivery and for self invoicing as a basis for direct payment by electronic funds transfer (EFT). EDI/EFT can eliminate several of the conventional documents (the delivery note, the supplier's invoice and the receipt for payment) thus simplifying, accelerating, and reducing the cost of the transaction.

13.3 Management For Distributed Systems

13.3.1 WHAT IS A DISTRIBUTED SYSTEM?

Sloman and Kramer [1] note that there is, as yet, no agreed definition of a "distributed system". "There is rather a spectrum of systems ... from centralized systems through to a set of diverse, physically dispersed, autonomous computer systems which are interconnected ... to permit the exchange of information. "DOMINO" ("Domain Management in Open Systems") is concerned with systems in which several autonomous computer processes and data stores, separated either physically or organisationally or both, work cooperatively by the exchange of data over a communications network to achieve some common goal.

13.3.2 THE NEED FOR MANAGEMENT

There are many issues which distinguish the management of distributed systems from that of conventional computer processes. Distributed systems management is particularly complex for the following reasons:

- Distributed systems cross organisational and legislative boundaries. The management of the application as well as of the underlying communication and processing resources will have to cooperate across these boundaries. No single partner controls the entire system, and the management styles of partner organisations may be very different.

- Systems may be built from diverse components, from basic microcomputers to large mainframes. These may provide similarly diverse services, for example from simple time-of-day service or monitoring of sensors to control of tools on the shop floor or sophisticated distributed database services. All of these have to interact and to be managed.

- The management interfaces provided by different vendors' equipment are likely to be diverse and incompatible. This makes it difficult to apply a consistent integrated approach to management.

- Systems may make use of wide area networks under the control of an independent organisation, such as a national PTT or other carrier.

- Components and services being managed are physically distributed and there will be genuine parallelism between components. This makes it difficult to obtain and maintain consistent global data, which are required both as the basis for management decisions and to synchronise management actions on different components.

The size and complexity of distributed systems makes it infeasible to treat each and every component independently for management purposes. Practical management must depend on grouping components (and users) into sets which can be managed together. The complexity of the management task makes it all the more essential to develop standards which will enable a systematic approach to be adopted.

13.3.3 MANAGEMENT BY FUNCTION

One approach to coping with the complexity of management in distributed systems is to partition the task according to areas of functional responsibility. This approach is being taken by ISO for the development of OSI communications system management standards [2].

ISO define the following areas of functional responsibility:

- Configuration management, including installation of both hardware and software components; creation of software components and their allocation to hardware; binding of interfaces; name management; control of the components of a server; and changes in all these as the system evolves over its lifetime.

- Performance management, principally the optimisation of performance to improve service to users, in terms of parameters such as throughput, reliability or response time; but possibly with other aims such as cost reduction or profitability of the service.

- Fault management, the detection, location and rectification of faults (which may require use of configuration management facilities).

- Security management, maintaining the security mechanisms of the system (access control, encryption, physical security, etc.) This aims to protect resources by preventing unauthorised access, monitoring exceptions, and taking appropriate action. The delegation of authority is of particular importance in commercial organisations.

- Accounting, permitting users to obtain information on usage of resources, and needed to allow suppliers of services to charge for their use.

13.3.4 OTHER MANAGEMENT STRUCTURES

Other ways of partitioning management responsibilities can provide alternative structures appropriate for some aspects of management:

- Organisational structure: for many purposes the boundaries of responsibility will correspond approximately to organisational boundaries. The management structure must reflect the independence of the partner organisations, and must permit negotiations and cooperations between equals. However, most organisations internally have a hierarchical management structure. They will probably wish to reflect this structure for functions such as accounting and resource management.

- Physical structure: many distributed systems are physically distributed and are based on interconnected LANs and WANs. Some aspects, such as fault management, are best partitioned to reflect this fact.

- Service structure: increasingly, large distributed systems are seen as sets of interacting services such as communications service, file service, electronic mail service, payroll service, etc. Different administrative and service staff may be responsible for managing these services, any of which may be distributed across physical and organisational boundaries.

- Security structure: systems can be partitioned to reflect mandatory security boundaries and structures, such as the set of resources permitted to specific sets of users. For example, users who access a system by dial-in lines may be limited to a subset of resources.

13.4 The Object-Oriented Approach To Management

13.4.1 OBJECT-ORIENTED ANALYSIS

Conventional systems analysis separates the description of an entity (attributes) from the functions which are needed to create, control and maintain it, although the two strands of analysis may be performed together. Data needs to be considered independently of specific queries or reports, to allow the database to be used flexibly. However, there is considerable common ground between functions required of different entities: for example creation, display and deletion.

Object oriented analysis brings together entities and functions: an "object" is an entity with certain well-defined behaviours. The object is said to be encapsulated: its interaction with other objects is well defined but its internal implementation and behaviour is not visible at this interface. Individual instances of objects are created from templates, also called classes or types. There may be different templates which implement the same interface.

Object oriented programming languages normally insist that none of the state of the object be visible externally. However, we follow the object oriented database (OODB) approach of defining attributes: internal state parameters visible at the interface [3]. This avoids the need to specify many different access operations to manipulate these data.

An attribute may be a simple data type (eg. integer or logical) or a structured type (eg. array, record or set in Pascal terminology). Typical attributes include the object's instance identifier; the identifier of the template from which it was created; and specific information such as error statistics, buffer size, or whether a device which the object controls is on-line, off-line or paused. The modularity of the object oriented approach fits well with the need to describe components in a distributed system where the interfaces between components, which may exist in different management areas, must be well known and stable but their implementation need not.

Objects, in a distributed system, comprise not only processes and data but also hardware, communications and even people. In a conventional system, management of the computer hardware and communications network is not normally considered part of the management function of, for example, a database administrator. In a distributed system it may very well be necessary to bring all these elements into the management picture.

13.4.2 INTERACTIONS BETWEEN OBJECTS

Experience in implementing distributed systems has shown that at least two kinds of interaction are required [4]. Asynchronous signalling permits an object to signal events to one or more other objects, and request-reply transactions permit one object to operate upon another. These interactions are made available by an object at named interaction points within its interface. Examples of interaction points supported by distributed system building tools include ports, channels, mailboxes and remote procedure call (RPC) names.

Any object may interact with any other object. Access rules (section 4.3) control this: they enforce the security policies of computer systems, and their specification will be constrained by security policies within an organisation.

13.4.3 MANAGING OBJECTS

Management is a specific kind of interaction between a managing object (or "manager") and a managed object. It entails obtaining information on the current state of a managed object; making decisions; and performing control operations on the object.

A managed object may be a tangible ("real world") entity, such as a workstation, processor, software module, data file or person. Equally it may be an abstraction: a representation of information about a real world entity. The following examples illustrate this:

- a maintenance engineer who is repairing a processor is manipulating the real world processor.

- a resource scheduling program manipulates a data structure which represents relevant facts about the processor.

- if the processor acts as a gateway between two networks, its set of routing tables is managed by a routing manager.

- thus there can be several system objects, of different types and being managed for different purposes, which correspond to the same real world object (in this case, the processor);

- the DOMINO model recognises three types of management interactions.

- requests for information are directed by the managing object to the managed object, and result in a reply.

- control actions are initiated by the managing object, to modify the behaviour of the managed object.

- notifications originate from the managed object, which sends unsolicited data to its managing object. An object can be managed if its definition includes an appropriate management interface, making available appropriate interactions. The manager must implement a complimentary interface.

13.4.4 MANAGEMENT FUNCTIONS

All objects must support generic management interactions which we define as follows.

- Create object - instantiate an object from a template, and initialise its attributes.

- Destroy object - remove the object from the system. There may be constraints: for example, it may only be possible to destroy an object when it is in a passive or "stopped" state.

- Read attribute - obtain the value of a single attribute in order to make management decisions.

- Write attribute - change the value of an attribute, for example a set-point or error limit, in order to cause the object to modify its behaviour. There may be constraints restricting which attributes can be written to and/or on the values which can be written to specific attributes.

- Notifications - operations initiated by the managed object, which acts on its manager by sending unsolicited reports. These may be, for example, error notifications or may be regular reports on the state of the object.

Creating and destroying objects can be complex processes. Creating is not really an operation on the object itself but rather upon a manager or factory object which creates other objects. It may involve actions such as loading of code or initialising a real world entity which the object controls. Destroying an object may require it to interact with its peers to reach a consistent state before it can actually be destroyed [5].

Some attributes may be set by a managing object. Others will be set only by the object itself. For example, a managing object may issue a command to bring a device on-line. The attribute which indicates that the device actually is on-line will be changed by the managed object when it detects that the real-world event has successfully completed. This attribute can be read by the managing object but must not be modified by it. There will be application specific operations which combine these primitive operations, typically reading and/or writing several attributes, altering the state of an object, or triggering off further inter-actions with other objects and finally returning a response to the initiator. For example, a boolean expression involving some attributes may be used as a guard on changing the values of others: this is similar to the OSI concept of filters [6].

It is possible for a manager to have the same management interface as the objects it is designed to manage. It may then perform management operations on itself. For example, a configuration manager may perform interface binding for other processes and also bind its own interface [7].

13.5 Using Domains To Structure Management

13.5.1 THE DOMAIN CONCEPT

A central problem for the management of distributed systems is that objects to be managed do not fall neatly within the boundaries of the organisations who build, use and maintain the system. An example has already been given (section 1) showing that both customer and supplier may have management functions for records in a supplier's database, and require appropriate access to them.

In the end, there is always a question of individual (human) authorisation. The supplier does not want to be involved every time a new data entry clerk is employed by the customer. The customer is given the right to sanction appropriate access to the database. This does not conflict with the supplier's own access rights: by identifying precisely what access each requires, the appropriate control and security can be achieved.

In essence, this is the concept of management domains. We define a domain as a set of managed objects to which a common management policy is applied. The set of identifiers of the managed objects is referred to as the object set of the domain.

Domains are not a new concept: they have been used informally both in system management and for specifying access control. They have the potential to provide a formal structure within which objects can be grouped for the purposes of management:

- to define carefully who has what kinds of access to which parts of the total system.
- to define who controls the different accesses required by different functions.
- to structure the delegation of management authority over sets of objects, to individuals or to sets of managers, to carry out activities such as configuration, security management and accounting.

In the DOMINO model, objects for management can exist only in domains since domains define the management relationships and policy. Creation of an object is therefore a domain operation: objects are created within a domain, and the operation is performed by the domain's managing object.

A Domain object must support operations to include object identifiers in its object set, and to remove them from it (as shorthand, we refer to these operations as "including" and "removing" the object). An object may be included in more than one domain. Removal of an object from a domain is only permitted if it remains a member of some other domain. An object may be moved from one domain to another: this is equivalent to first including it in the new domain and then removing it from the original one. None of these operations affect the state of the object itself.

The following examples illustrate the domain concept at work:

- a set of files in a directory is managed by the owner of the directory. Other users may have specific rights to access the files.

- an enterprise-wide E-mail service is managed by a number of systems programmers and operations staff who are responsible for configuring and maintaining specific parts of the overall service.

- a security administrator controls access to a set of objects (files, programs, high-security printers, etc), and gives users specific access rights to these objects.

- a management role in an organisation can be modelled as a domain (the "Manager Domain") whose members have management rights over another domain (the "Managed Domain") containing the objects (facilities, people) to be managed. An individual is given a management role by being included in the Manager Domain.

One of the main motivations for using domains is to structure management. Therefore it is necessary to define the relationships which may exist between different domains. There are three kinds of relationships: mathematical set relationships; access rule relationships, defining what operations objects in one domain may perform on those in another; and protocols for interaction between autonomous managers.

13.5.2 SET RELATIONSHIPS

Two domains are disjoint if their object sets are disjoint (there are no objects which are in both domains). Mechanisms are needed to permit disjoint domains to interact.

Two domains are overlapping if one or more objects are members of both. For example, the management of a gateway connecting two networks may be shared between the management centres of the two networks. Overlap is contentious because it means that more than one manager has management rights (responsibilities) within the domain. In many cases this can be overcome by creating a new domain, with a single manager, for the objects in the intersection. A special case of overlapping occurs when the objects in one domain are a subset of the objects in another.

Implicit overlap may occur where separate domains contain objects which are created from different templates but which reference the same real world entity. For example, if the processor in the example of section 13.4.3 is taken out of service in the maintenance domain it also becomes unavailable in the scheduling domain. Implicit overlap is likely to occur where management is partitioned functionally, and careful design needed to coordinate management in this situation.

A subdomain is a domain object within another domain (it is not a subset of the enclosing domain). The normal domain definition applies: a common management policy is applied to the objects in the subdomain. This may be different from the policy applied to the objects in the enclosing domain. The use of subdomains extends the domain concept in a very powerful way, since they provide the principal method of structuring management. Subdomain structures can be useful for purposes other than the delegation of authority. A manager may define arbitrary sets of objects which are related, for example, for naming purposes. Many tree structured file systems work this way using directories (domains) and sub-directories (subdomains).

13.5.3 ACCESS RULE RELATIONSHIPS

Management is a specific kind of interaction and, like others, requires control. Access rules for management specify the responsibilities of managers. They identify the domains which managers are authorised to manage and define what operations they may carry out.

A management access rule is a ternary relation which specifies a domain of managers; a domain of managed objects; and a set of permissions. The operations permitted must be a subset of those defined by the managed objects' interfaces.

An operation may require more than one access permission. For example, to include an object in another domain requires permission both to add to the object set of the target domain and to use the identifier of the object in this operation. Moving an object from one domain to another is a compound operation, first including the object in the destination domain and then removing it from its existing one, and requires permission for both operations.

Access rules themselves need to be maintained (created, deleted and modified) and these operations will in turn be subject to access rules.

13.5.4 PROTOCOLS

Interaction between independent managers is essential in the management of distributed systems, for example to exchange management information, establish access rules, and negotiate over any conflicts. There are two conceptually different ways to implement this:

- one manager may be given controlling responsibility over a domain. Other managers wishing to interact with objects in the domain must do so via the controlling manager. This gives a high degree of control to the controlling manager, at the expense of extra work.

- the controlling manager may create a new domain, as either a sub-set or a subdomain, and give another manager direct management access to it. This saves work but maintains less control.

It is a policy decision which approach is adopted. In either case, however, some interactive protocol between managers is required so that they can engage in preliminary negotiation of the terms on which interactions can be performed and can set up appropriate access rules. Such protocols go beyond the definition of mathematical relationships and access rules, and are the subject of further study.

13.6 The DOMINO Project

13.6.1 SPONSORSHIP

DOMINO is a three year programme sponsored by the Information Engineering Directorate of the Department of Trade and Industry and the Science and Engineering Research Council. The partners are Sema Group; British Petroleum; and Imperial College.

13.6.2 SEMA GROUP

Sema Group was formed in 1988 from CAP Group plc in the UK and SemaMatra in France. Sema's business is to apply IT for the benefit of customers in industry, commerce, finance and government. It employs over 6000 staff in Europe, North America and the Far East.

Through its Communications Consultancy group, Sema provides network consultancy services to both private and public sectors. They contribute to international standards development through participation in Open Systems Interconnection (OSI) working groups and by other means.

Sema act as overall project manager for DOMINO, and have primary responsibility for Quality of Service (QoS) and accounting specifications and toolset development, and for enhancements to existing OSI standards.

13.6.3 BRITISH PETROLEUM

The BP Group is a world-wide group of major energy and resources businesses. The size and international nature of its business places exceptional demands on its information systems and upon its communications expertise. BP is already using domain models in the management of its world-wide communications network; and is developing the role of distributed systems which are, or will become, crucial to its commercial and industrial activities both in Europe and world-wide. BP recognises the need to control the complexity of its large scale distributed systems and, as a major user, is committed to the Open Systems concept.The BP Research Centre exists to anticipate and meet the needs of the Group through research, development and application of emerging technologies. BP participates in DOMINO through the Centre's Information Technology Research Unit which is a centre of expertise for the Group in network concepts, object-oriented systems, and human-computer interfaces.

BP have principal responsibility for development of the prototype graphical toolset for the management of domains, which is one of the major deliverables of DOMINO, and also an important role in ensuring a sound business basis for the project.

13.6.4 IMPERIAL COLLEGE

Imperial College's Department of Computing has an established record in developing the concepts and providing software tools for designing, constructing and managing distributed systems. A major emphasis of the group has been on configuration management: the Conic toolkit, developed in the Department, is already in use in a number of industrial as well as research environments. The group has close links with industry and has been involved in previous collaborative projects with BP and, among others, with British Coal.

The Imperial College group have primary responsibility for developing and formalising the concepts and protocols on which DOMINO will build, and provide technical direction for the project.

13.6.5 AIMS

The overall aims of DOMINO are to use the domain concept to structure the requirements for management; and to create prototype tools to enable management functions to be appropriately and effectively carried out.

By formalising the use of domains as a uniform and well defined grouping tool, DOMINO will provide an integrated approach to the management of distributed systems.

13.6.6 STRATEGY

We are experimenting with various implementation strategies for both managed objects and domains, using object-oriented software such as Smalltalk and Imperial College's CONIC configuration management interface. We shall develop prototype tools for specifying and manipulating domains and other managed objects and demonstrate their use.

We shall apply the domain concept to functions such as accounting and security management, which are qualitatively different in the commercial environment from either an open (university-type) environment or a military one [8]. The use of domains in formulating access rules will be explored.

A major area for study is the specification and implementation of Quality of Service (QoS) in a network environment, and in particular the applicability of domain structuring to QoS management is one of the areas currently being addressed by OSI, and DOMINO will provide a means for the development of the UK contribution in this important topic.

13.6.7 FORMAL DELIVERABLES

(a) Domain Framework

Definition of a domain management framework for structuring management of large distributed systems - Integration of domain management framework into Open Distributed Processing and OSI Management standardisation activities - Definition of domain management interaction protocols.

(b) Security Management

Provision of techniques for specifying domain based security in terms of access rules and security boundaries - Defining techniques for delegating authority in large, complex, autonomous organisations which may interact with each other.

(c) Quality of Service (QoS) Management

To consider the specific requirements for the establishment of an agreed Quality of Service between the participants in a distributed systems enterprise - To establish a generic framework for the specification of QoS in the distributed systems environment - To develop specific techniques for the monitoring, control and notification of QoS in distributed systems.

(d) Accounting

To develop an architecture for multi-domain accounting practices - To apply the architecture to specific examples of distributed systems environments, eg. the pan-European research network (CO- SINE).

(e) Management Interface and Tools

To develop prototype graphics-based interactive tools for:

- specifying, developing and analysing management domains;
- monitoring domains through simulation and animation;
- controlling and manipulating domains.

To investigate the potential for porting prototype tools to other architectures and for commercialisation of the toolset.

13.6.8 BENEFITS

The project is publicly funded and results will be available in the public domain. They will provide a framework within which new products and services can be developed, giving the UK a chance to gain a lead in products and services to the benefit both of suppliers and of users. Results will contribute to the work of standardisation organisations, particularly in OSI Management and Open Distributed Processing (ODP). The domain concepts are already making a contribution to standardisation processes, but need to be refined and tested. At the same time, the partners expect to benefit by earlier access to the project results and through expertise gained by being closely involved in the developments. Sema and Imperial College, through their close links with clients and other industrial sponsors respectively, will transmit the benefits into the private sector, and this will also take place through BP's relationships with other organisations in its commercial activities.

While the project itself is not intended to generate directly saleable products, it will point the way to commercialisation of its results.

References

[1] SLOMAN, M.S., & KRAMER, J. (1987) : "Distributed Systems and Computer Networks", Prentice-Hall.

[2] KLERER, S.M. (1988) : "The OSI Management Architecture: an overview", IEEE Network, 2, pp 20-29.

[3] PECKMAN, J., & MARYANSKI, F. (1988) : "Semantic Data Models", ACM Computing Surveys, 20, pp 153-188.

[4] MAGEE, J., KRAMER, J., & SLOMAN, M.S. (1989): "Constructing Distributed Systems in Conic", IEEE Trans. Software Eng., 15, pp 663-675.

[5] KRAMER, J., & MAGEE, J. (1988) : "A model for change management", Proc. Workshop "Distributed Computer Systems in the 1990s", Hong Kong, Sept. 1988; IEEE Computer Society.

[6] ISO (1989) : "OSI Management Services SMI Part I: Management Information Model", ISO/JTC1/SC21 proposed DP 10165-1.

[7] TWIDLE, K., & SLOMAN, M.S. (1988) : "Domain based configuration and name management for distributed systems", Proc. Workshop "Distributed Computer Systems in the 1990s", Hong Kong, Sept. 1988; IEEE Computer Society.

[8] MOFFETT, J.D., & SLOMAN, M.S. (1988) : "The source of authority for access control in commercial systems", Computer, 21,2, pp 56-69

CONCLUSIONS

STRATEGIC DATA PLANNING IN A DISTRIBUTED ENVIRONMENT

David Gradwell
Data Dictionary Systems Limited

14.1 Introduction

The notion of the corporate database has been with us for nearly twenty years now. In that period we have seen database technology mature and some companies build very successful corporate databases upon which their businesses now depend for growth and flexibility.

Many other organisations, however, have built only departmental systems or often just "systems" that do not fit together. This is the classical data management problem that conventional strategic data planning addresses.

How then is the problem changing ? Is it getting better or worse ?

There are two sets of drivers that are forcing change on how we approach data management, turning it from consideration of how to build corporate databases to how to build distributed databases. These drivers are advances in technology and changes in business. The combined pressures are forcing data management staff to undertake Strategic Data Planning in a Distributed Environment.

First let us consider the technology drivers.

14.2 Technology Drivers

Application logic is moving on to the PC or workstation. (Some people reserve the term "workstation" for large screen UNIX boxes, but the distinction matters little for this paper, so I shall use the two interchangeably to cover all intelligent desk based hardware, including IBM PCs. PS/2s, IBM Compatibles, Apple Macintoshes, Sun Workstations and the like.)

There is now a firm belief that CPU power available on a PC or workstation is typically a factor of ten (some say twenty) cheaper than on a large mainframe. Even though some may argue the exact figures, there is therefore considerable pressure to put applications on small machines. Their databases then naturally stay on the same machine or large minicomputers if possible.

All of this makes database application development possible without the infrastructure needed for managing a large mainframe database. However, such gains are at the cost of failure to be able to share data. This independence leads to failure to fit applications together. The author is aware of several organisations who had, four years ago, got data administration well in hand, only to have their policies destroyed by the availability of cheap but non-integrated mini- or micro-based packages. However, there are some positive developments that may ultimately give us the benefit of lower cost workstations, lower cost development and corporate-wide data sharing.

Database management systems are becoming network servers. Oracle and Ingres can run on many platforms. A user on one system can access data on any other on the network. Oracle or Ingres users can also access DB2 databases. Figure 1 overleaf gives an idea of the potential of using different technologies with the mainframe as a database server.

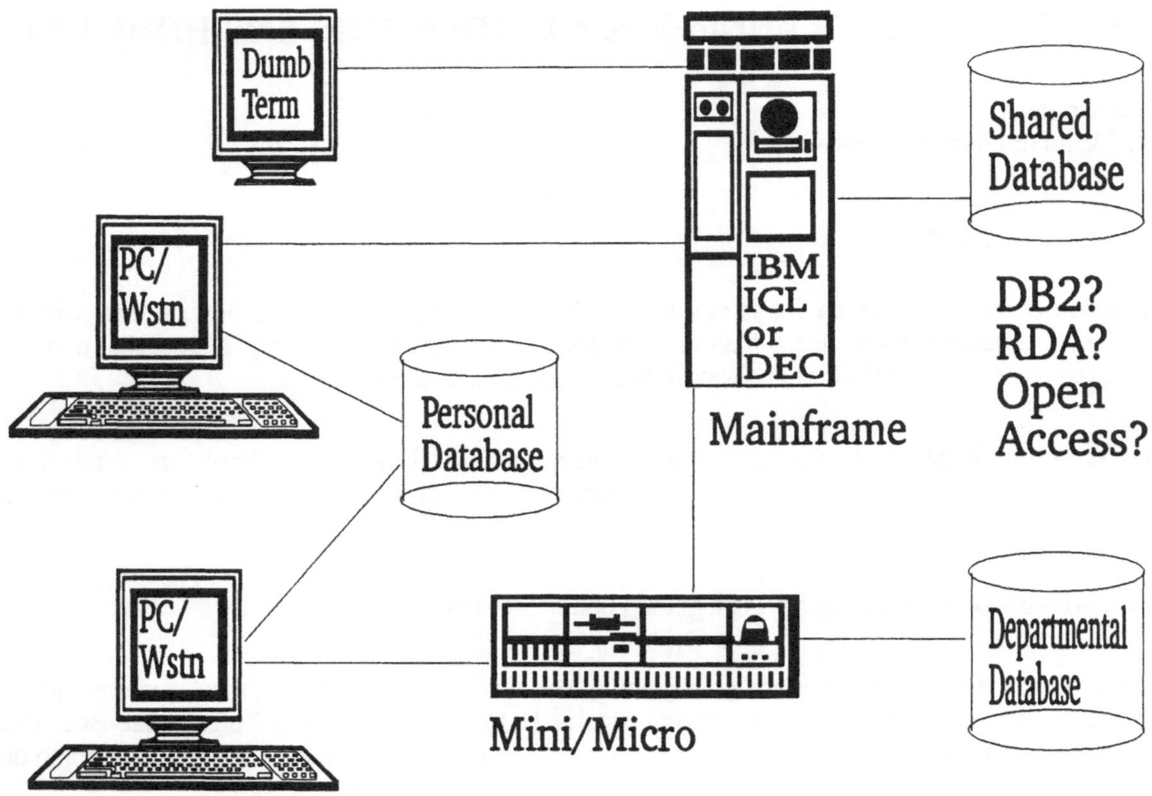

Figure 1 : The Mainframe As A Database Server

Apple have released a product called CL/I that allows a Macintosh application to access data on a wide variety of relational databases (eg, DB2, Oracle, Ingres, Sybase, Rdb) anywhere in the network.

Application development using the Oracle and Ingres 4GL's or using C (or C++) and SQL with a standard windows environment is becoming more portable. Developments in the UNIX/POSIX environment are speeding this along.

All these developments give us the ability to both build applications on PCs or workstations and also to share data. Better still, the shared database can be distributed across several machines and can be put on the size of box that is the most cost-effective. We only need to use mainframe database technology if we have a large quantity of data accessed by many users. Applications can start small and grow by moving the database without affecting the applications.

This must surely have an impact on mainframe prices as the location of the database ceases to be as important and we can buy our "database server MIPS" how we choose.

More pressure for this direction is coming from International Standards work on Remote Database Access, expected to result in an ISO standard by about 1992. There is also a group of vendors who have banded together to form a group called "Open Access" to promote interconnection between their database management systems.

Thus the technology for developing applications locally and accessing data across many sites already exists now and will get more flexible in the next two to three years. Within five years it will become the norm.

14.3 Business Drivers

The need to manage the organisation effectively leads mangers to assemble a wide range of information on which to base their decision making. PC based tools offer great promise until the unfortunate manager discovers that the tool is only as good as the data he can acquire. Worse still, the data that is available comes from many systems, is inconsistent and needs re-keying. His "corporate database" often holds only a fraction of the information needed.

It is not long before such managers realise that their data processing systems are in more confusion than they realised before. The gaps between systems become glaringly obvious as a manager struggles with three terminals on his desk to get information out of two different database technologies, a general ledger with its own file structures and a package sales system!

Yet the need for the information to plan products, pricing, capacity and human resources grows as Government privatises and commerce faces up to 1992. The business pressures are certainly there. So is the information needed, if only we could get at it and understood what it meant.

14.4 Assessing The Need

14.4.1 WHAT TO LOOK FOR

In assessing the need for Strategic Data Planning in a distributed environment, we should look at:

- the degree of organisational cohesion;
- the reasons for data distribution;
- the opportunities for data sharing;
- the business problems that require data exploitation to solve them.

14.4.2 ORGANISATIONAL COHESION

The strategic data planner must be sensitive to the degree to which the organisation holds together.

Consider first whether the organisation has one or two over-riding objectives, eg, "make money by flying passengers" or "transport passengers by train within the constraints of Government Policy" or whether it has a range of diverse and possibly conflicting objectives. Examples in the latter category might be decentralised conglomerates where the only common point is profits returned to the holding company or a Government ministry with a wide spread of responsibilities and activities.

Look at the chain of command. The organisation may be tightly managed and directed by one management team. In this case there may well be a clear corporate strategy and a suitable environment for strategic data planning. Another organisation with a similar structure on paper may not actually be managed as a whole but as separate units whose managers have little or no control over each other and no overall direction. In such an environment strategic data planning may be a waste of time unless it is limited to areas where there is a common understanding of the need. Thus there may be particular data areas that are common and acknowledged to be common.

Figure 2 shows two dimensions for assessing an organisation.

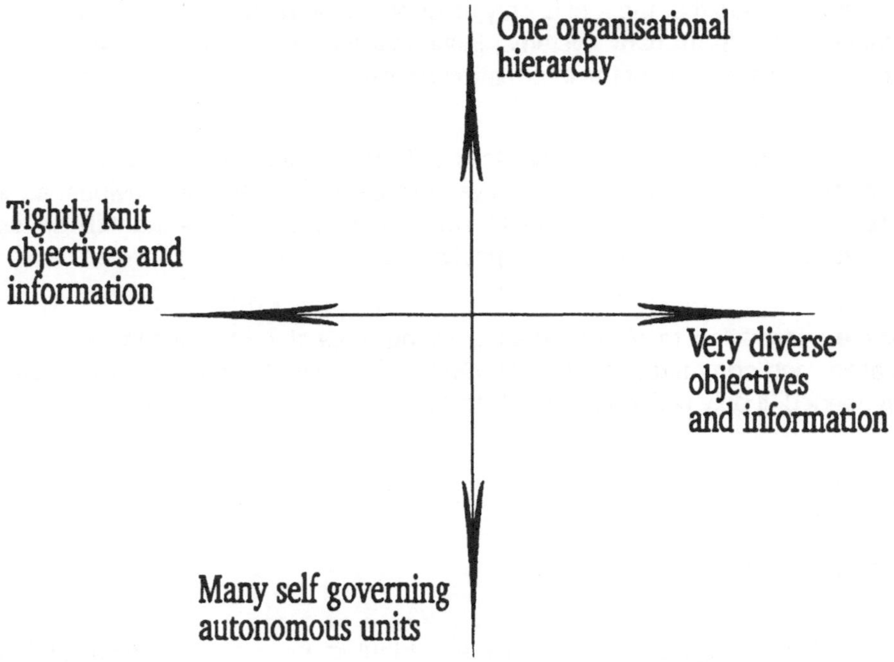

Figure 2 : Dimensions Of Organisational Cohesion

14.4.3 REASONS FOR DATA DISTRIBUTION

The degree of data distribution or centralisation that appears within an organisation is the result of the level of organisational cohesion, problems within Information Technology and the geographic spread of the organisation.

Organisational fission can result from the establishment of separate profit centres or subsidiaries. This may be a valid business strategy but will often destroy the ability to share data unless central management take responsibility for the data strategy and the impact of its costs on profit centre performance. If the split between profit centres is complete there will of course be no motivation for data sharing. The data strategist has to realistically assess whether there is any business case for data sharing in such an organisation or whether the management approach is to leave each profit centre to sink or swim with no support (even in information terms) from the others. This is very much a management culture issue. In many UK companies today decentralisation is in vogue. Such an approach will often be right but may destroy the organisation's ability to function as a whole. Therefore, the strategic data planner must understand whether his organisation is greater than the sum of its parts and if so how. Further, the key corporate managers must share this vision.

A different kind of fracture is caused within data processing community itself. Where projects are funded entirely by line managers from their profit centre, resources are rarely available for cross-project coordination. Attempts to schedule the implementation of projects so that they build upon each other will fail unless managed from the centre. The cost pressures mentioned earlier push development and operation of systems on to separate machines. "Small machines are cheaper but each is too small to run more than one system" is a cry often heard. It is easy to proceed to develop many small unrelated systems.

Geography clearly also contributes, both in terms of distance and as a means to achieve isolationism. Geographically distributed units may try to be totally autonomous. Again, look at the organisational cohesion. Contrast an airline or a software development and marketing organisation with an advertising consultancy. The airline must hold together in information terms if its planes are to fly. The software company must be managed as a whole although less time critically. An advertising consultancy is often run as a number of separate individuals or teams needing little central information, ... until a multinational client comes along!

Thus, if the strategic data planner is to be successful he must identify the degree of cohesion in his organisation, be aware of the approach to information technology development and understand the impact of geography on the business and its data. He must determine what data is corporate, which systems depend on that data and ensure that the key line managers share his vision.

14.4.4 ASSESSING OPPORTUINITIES FOR DATA SHARING

If an organisation has no cohesion and all data can be managed locally with no need for any data sharing, there is no need for strategic data planning. However, few organisations are that simple, even if they think they are! There will at the very least usually be financial information such as budgets, commitments, expenditure and income that must be known on an organisation wide basis.

Thus the key to successful strategic data planning is to assess what opportunities there are for data sharing to the benefit of the business. It is important to concentrate on the business benefits because these are what must be used to justify any resulting developments.

There may be constraints on what is achievable. There may be legal constraints such as the Data Protection Act and the Financial Services Acts. The need for "Chinese Walls" is quite widespread.

There will of course be practicalities such as where does the data originate, who uses it and where are they located, what are the access rates and how much data is to be stored? All of these factors will determine where data is to be stored, whether it has to be duplicated and indeed whether sharing it is practical in performance terms. However, I have become somewhat of a cynic about performance issues. If the business is currently sharing data by re-keying data from photocopied printouts there must be a better way!

The likelihood is that the management and organisational problems will far outweigh the performance issues for any except the largest volumes.

Thus we return to the business issues. Do managers want to pull together? Do they want to be islands unto themselves? Gauge the feelings of the managers. Determine if the business really does want to share data.

And if the answer is no? Perhaps the effort should go on something else.

14.5 How To Do It

To look on the more cheerful side there will of course be many organisations that value their information highly and who wish to exploit it for all it is worth. In these organisations we need to develop the conventional approach to data management to take account of the increasing level of data distribution arising because of the pressures discussed earlier.

The steps in strategic data planning in a distributed environment are little different from strategic data planning in a centralised environment. They are to:

- analyse the business objectives, problems, opportunities and information needs as part of normal strategic planning;

- construct a high level data model and a systems map to show how data is or might be shared;

- analyse the distribution of data by system, by organisational unit and by geographic location;

- build a business case for any data sharing that seems cost justifiable or justifiable in terms of the positive impact it will have on the organisation;

- develop a data storage strategy and a detailed architecture, setting out what data will be stored on what machines and using what database technology;

- initiate projects in the usual way or redirect existing projects to conform to the architecture.

Standard data analysis and data management techniques do of course apply in the more distributed environment. Everything you ever learnt about data modelling holds true. Of course the situations are more complex. There are more varied view points to accommodate, but the principles are the same.

In particular, project data models must be carefully co-ordinated with business area, geographic area and corporate data models. But this is not different from normal corporate data administration.

Great care must be taken with the granting of access rights and the controlling of update responsibilities in a distributed environment. Analysis of the entity life history of each major entity is very valuable here. The key problem is that ownership of information about a particular entity may change as the entity proceeds through its life. This happens in non-distributed systems too, but is often not as acute.

14.5 Barriers And Obstacles

14.5.1 TECHNICAL BARRIERS AND OBSTACLES TO SRATEGIC DATA PLANNING IN A DISTRIBUTED ENVIRONMENT

It is very easy to buy a different database management system or operating system or hardware box for each project. In the current state of remote database access technology this approach makes it very difficult to share data. Even when the technology matures it will still be highly desirable to plan what data will be held on what machines corporately. If a new application comes along that needs its data from two systems on separate machines it will be expensive to implement. If the two systems had shared databases to begin with the cost would have been minimal.

The safe option is now to buy DB2. However, this is an expensive approach for departmental systems that could run happily on a cheap UNIX box. Departments and projects have a strong preference for small machines that they can own and control and whose costs will not create a large hole in the budget.

There is thus no clear "right answer" to this problem. Thus data sharing is not easy unless planned in an overall, cross-departmental context.

14.5.2 BUSINESS BARRIERS AND OBSTACLES TO STRATEGIC DATA PLANNING IN A DISTRIBUTED ENVIRONMENT

As discussed earlier, devolution of responsibility is often an impediment to corporate wide data sharing. If the devolution is of just a particular function (eg, production or marketing) then data sharing is still vital. If the devolution is of profit responsibility and the devolved unit contains all the functions needed for a complete business it will not usually make sense to share much data outside the unit.

Finally, the meaning of data does of course change from location to location, especially across countries. For example, the legal definition of a "company" is different is each of the countries of the European Community and expressed in different languages. An EC manager wishing to plot a graph of his company's turnover faces many problems, not least of which is getting consistent definitions of a "sale" in to use in all countries.

14.6 Achieving Culture Change

Strategic Data Planning in a Distributed Environment is without point unless it yields results. Yet this can be a long process. The organisation has to grow from the perception that "it is not possible" to a shared understanding of the value and meaning of its data. This can only be built on the development of successful systems that really do share data to the benefit of the business.

Thus it is important to choose early projects that will:

- show the importance of cross-site, cross function data sharing;
- demonstrate to key managers that their staff can actually extract the data they need from corporate databases and that it is right and means what they think it does;
- succeed at a reasonable cost and within a reasonable timeframe.

It is crucial to educate line managers about what data is available, what it means, how good the quality of the data is and how to access it. This will help them to exploit the data that is available. It will also lead to a growing understanding of why systems should be built to share data.

14.7 Conclusions

We have seen that the problems that face a strategic data planner in a distributed environment are not different from those encountered in normal data management. However, all the difficulties are magnified somewhat.

Industry trends towards devolved management and IT trends towards development of applications to run on PCs and workstations means that all our data management problems are becoming distributed data management problems.

The first step forward is to ensure that your data management infrastructure exists and is running well. Project co-ordination procedures must be in place and effective at the strategic planning, the budgeting and the technical analysis and design levels.

Selection of those business problems that will give the greatest benefits to the business is key. We can then demonstrate that distributed data management can indeed turn business problems into opportunities. However, we have to be careful to avoid what one colleague called the "insurmountable opportunity" and concentrate our efforts where results can be achieved.